THE UNIVERSITY OF
WINCHESTER

Martial Rose Library
Tel: **01962 827306**

2 1 JAN 2013

To be returned on or before the day marked above, subject to recall.

CAMBRIDGE STUDIES IN EIGHTEENTH-CENTURY
ENGLISH LITERATURE AND THOUGHT 5

The Body in Swift and Defoe

This original book takes a new look at problems surrounding the physical, material nature of the human body in eighteenth-century England, in particular as represented in the works of Jonathan Swift and Daniel Defoe. It examines the role that literary invention (with its rhetorical and linguistic strategies) plays in expressing and exploring the problems of physicality, and deals with issues such as sexuality, cannibalism, scatology and the fear of contagion. Swift and Defoe are seen as writers confronting the essentially modern problem of what it is to be human in a rapidly developing consumer economy, where individual bodies, beset by poverty and disease, are felt to be threatened by the enveloping masses of urban crowds. In an eclectic synthesis of recent approaches, Carol Flynn works into her study the insights provided by biographical and psychoanalytic criticism, Marxism and social history, studies of eighteenth-century philosophy, and feminist readings. Her challenging approach reviews the cost of being human, the "expense" of material as opposed to spiritual life in eighteenth-century society, as it is revealed in its literature.

CAMBRIDGE STUDIES IN EIGHTEENTH-CENTURY
ENGLISH LITERATURE AND THOUGHT

General Editors   Dr. HOWARD ERSKINE-HILL, Litt.D., F.B.A., *Pembroke College, Cambridge*
and Professor JOHN RICHETTI, *University of Pennsylvania*

Editorial Board   Morris Brownell, *University of Nevada*
Leopold Damrosch, *Harvard University*
J. Paul Hunter, *University of Chicago*
Isobel Grundy, *Queen Mary College, London*
Lawrence Lipking, *Northwestern University*
Harold Love, *Monash University*
Claude Rawson, *Yale University*
Pat Rogers, *University of South Florida*
James Sambrook, *University of Southampton*

The growth in recent years of eighteenth-century studies has prompted the establishment of this series of books devoted to the period. The series is designed to accommodate monographs and critical studies on authors, works, genres, and other aspects of literary culture from the later part of the seventeenth century to the end of the eighteenth. Since academic engagement with this field has become an increasingly interdisciplinary enterprise, books will be especially encouraged which in some way stress the cultural context of the literature, or examine it in relation to contemporary art, music, philosophy, historiography, religion, politics, social affairs, and so on. New approaches to the established canon are being tested with increasing frequency, and the series will hope to provide a home for the best of these.

Titles published
The transformation of The Decline and Fall of the Roman Empire,
by David Womersley
Women's place in Pope's world, by Valerie Rumbold
Sterne's fiction and the double principle, by Jonathan Lamb
Warrior women and popular balladry, 1650–1850, by Dianne Dugaw
The body in Swift and Defoe, by Carol Houlihan Flynn

Other titles in preparation
Plots and counterplots: politics and literary representation, 1660–1730,
by Richard Braverman
The eighteenth-century hymn, by Donald Davie
Sentimental comedy: theory and practice, by Frank Ellis
Henry Fielding and the language of morals, by Roger Fallon
Richardson's Clarissa *and the eighteenth-century reader,* by Tom Keymer
Robert South (1634–1716): an introduction to his life and sermons, by Gerard Reedy
Reason, grace and sentiment: a study of the language of religion and ethics in England, 1660–1780, by Isabel Rivers
Defoe's politics: parliament, power, kingship and Robinson Crusoe,
by Manuel Schonhorn
Disturbing the soul: a study of eighteenth-century sensibility, by Ann Jessie Van Sant
Space and the eighteenth-century English novel, by Simon Varey
The rhetoric of Berkeley's philosophy, by Peter Walmsley

The Body in Swift and Defoe

CAROL HOULIHAN FLYNN
Tufts University

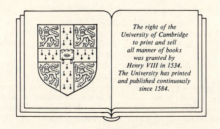

The right of the
University of Cambridge
to print and sell
all manner of books
was granted by
Henry VIII in 1534.
The University has printed
and published continuously
since 1584.

CAMBRIDGE UNIVERSITY PRESS
CAMBRIDGE
NEW YORK PORT CHESTER MELBOURNE SYDNEY

For my parents
Mildred and Arthur Houlihan

Published by the Press Syndicate of the University of Cambridge
The Pitt Building, Trumpington Street, Cambridge CB2 1RP
40 West 20th Street, New York, NY 10011, USA
10 Stamford Road, Oakleigh, Melbourne 3166, Australia

First published 1990

Printed in Great Britain at
The University Press, Cambridge

British Library cataloguing in publication data
Flynn, Carol Houlihan, 1945–
The body in Swift and Defoe.–(Cambridge studies in eighteenth-century English literature and thought; 6)
1. Fiction in English. Defoe, Daniel, 1660 or 1–1731–critical studies 2. English literature. Swift, Jonathan, 1667–1745–Critical studies 823'.5

Library of Congress cataloguing in publication data
Flynn, Carol Houlihan, 1945–
The body in Swift and Defoe / Carol Houlihan Flynn.
p.   cm. – (Cambridge studies in eighteenth-century English literature
and thought: 6)
Includes bibliographical references.
ISBN 0–521–38268–8
1. English literature–18th century–History and criticism.
2. Body, human, in literature.   3. Sex in literature.   4. Swift,
Jonathan, 1667–1745–Criticism and interpretation.   5. Defoe,
Daniel, 1661?–1731–Criticism and interpretation. –I. Title.
II. Series.
PR448.B63F5   1990
820.9'36'09033–dc20–89–36869CIP

ISBN 0 521 38268 8

GG

Contents

Acknowledgments

One of the most rewarding aspects of finishing a book is thanking, finally, the many friends and colleagues who have shared in the writing process. This book has been seven years in the making, and has, through the years, been read and reread in various versions. It began at New York University, where it was known as "Crazy Carcasses" and "Physical Economy." I owe both the faculty and students in the English Department a debt of gratitude for listening to and contributing to the initial cluster of ideas that evolved into this book. They asked and answered important questions. My colleagues Denis Donoghue, Dustin Griffin, John Maynard and Mary Ann Shea were particularly helpful, offering close readings and many critical insights, for which I will always be grateful. I would also like to thank the Mellon Foundation for a grant that enabled me to take a semester off from teaching in 1985 to complete the first version of the text. The book continued at Tufts University, where it was known as "The Dearness of Things" and, finally, "The body in Swift and Defoe." The students and faculty alike offered invaluable support as critics and collaborators. My colleagues Alan Lebowitz, Sheila Emerson and Ann Van Sant in particular have given freely of their time and attention in careful readings. I would like to thank them for their intellectual and emotional support.

Colleagues and friends, in and out of eighteenth-century studies, have contributed in countless ways to this book. I would like to thank Nancy Armstrong, Margaret Doody, John Dussinger, Jan Fergus, Dennis Flynn, Miriam Hansen, Paul Hunter, Peter Linebaugh, Felicity Nussbaum, Ronald Paulson, Claude Rawson, Roy Roussell, Shirley Samuels, Mark Seltzer, Patricia Meyer Spacks, David Tarbet, Jan Thaddeus, John Traugott and William Warner for their generous and searching criticism through various stages of this work. I am particularly indebted to John Richetti, the co-editor of the Cambridge Studies in Eighteenth-Century English Literature and Thought. He was one of the first readers who understood what I was trying to do, and offered along the way the language that would help make my argument. His critical support has meant a great deal to me. I would also like to thank my editor, Kevin Taylor, and Karl Howe and Trudi Tate at Cambridge University Press for their work on this book. Charles Trocano took painstaking efforts in proof-reading and preparing the index for which I am especially grateful.

The staffs of the British Library, the New York Public Library, the Boston Public Library, and the libraries of Tufts University, New York University, Boston University, Harvard University and Yale University were most helpful to me. I thank them all for their able assistance. I am particularly grateful to Richard Wolfe of the Rare Book Library at Harvard Medical School for his indefatigable efforts on my behalf. Finally, I thank my children, Partick and Molly Flynn, for their love, support and tolerance. They are my best critics.

Abbreviations

The following abbreviations are used throughout in references to Defoe's major texts:

CL:	*Conjugal Lewdness; or, Matrimonial Whoredom, A Treatise concerning the Use and Abuse of the Marriage Bed,* ed. Maximillian Novak, Gainesville FL, 1967.
DP:	*Due Preparations for the Plague as well for Soul as Body,* ed. George Aitken, London, 1905.
JPY:	*A Journal of the Plague Year,* ed. Louis Landa, Oxford, 1969.
MF:	*Moll Flanders,* ed. G. A. Starr, Oxford, 1981.
RC:	*Robinson Crusoe,* ed. J. Donald Crowley, Oxford, 1981.
R:	*Roxana,* ed. Jane Jack, Oxford, 1981.

When textual references follow logically, I have merely given page numbers.

The following abbreviations are used throughout in references to Swift's major texts:

Corr:	*The Correspondence of Jonathan Swift,* 5 vols., ed. Harold Williams, Oxford, 1963–65.
GT:	*Gulliver's Travels, Prose Writings,* III.
JS:	*Journal to Stella,* 2 vols., ed. Harold Williams, Oxford, 1948.
Poems:	*The Poems of Jonathan Swift,* 3 vols., ed. Harold Williams, Oxford, 1937.
PW:	*Prose Writings,* 14 vols., ed. Herbert Davis *et al.,* Oxford, 1939–68.
Tale:	*A Tale of a Tub,* ed. A. C. Guthkelch and D. Nichol Smith, Oxford, 1958.

Introduction

"The Dearness of things": the body as matter for text

All humane things are subject to decay.   Dryden on Flecknoe[1]

The undertaker, after three days' expectance of orders for embalment without receiving any, waited on the lord Jefferies, who pretending ignorance of the matter, turned it off with an ill-natured jest, saying, "That those who observed the orders of a drunken frolick deserved no better; that he remembered nothing at all of it; and that he might do what he pleased with the corpse."
                                        Johnson on the death of Dryden[2]

Once Locke reduced, almost inadvertently, thought to matter in an attempt to address the more insistent materialism of Hobbes, it was inevitable that the body would intrude upon the most sanguine attempts to render form and meaning out of substance. The body had always complicated the very human desire for spiritual certainty. Idealists for centuries scourged it, refined it, shed it altogether in attempts to link it into larger patterns of coherent meaning. But after Hobbes, after Locke, and in spite of Descartes, the body, at least in eighteenth-century England, would not go away easily. It became instead matter difficult, perhaps impossible, to idealize – matter in the way. The epistemological bind of the age, the confinement of thought to matter that could only be patterned self-consciously, made knowing the body at best problematic. The urban bind of the age, the confinement of too many bodies into crowded, diseased cities, made not knowing the problem of the body impossible.

When Defoe and Swift employed strategies to contain or escape from the body, they reflected the struggle against materiality that characterized their age. Both writers understood the difficulties of knowing a self trapped in a world of sensation. If it is possible to "see" matter at all, it

[1] John Dryden, "Mac Flecknoe," *The Works of John Dryden: Poems 1681–1684*, ed. H. T. Swedenberg, Berkeley CA, 1972, p. 54, line 1.
[2] Samuel Johnson, *Lives of the English Poets*, 3 vols., ed. George Birkbeck Hill, New York, 1967, I, p. 391.

1

becomes impossible to see beyond it into larger patterns of organization that keep dissolving when stared at long and hard. Whether considered as a vehicle of perception, an instrument of sexuality, or a part of a larger political structure, the body intrudes as material that can only be managed through language self-consciously, often ironically, and always energetically employed.

Although I am going to confine my argument to the works of two major Augustans, I would like to introduce the dilemma they share with the work of a later figure, one known as the last Augustan. In his *Lives of the English Poets* (1779–81), Johnson was still grappling with the problems that Defoe and Swift clarified so much earlier for their century. I bring in Johnson for a personal reason. In reading the "Life of Dryden," I began thinking about the matter of this book. The farce that informed Dryden's undignified death became for me the point of speculation that has become this book. But in broader terms, the "death" touches upon the themes that dominate the century, concerns about corporeality that Defoe and Swift return to obsessively in their work. Johnson dwells relentlessly on the fact of the body in his *Lives of the English Poets* as he persistently reduces spirit to body, literary aspirations to carcass. His account of the death of Dryden particularly insists upon materiality as it undercuts traditional attempts to transcend the matter at hand.

Dryden's fate points to one Defoe and Swift confront in their fiction: the dilemma of the writer contained by matter that must be controlled. Defoe's most desperate writer, H.F., trying to order the materials of the plague year, becomes subsumed by the pit itself, while Swift's "poet" as well as his self-reflexive hack end up implicated in materials they are unable to order, and resign themselves to emptying their veins into a corporate audience hungry for similes. The story of Dryden's death is a sensational one, what H.F. would call a "speaking sight," a spectacle of the body typical of the eighteenth century, when private fears became public theatre in the street. And the story is a dubious one, an undetermined narrative impossible to ascertain, but equally impossible to ignore. In their assaults on the body, both Defoe and Swift become, at times, ironically indirect, hiding behind anecdotes that trail off, materials that might be false or forged. Just so does Johnson disclaim his "wild story," which comes from "a writer of I know not what credit." But in spite of his skepticism, Johnson tells his story, for it exploits a dilemma he understands too well, the problem of being contained in a body that mortifies spirit and turns ritual into farce.

Johnson particularly attends to the physical fact of Dryden as disorderly material in the way. His very carcass presents an immediate problem of disposal that reproaches the viewer. Although his corpse is put into a velvet hearse, to be accompanied by eighteen mourning coaches, such a display is not enough. "What," cries the drunken Lord Jeffreys, shall Dryden, "the greatest honour and ornament of the nation, be buried after this private manner!" Proposing a spectacular funeral at Westminster Abbey, he falls on his knees to beseech Dryden's widow for the body. Presented with the sight of the nobleman and his company on their knees, she faints away, and when she recovers her speech, cries "No, no!" Jeffreys interprets her words his way: "my Lady is very good, she says, Go, go!" and he carries off the corpse to an undertaker in Cheapside.

If the corporeality of the laureate has not already been made evident, it becomes impossible to deny once removed from its domestic space. To the bewildered undertaker, it becomes a nuisance, for once Lord Jeffreys sobers himself, he disclaims his plan to honor Dryden as the result of a "drunken frolick." While the widow and son remain inconsolable, the body itself, "subject to decay," goes off, becoming so offensive that the undertaker threatens to set the corpse itself before the widow's door.

Friends of Dryden rescue his body, but not his dignity, for after a belated service in the Abbey, Mr. Charles Dryden sends a challenge to Lord Jeffreys, but receives no satisfaction. His Lordship leaves town, leaving Mr. Charles Dryden robbed of the "satisfaction of meeting him, though he sought it till his death with the utmost application." As Farquhar, one of Johnson's sources, suggested, the funeral itself, thwarted duel notwithstanding, was spoiled enough by the mock heroics of the situation: "The quality and mob, farce and heroics; the sublime and ridicule" mix "in a piece."[3]

Johnson confesses that he "once intended to omit" the dubious story, since only in a letter of Farquhar's can he find any evidence of the "tumultuary and confused" circumstances surrounding Dryden's funeral. He includes it nonetheless, adding a nervous speculation about the change of manners for the better. Johnson is talking to himself, I suspect, when he affirms gruffly, one eye on his own posterity, that a young drunken lord of his own age "would be jostled out of the way, and compelled to be quiet" if he dared to violate "the pompous regularity of a magnificent funeral." He would in fact "be sent roughly away, and what is yet more to the honor of the present time, I believe that those who had subscribed to the funeral of a man like Dryden, would not, for such an accident, have withdrawn their contributions." "A man like Dryden," a man "like" Defoe and Swift, Johnson sniffs the air and hopes it has changed, but the idea of the body going off remains. It is an idea that dominates the literature of the century, one expressed frequently in forms that afford some relief in the telling.

The dislocation that Dryden's body inspires, the disorder that Defoe's

[3] Birkbeck Hill notes that Farquhar "ridiculed the mixed ceremony": the pomp of ceremony "was a kind of rhapsody, and fitter, I think, for Hudibras than him." *Ibid.*, I, p. 392.

H.F. declares "*very, very very* dreadful," becomes of necessity articulated. The complicated drama of the missing body, a melodrama turning to farce as rapidly as laureateship turns to mortified material, includes the problem not just of corporeality, but of crowded corporeality in a tragic world that quickly turns bathetic as soon as the grounds of mortality are taken into account.

Dryden going off is not going, at least in the version Johnson supplies, to heaven. He is not even going to Westminster Abbey without a struggle. When Johnson reduces his poet's end to a slightly ridiculous, overfed body, he is not reducing hack to matter (as Dryden himself did to the portly Thomas Shadwell), but cutting down the pretensions to spirit of one of his favourite poets. For Johnson, only Milton and Pope can share the greatness that was Dryden's, and Pope – we learn from Johnson – died of overeating lampreys cooked in a silver saucepan. Such satiric reduction tells much of their subjects, poets all trying to order the demands of the flesh, the call of appetite. That Johnson allows them no out suggests an intransigence that comes with the territory. For the body becomes for Defoe and Swift – and Johnson – material that resists literary transformation and can only be used if it is recognized as all there is, as Mandeville would say, what we "*really are*."[4] With pains the matter of the body can be made literary material, but the transformation is of necessity costly and often ironic, taking account of a metamorphosis that cannot occur without a struggle.

This cost dominates the work of both writers. Swift alludes to it in the notes for his essay on "Maxims Controlled in Ireland." First on his list of "Maxims Examind" is the "*Dearness of things* Necessary to Life" (*PW*, XII, p. 309). His scribbled maxim approaches most economically the problem that the body presented – and still presents. "Dearness" cuts both ways, suggesting expense and esteem, cost and affection. In his complicated sexual strategies, Swift approaches dear things (he frequently addressed Stella and her companion Dingley as "md," my dears) only to run away from the expense of spirit and body they represent. In his larger political struggles, attempting to solve more grossly apparent problems of the poor bodies that fill his Irish tracts, Swift reveals an exasperated desire for riddance – on a grand scale – of the urban problems impossible to ignore. He exposes at the same time his own soul lacerated by a hard, ungiving need that he forces upon his reader. When he, like Defoe, looks

---

[4] Mandeville, *The Fable of the Bees*, ed. Philip Harth, Harmondsworth, 1970, p. 77. Two recent studies dealing with the body examine not so much what we *are*, but more precisely what and how we are *not*. In *The Tremulous Private Body: Essays on Subjection*, London, 1984, Francis Barker argues for the "absence" of the ultimately subjected body in the seventeenth century, while Frederic V. Bogel in *Literature and Insubstantiality in Later Eighteenth Century England*, Princeton, 1984, finds that assertions of materialism mean that we begin in the latter half of the eighteenth-century to fear that we don't really matter. See also Elaine Scarry, *The Body in Pain: The Making and Unmaking of the World*, New York, 1985.

to things "Necessary" to life, by necessity he attempts to pare away at desire that always remains suspect. His final solution, remarkably close to Defoe's, is to run from the problem altogether, hiding out on (nearly) deserted islands.

Defoe, always conscious of the physical burdens of the consuming bodies he imagines, repeatedly makes "dear" his characters' fictional solutions. Like Swift, he calls attention to the expense of an economy that he dreams of managing. Unlike Swift, he enters into the fictional consciousness of characters, particularly feminine characters, whose fortunes invalidate the "necessary" schemes he makes up on the run. Both writers reveal a consciousness of their dilemma, an urgency bordering on despair, and ultimately a dependence upon the literary process itself as a means to clarify, if not solve, their most physical circumstances.

This study will look at three specific ways in which Swift and Defoe, speaking for their age, addressed the problems of the body. Locked into unidealized substance that resists form, the passive receiver of sensation receives information which cannot be ordered. The need to idealize, to perceive providential patterns that would inform matter with meaning, is undercut consistently by the opaque, illusive nature of a reality that resists perception itself. Any meaning must be made by immersion into the matter itself, a process that produces an even more radical uncertainty of expression. Defoe makes the epistemological struggle his subject; Swift makes his assault on the problem his meaning.

The body for both writers takes on larger cultural meanings as it reflects not just problems of personal identity, but problems of sexual connection. Sexuality leads into childbearing and into death, into new "useless mouths," new "burthens in the belly" that cannot be experienced without pain. Both men reflect a fear of sexuality that they attempt to contain through their attempts to order a physical economy. But the problem of sexuality lies in its resistance to order, its irrational assertion of desire over "reason," and yet paradoxically of material over spirit. Both writers are particularly attentive to the problem of feminine sexuality. While seeking ways of containing the appetite in his tracts and in his fiction, Defoe creates characters driven by desire and necessity to express themselves through bodies that eventually betray. Swift's own struggle against appetite drives him to demystify "the sex," while containing it through teasing nursery games that he controls. Sexuality eventually becomes something that one can only run from, as both writers place their male characters on isolated islands to secure them from desire.

Bodies beget bodies, growing in a physical economy difficult to manage, "useless mouths," more material getting in the way. Defoe and Swift address the problem of the city filling up with bodies, proposing in their

tracts and fiction radical solutions to reduce the strain that too many
bodies put on their economy. Defoe looks to the plague itself as a purge
of the body politic, carrying off need with the bodies in the way, while
Defoe and Swift employ the "cannibal" to "eat up" the superfluous
material that implicates them in the struggle against corporeality. The
vision they present is ultimately political, disclosing a keen, often bitter
awareness of the intransigence of materials that may be impossible to
manage. When they create a world in which one bites or is bitten, where
cannibalistic strategies are necessary for severely diminished survival,
they are taking measure of a society dedicated to the consumption not
just of goods, but of flesh, a society crowded with need that will not go
away.

The problem of the body becomes one of the central concerns of the
eighteenth century, dominating the work not just of Defoe and Swift, but
of – to name a few – Smollett and Sterne, Fielding and Richardson,
Boswell and Johnson, Pope and Hogarth, Burney and Thrale. I concentrate here on Defoe and Swift, both writing about the same subject at the
same time, to emphasize the interconnections between two writers often
viewed as dissimilar in their visions. In his study, *The Country and the
City*, Raymond Williams separates the "urbane" and "conventional" Swift
isolated in "polite literature" from a Defoe able to see the "darker reality"
of the "actuality" that was London.[5] The distinction Williams makes may
be too neat. "Polite literature" hardly insulates its writer from reality,
particularly when it is produced with the rude, impolite energy Swift
refuses to repress. Both Swift and Defoe were able to see "darker realities"
of their culture. The problems they encountered every day in the streets,
problems that the gentry might try to ride over in their soft cushioned
chairs, problems that lace and silk couldn't cover up, remained material
that they forced upon their readers. Using as much as possible their
own language, the language of the burthen in the belly, of the offensive
materials in the way, of the cannibal devouring its kind, I would like to
attend to their vision of bodily confinement and bodily need. Both writers
saw, consciously and clearly, material issues of sexuality and poverty that
we still have not yet been able to solve, we moderns equipped with our
own optics, our own conscious language, our own schemes of interpretation. In their insistence upon the materiality of things in their refusal to
idealize that which could not be incorporated into providential patterns
or political structures without a struggle, Defoe and Swift speak loudly
enough to be heard in their own words.

What I propose in this work is a revision of the century's sexual and
political considerations. It is generally agreed that the modern world was
taking on its familiar, alienating form in this period. Notions of com-

[5] Williams, *The Country and the City*, Oxford and New York, 1982, p. 144.

munity were breaking down, religious and political certainties had long given way to nervous assertions of an individualism that separated private from public desires. Both formally and informally, agencies of obligation and responsibility were being reorganized under various pressures that hierarchical, capitalistic, and patriarchal structures exerted upon men and women squeezed by circumstance. What interests me is the degree of *consciousness* that victims and victimizers alike demonstrate of the structures of their changing society. Over and over Swift and Defoe reveal an awareness of the brutal, frightening inequities in their social, sexual, and political system. Awareness, however, would not seem to extend into political analysis that could be separated from a materiality too difficult to transcend or solve. In the work of Defoe and Swift we can see that the problem of *being material* – material resistant to schemes providential and scientific – determined practical and fictional strategies that take on a certain poignant consistency when they are viewed as attempts to work within a condition both confining and decadent. For all things were seen as subject to decay, including schemes to exert authority in both sexual and political economies devised to make use of material that threatened men and women alike. A sense of frustration informs many of the attempts to rationalize, utilize, and eventually get rid of the bodies that bind.

The discourse is neither unreflecting nor uncaring in its expression of an often thwarted desire to overcome a materiality that threatens to become all that there is. By virtue of their energetic exertions, Swift and Defoe achieve a fleeting degree of liberation. In demanding that attention be paid to the dearness of things necessary to our lives, they achieve, in the moment of discourse, grace.

1

Dull organs: the matter of the body in the plague year

'Tis a speaking Sight, says he, and has a Voice with it, and a loud one, to call us all to Repentance; and with that he opened the Door and said, Go, if you will.
A Journal of the Plague Year, p. 61.

He look'd into the Pit again, as he went away, but the Buriers had covered the Bodies so immediately with throwing in Earth, that tho' there was Light enough, for there were Lantherns and Candles in them plac'd all Night round the Sides of the Pit, upon the Heaps of Earth, seven or eight, or perhaps more, yet nothing could be seen. *A Journal of the Plague Year*, p. 62.

One of the central concerns of the *Journal* is epistemological. Defoe's narrator, the curious, skeptical H.F., spends much of his time trying to interpret the phenomenon of the plague year. He addresses problems of perception – how can he see anything at all – and problems of interpretation – how can he understand what he is trying to observe. In his compulsion to make sense of the materials in his way, he demonstrates the problem of his age, the difficulty of reconciling a yearning for large patterns to the resistance the materials themselves bring. H.F. stands as a man of religious faith crossing warily over into the age of enlightenment, a man who consults his bible to plan his course but demonstrates at the same time that providential patterns cannot quite hold the plague in place. His struggle to find meaning in the plague pit itself reveals his difficulty. H.F. as measurer of the pit, seeking enlightenment from the "speaking Sight . . . tho' there was Light enough," can only see so far into material that keeps shifting out of comprehensible shape.

H.F. reflects an uncertainty shared by Defoe's contemporaries, moderns lost in a Lockean world difficult yet necessary to read. Even as he cannot understand the materials of the plague year, H.F. can no more resist its unwieldy matter than Locke's model of the understanding can resist its simple ideas, no more "than a mirror can refuse, alter or obliter-

8

ate the Images or *Ideas*, which, the Objects set before it, do therein produce."[1] While Locke did not insist that the understanding was entirely
passive, he did demand that attention be paid to the difficulty of making
sense out of experience. External sensation might illuminate the understanding as light entering the dark room of understanding through little
windows, but once the "picture" enters the dark room, it may not "stay
there, and lie so orderly as to be found upon occasion" (*Essay Concerning
Human Understanding*, II, xi, 17, p. 163). Instead, the mind "exerts several
acts of its own," combining simple ideas into compound ones, bringing
two ideas together for comparison, and, most dangerously, "separating
them from all other *Ideas* that accompany them in their real existence,"
creating unstable abstractions (*Essay*. II, xii, 1, p. 163). In his attempt to
inquire reasonably into the matter of existence, Locke just as reasonably
dismantled a structure of thought that observers like H.F. depended
upon, and left them with a material world in flux. Pictures once perceived
will not "stay there, and lie so orderly as to be found upon occasion," but
wander in and out of focus. Thought becomes a matter of seeing, while
the soul, possibly, becomes matter itself: "It being, in respect of our
Notions, not much more remote from our Comprehension to conceive,
that GOD can, if he pleases, superadd to Matter a Faculty of Thinking,
than that he should superadd to it another Substance, with a Faculty of
Thinking" (*Essay*, IV, iii, 6, p. 541).

Locke appears not to have experienced the confusion he inspired in
contemporaries who seized upon the radical implications of his ideas. For
him the possibility of error could be avoided as long as the mind could
flood itself with light, for light is "that which discovers to us visible
Objects." The cause of obscurity, on the other hand, "seems to be either
dull Organs; or very slight and transient Impressions made by the
Objects; or else a weakness in the Memory" (II, xxix, 2–3, p. 363). It all
sounds reasonable enough, but for an observer like H.F., obscurity,
rather than clarity, confusion rather than distinct understanding, dominate the experience of the plague year. "Enlightenment," suggests Lester
King in his study of eighteenth-century medical theory, enables us "*to see
things in a clearer light*."[2] Yet seen most clearly in the plague year are the
bodies, opaque material that obscure any meaning larger than their
corporeal presence. "'Twas Mr. Locke," Shaftesbury argued, rejecting his
tutor's philosophy, "that struck at all fundamentals, threw all order and
virtue out of the world, and made the very ideas of these (which are the

[1] John Locke, *An Essay Concerning Human Understanding*, ed. Peter H. Nidditch, Oxford,
1979, II, i, p. 118. I am indebted to John Richetti's *Philosophical Writing: Locke, Berkely,
Hume*, Cambridge MA, 1983; Ernest Tuveson's *Imagination as a Means of Grace*, New York,
1974; and John Yolton's *John Locke and the Way of Ideas*, Oxford, 1968, in this discussion.
[2] *The Road to Medical Enlightenment: 1650–1695*, London, 1970, p. 11.

same as those of God) *unnatural,* and without foundation in our minds."[3]
H.F.'s journal represents such a world fundamentally disordered as it
records his attempts to see with dull organs past and through material
that envelops a most tenuous spiritual reality.

It is difficult to situate Defoe's place in this process. His own ability to
enter into the struggles of his narrators provides him with the tools to
build a "realistic" novel that thrives upon his subjectivity. Yet he hides
behind flawed narrators who protect him from any truth that their narrative might seem to uncover. This is partly, I think, because Defoe is unable
to separate himself from the authorities that his fictions rather unsystematically subvert. The laureate of capitalism entices his readers to celebrate
the exploits of thieves and whores and pirates. Once he has won their
confidence, however, he retreats. In opaque and often undetermined
endings, he abjures whatever truth he has discovered in his fictional
exercise. In the same way, perhaps the most accessible writer of prose
fiction, a plain dealer depending upon the accessibility of his plain style,
creates a narrator frustrated by problems in perception and articulation.
His problems make vivid, concrete, and convincing the "journal" of a
plague year that exists improbably in an imagined-to-be-real history. Just
as he undermines, and then covers over, the flaws in a political and social
system that he is determined to support, in his *Journal* he subverts the
possibility of knowing the *"very, very, very* dreadful" particulars of an
experience that in spite of its obscurity becomes clarified – until he undoes
the clarification. Through it all Defoe manages to jump free of either
position as he doggedly continues to create fictions that *could be* real.

H.F.'s flawed perception becomes the matter of Defoe's text, a record
repeatedly interrupted by the narrator's problems of interpretation. We
can see H.F. attempting to "see things in a clearer light" when he tries to
comprehend the meaning of the great plague pit at Aldgate. Immediately
before recording his visit to the plague pit, H.F. begins to tell the story of
the three men of Wapping, a history which "will be a very good Pattern
for any poor Man to follow," but suddenly, just about ready to deliver an
exemplary moral tale, he breaks off, "having yet, for the present, much
more to say before I quit my own Part." H.F.'s refusal to continue a
moral tale, a pattern that he won't "vouch" for in its particulars (p. 58), is
significant here, introducing a consistent trope in the *Journal.* Over and
over H.F. offers enlightenment only to back away, insisting instead upon
the impossibility of applying patterns to discrete, contradictory particulars, those Lockean pictures that fail to "stay there" and remain orderly.

Taking up his "own part," H.F. leaves his "very good pattern" to run

[3] Tuveson, *Imagination,* pp. 51–2. See also John Dussinger, "'The Lovely System of Lord
Shaftesbury': An Answer to Locke in the Aftermath of 1688?" *Journal of the History of Ideas,*
42, 1 (1981), pp. 151–8.

himself "into apparent Danger" to stare hard into the pit itself, locus of
anxiety in his narrative. "I could not resist my Curiosity to go and see it,"
he explains, as he describes the difficulty he found in taking the measure
of "this dreadful Gulph . . . for such it was rather than a Pit." The qualifi-
cations begin almost immediately. At first it seems "about 40 Foot in
Length, and about 15 or 16 Foot broad; and at the Time I first looked at
it, about nine Foot deep; but it was said, they dug it near 20 Foot deep
afterwards." Once the pit begins to fill with bodies, it changes its dimensions again, for the bodies themselves become part of the pit, part of the
matter that turns into the container itself. By the time H.F. writes his
account, any trace of the pit has vanished, although "there may be some
antient Persons alive in the Parish . . . able to shew even in what Part of
the Church-Yard, the Pit lay, better than I can," for they will be able to
"see" with their memories matter so mutable that even the "Mark" of it
can disappear (pp. 58–60).

In an attempt to understand the nature of the pit, H.F. makes a second
visit, defying a strict order to prevent such investigations, and this time,
he returns in the night:

I was not content to see it in the Day-time, as I had done before; for then there
would have been nothing to have been seen but the loose Earth; for all the Bodies
that were thrown in, were immediately covered with Earth, by those they call'd
the Buryers, which at other Times were call'd Bearers; but I resolv'd to go in the
Night and see some of them thrown in.

The pit is more than loose earth, more than the bodies filling up the hole,
more than the hole itself always changing shape. The pit is the process of
the pit, the bodies falling through mid-air. This insistence upon the kinetic determines much of H.F.'s reporting. Since the plague itself is always
moving, never determined, known only in its erratic outbreaks, the movement itself becomes the account, recorded on the run in cries, screeches,
and wails. Once recorded, however, once fixed, the movement loses its
kinetic significance. "It is impossible to say any Thing," H.F. frequently
reminds his reader, "that is able to give a true Idea of it to those who did
not see it, other than to say this; that it was indeed *very, very, very* dreadful,
and such as no Tongue can express."

The Sexton of the Church-Yard, "a good religious and sensible Man,"
spokesman for a past that Defoe cannot recover, takes a different view
of the powers of the tongue. For him, the pit affords didactic pleasure as
a "speaking Sight." With a Voice, a loud one, "to call us all to Repentance,"
the pit becomes not only comprehensible, but a phenomenon that can be
articulated through metaphor. H.F. is partly responsible for the Sexton's

description of the pit, for when it becomes clear that his own reason for wanting to visit the pit, his "own Curiosity," does not convince the Sexton that he deserves entry, H.F. suggests that "perhaps it might be an Instructing Sight, that might not be without its Uses" (pp. 60–61). His use of litotes and his strategical dependence upon religious topoi to justify a secular motive undercuts whatever moral H.F. is intending to take home from his speaking Sight, but his reason convinces the Sexton to let him through the door.

The sight speaks cryptically. So much local activity intrudes upon the text that the reader, like H.F., is hard pressed to make sense out of such a fleeting sermon. H.F. seems to spend most of his time trying to interpret the actions of an agonized mourner standing at the pit's edge. Is he a poor delirious creature getting ready to throw himself into the pit; is he a person infected and desperate, or a person distempered in mind? Once it is determined that the man has followed his wife and several children, "all in the Cart," his mourning is cut short by the action of the pit itself: "but no sooner was the Cart turned round, and the Bodies shot into the Pit promiscuously, which was a Surprize to him." The mourner swoons and is taken to the Pye-Tavern to recover, but suddenly H.F. shifts his narrative back to the pit:

but the Buriers had covered the Bodies so immediately with throwing in Earth, that tho' there was Light enough, for there were Lantherns and Candles in them, plac'd all Night round the Sides of the Pit, upon the Heaps of Earth, seven or eight, or perhaps more, yet nothing could be seen.   (p. 62)

"Tho' there was light enough," once the bodies stop shooting promiscuously through the air, H.F. can only see "Heaps" of matter, nothing more, nothing less.

The bodies in the plague year, matter impossible to transcend, impossible to ignore, determine H.F.'s text. To explain them at all, he must resort to cliché: they are a "speaking Sight," or later, they are all "huddled together into the common Grave of Mankind . . . Poor and Rich . . . together," but the fact of the bodies remains. "Sixteen or seventeen Bodies . . . some were wrapt up in Linen Sheets, some in Rugs, some little other than naked, or so loose, that the Covering they had, fell from them, in the shooting out of the Cart, and they fell quite naked among the rest." The sight "almost overwhelm[s]" him, sending him away "with my Heart most afflicted and full of the afflicting Thoughts, such as I cannot describe" (pp. 62–3). Although he discloses an inability to describe what he has seen, once he is away from the pit itself, safe from the materials that so disturb him, H.F. can find the language to justify their place in God's plan. At the Pye-Tavern, he tells the blasphemers who taunt and ridicule the mourning man that God has preserved them from the plague so that he might reprove them for their "audacious Boldness" (p. 65). Indeed, when the blasphemers are for their sins, every one of them, "carried into the great Pit," H.F appears relieved that such wickedness should be punished. But particular acts of God's vengeance are rare in this tale, and H.F., after indulging his desire for patterns, "must go back here to the particular Incidents" (pp. 67–9) that complicate his tale.

This return to "the particular" determines the fragmentary nature of a text invaded by sensational incidents. Rodney Baine argues that Defoe was "striving in an age of sensuous epistemology to re-establish the reality of an unseen world."[4] This may be true of the Defoe who wrote his providentially patterned narrative, *The Storm*, and partly true of the Defoe who wrote *Robinson Crusoe*. But the Defoe writing H.F.'s journal removes himself from his narrator's obsession to find truth behind flawed materials. He demonstrates instead a more detached interest in the problem of knowing, a problem that can only be resolved in the act of writing itself which becomes a process of making truth for the moment. In this way he is more like the Defoe of a dissenting childhood who set out to preserve the scriptures from being seized by authorities of the established church. He "worked like a horse, till [he] wrote out the whole Pentateuch" in shorthand, but then gave out, "so tired, I was willing to run the risk of the rest."[5] The Defoe writing the *Journal*, perhaps weary of applying providential patterns to narratives that strain under their weight, is willing to "run the risk" of allowing the stubborn materials to exist as he finds them.

The providence tradition

H.F.'s reluctance to forgo the pleasures of providential allegory stems from an understandable need to organize and idealize the particulars of experience. It cannot be denied that the materials of reality make more sense when they are placed in providential patterns. Even earthquakes have their uses, while rainbows remind us continuously of God's mercy in drying out a drowned world. "I had rather consider the *Rain-bow* as the *Reflection* of God's mercy, then the Sun's Light," claimed Thomas Manningham as he tackled natural philosophy, that "great *Diana* of this *Mechanick* age."[6] The word "rather" tells much, for what mattered is what stood in the way of such preferences, a material world ordered not by God, but by Newton and Locke, and one that resisted spiritual patterns

[4] *Daniel Defoe and the Supernatural*, Athens GA, 1968, p. v.
[5] James Sutherland, *Defoe*, Philadelphia and New York, 1937, p. 15
[6] Michael Hunter, *Science and Society in Restoration England*, Cambridge, 1981, p. 175.

of a more reassuring nature. Not that Newton and Locke insisted upon the implications of their thought. While Newton maintained his own orthodoxy by attacking Locke for being a Hobbist, Locke wrote treatises defending the reasonableness of a Christianity threatened by his doctrine.[7] Less comfortable with dislocation than Newton or Locke, compilers of providential interventions of spirit on to matter resisted disorder with records of the way God could shape his world. Recording providences established the logic of a universe ordered by an intervening God and preserved it from the "particulars" of experience Locke insisted upon.

As Paul Hunter suggests, by the late seventeenth century, the "providence tradition" had taken on a polemical caste both poignant and vigorous. William Turner, "distributing his several hundred stories under 150 headings," records providences because it *"seems to be one of the best Methods that can be pursued, against the abounding* Atheism *of this Age."*[8] Just the idea of 150 separate headings discloses a zeal almost hysterical and suggests that it takes a great many categories indeed to make the materials of experience fit any pattern at all. Of course, the impulse to make things fit bears with it a strain at any period. John Rowe, for instance, in an earlier collection of the revelations of the *Wonderfull hand of God* (1653), recording the collapse of the Paris Garden, is distressed to note not the maiming and killing of hundreds of sinners, but the escape of one transvestite, a "man in womans apparell" who "lay panting for breath" until a fellow actor preserved him. Rowe can only hope that God "hath reserved the great and full recompense for another day and place."[9]

In the late seventeenth century, buttressing faith against materialistic corrosion, the compilers of acts of providence demonstrate an uneasiness difficult, if not impossible, to relieve.[10] H.F. reflects this uneasiness when he tries to apply providential patterns to what confronts him in the street. The "Finger of God" (p. 244) may write across the page of his journal, but it is difficult to read what it leaves behind.[11] Does the plague unite a difficult, disparate people through the fear of death? Yes, H.F. is certain

[7] John Redwood discusses the attacks and counter attacks on Locke and Newton as atheists in *Reason, Ridicule and Religion*, Cambridge, 1976. See also Margaret Jacob, *The Newtonians and the English Revolution*, Ithaca, 1976.

[8] Paul Hunter, *The Reluctant Pilgrim: Defoe's Emblematic Method and Quest for Form in Robinson Crusoe*, Baltimore, 1966, pp. 62–6. See also the "Providence" chapter of Keith Thomas, *Religion and the Decline of Magic*, London, 1971; Louis Landa's introduction to *A Journal of the Plague Year*, pp. xvi–xxiv; and Everett Zimmerman, *Defoe and the Novel*, Berkeley and Los Angeles, 1975, pp. 107–25.

[9] Cited in Russell Fraser, *The War Against Poetry*, Princeton, 1970, pp. 24–5.

[10] See Melvyn New's "'Grease of God': The Form of Eighteenth-Century Fictions," *Publications of the Modern Language Association*, 91, 2 (1976), pp. 235–43.

[11] Max Byrd discusses "our feeling of lost control," in the *Journal* in *London Transformed: Images of the City in the Eighteenth Century*, New Haven, 1978, p. 40.

here, the threat of death brings together Anglican and dissenter alike. "Another Plague Year would reconcile all these Differences," he assures the reader, for "a close conversing with Death, or with Diseases that threaten Death, would scum off the Gall from our Tempers, remove the Animosities among us, and bring us to see with differing Eyes, than those which we look'd on Things with before" (p. 176). But significantly, to receive the gift of vision, we need "another" year, and will always need another year, for once the plague lifted, "the quarrel remain'd" (p. 235). As Homer O. Brown notes, "it is Defoe's insight that the essential characteristic of a symbolic death is that it is only symbolic and must be repeated *endlessly* . . . providence is sight cast forward, into the not yet."[12]

The plague year body itself refuses to be organized, spoiling not just large models of social and aesthetic harmony, but violating in its particularity reasonable expectations of what a body should be "like." In its disfiguration it becomes an emblem of disorder that complicates the search for emblematic form.

Ideally, the body discloses harmonious, divine proportion, matter made in God's image. In his study of the body in Renaissance literature, Leonard Barkan examines the ways the ideal of bodily proportion provided a representational model richly symbolic that could be applied to individual, social and governmental ideals of hierarchy and order. He observes that by the mid-seventeenth century, this idea of proportion had broken down. In spite of the popular adoration of harmonious "nature," by the eighteenth century, the body, unresolved, ill formed, blocks the way to an understanding, let alone an appreciation, of nature regularized.[13] The idealized human frame was breaking down to become fixed in its infirmities. While John Ray, a most generous physico-theologian, extolls "the admirable Art and Wisdom that discovers itself in the make and constitution, the order and disposition, the ends and uses of all the parts and members of this stately fabrick of Heaven and Earth," praising the body for "nothing in it deficient, nothing superfluous, nothing but hath its End and Use,"[14] dissident reports were being filed. H.F., too scrupulous an observer to overlook irregularity, reports the condition of a grieving relation of a plague victim, one so overcome with depression that "by Degrees, his Head sunk into his Body, so between his Shoulders, that the Crown of his Head was very little seen above the Bones of his Shoulders." Losing his voice and his mind, the man can eventually not keep his head erect "unless held up by the Hands of other People" (p. 120), and is unable to lift up his eyes. This almost casually inserted

---

[12] "The Displaced Self in the Novels of Daniel Defoe," *English Literary History*, 38 (1971), p. 579.

[13] *Nature's Work of Art: The Human Body as Image of the World*, New Haven, 1975, p. 280.

[14] Michael Hunter, *Science and Society in Restoration England*, p. 176.

"particular" of the plague year unsettles ideas of providential schemes in an example of circumstantial deformation that defies any pattern it could fit.

In nullius verba: the scientific dilemma

H.F. does not confine his search for order to a strictly religious methodology. Eager to apply secular solutions to material problems, he spends much of his time attempting to discover a scientific structure able to hold the plague in place. But science disappoints whatever expectations it arouses, leaving H.F. as skeptical of the "Doctors'" theories as he is of his own.[15] When he turns to scientific structures to explain his experiences, H.F. becomes a literary virtuoso, a collector of tales and a measurer of the distresses of his times. Careful to explain their flaws, he collects his materials nonetheless, observing circumstances and recording anecdotes, with the idea that the collection will eventually point to a truth. If enough stories are sifted through, something will shake into place: a form, a meaning, a theory. This faith in the knowledge behind matter that sends H.F. to the pit to observe the "speaking Sight" is the faith that sent the naturalists of the Royal Society out into the world to discover new animals and plants that would give up their "meaning" to their collectors. Yet at the time Defoe records the search for patterns, he comes up against the limitations of collecting. Too much unassimilated matter, too many bodies, confront him, swelling his narrative and blunting his point. The experience of the pit itself dissolves, overwhelmed by the materials that quickly cover up what exists only in process.

H.F.'s failure to render meaning from his materials is a casualty of the enlightened scientific method of his and Defoe's time, a method that could prove disappointingly inadequate. When the problem of context loomed large, collecting for its own sake could lead nowhere. In his study of Restoration science, Michael Hunter cautions against taking at face value the programmatic visions of the New Science. Baconianism, for

---

[15] Walter G. Bell, *The Great Plague in London in 1665*, London, 1951; Charles F. Mullett, *The Bubonic Plague and England*, Lexington KY, 1956; and J. F. D. Shrewsbury, *A History of Bubonic Plague in the British Isles*, Cambridge, 1970, all emphasize the puzzling nature of the plague's eventual disappearance. However, William McNeill, in *Plagues and Peoples*, Garden City NY, 1976, suggests that although "reason" did not cause solutions to the plague itself, a belief in reason brought about, eventually, reasonable solutions. Guy Williams supplies perhaps the most lurid indictment of the medical and scientific progress of the century in *The Age of Agony: the Art of Healing*, London, 1975, but his anecdotes are repeated by John McManners, Lester King, Richard Schwartz, Joseph Levine, Michael Hunter, and Richard Shryock in their discussions of enlightened conditions. For a more positive estimation of eighteenth-century conditions, see E. M. Sigsworth, "Gateways to Death? Medicine, Hospitals and Mortality, 1700–1850," in *Science and Society, 1600–1900*, ed. Peter Mathias, Cambridge, 1972, pp. 97–110.

instance, could inspire random collecting "in subjects where it was uncon-
structive enabling those lacking in imagination to make a virtue of their
abstention from philosophical speculation." Neutral empiricism could
replace rationalism while displacing the idea of meaning.[16] Even when a
collector of facts and matter worked according to plan, the theory might
not fit the material. Dr. John Woodward, a model collector in the empirical vein, amassed pieces of antiquary and fossils assiduously for his and
God's ends, wanting only to certify the historical reality of a forged shield
he believed authentic and to prove the certainty of God's influence
expressed in the fossils of fish found upon the mountain tops. But in both
instances, his theories failed to serve materials that remained, ultimately,
unassimilated. As Joseph Levine suggests in his evocative study of Dr.
Woodward's famous shield, there were "not enough comparable objects
yet to be seen."[17]

Optics: dull organs writ large

The problem was not just one of context, but of perception itself. Optical
improvements promised new possibilities, better ways of looking at matter. Addison praised the microscope for revealing a sublime world that
reflected an immense, magnificent nature while populizers like Henry
Baker and George Adams assured their readers that "the more we
enquire into nature, the more excellent she appears." John Hill went so
far as to predict that the microscope could render "the whole life one
continual act of adoration."[18] The adoration was not only enthusiastic,
but premature. Early microscopes led observers to construct elaborate
theories from incomplete evidence supporting hypotheses that would
actually contradict their findings. Scientists were confronting two separate problems at the same time: how to see correctly through a lens subject
to an average distortion of 19 percent and how to interpret what met the
eye. As Locke warned, discounting the benefits of both microscopic and
anatomical investigation, "though we cut into the inside, we [still] see but
the outside of things and make but a new superficies to stare at."[19] Such
sensible skepticism deflates the visionary component of the new science,
the desire to explicate matter itself.

[16] Michael Hunter, *Science and Society in Restoration England*, p. 17.
[17] Joseph Levine, *Dr. Woodward's Shield: History, Science, and Satire in Augustan England*,
Berkeley and Los Angeles, 1977, p. 287. Levine discusses the great race to discover new
species of plants and animals, p. 49.
[18] William Powell Jones, *The Rhetoric of Science*, Berkeley and Los Angeles, 1966, pp. 16–17.
See also Marjorie Nicolson's classic *The Microscope and English Imagination*, Smith College
Studies in Modern Language, XVI, 1934–35.
[19] Stanley Joel Reiser, *Medicine and the Reign of Technology*, Cambridge, 1978, pp. 72–6;
Richard H. Shryock, *Medicine and Society in America: 1660–1860*, New York, 1960, p. 52.

Trapped on the superficies of things, no matter how refined through optical distortion, the scientific visionary depended ultimately upon intuition and common sense. Harvey's well-known recognition of the heart's function, a discovery possible only when the hydraulic pump could demonstrate its function, illustrates the fundamental problem of perception. Before Harvey and his pump, the heart resisted penetration to remain just another opaque surface to stare at. Harvey's intuition animated the indecipherable material, but what of the less informed, or perhaps more wildly imaginative observers of the same phenomenon? As late as the end of the eighteenth century, a medical lecturer informed his class that "they could see anything they fancied in the objects examined through the microscope . . . microscopic anatomy was essentially based on imagination." The field was open for speculation.[20] Lenses that could both extend and distort the powers of observation allowed great room for error as well as for improvement.

A later scientific observer, Samuel Johnson, would exploit the problem of perception in *Rasselas* where he endowed his mad astronomer with acute vision and a hyperactive imagination larger than his field of vision. No less skeptical, H.F. seems to distrust what help a microscope would bring to the problem of knowing the plague. He hears only that plague breath condensed on a piece of glass might be observed under the microscope to shelter "strange monstrous and frightful Shapes, such as Dragons, Snakes, Serpents, and Devils, horrible to behold." H.F. questions the truth of this assertion, but still it remains a questionable truth expressed, one more fact to be absorbed into the narrative. Such imaginative leaps fall flat into the matter of things, for as H.F. direly suggests, the real problem of perception was not to recognize dragons and devils, but to be able to distinguish the sick from the well. Insisting here that we consider the plague as arising from natural causes, H.F. resorts to a most whimsically empirical solution to the problem of knowing the sick. His friend Dr. Heath was of the "Opinion, that it might be known by the smell of their Breath; but then, *as he said*, who durst Smell to that Breath for his Information? Since to know it, he must draw the Stench of the Plague up into his own Brain, in order to distinguish the Smell!" The absurdity of such a solution characterizes those times when H.F. employs science only to undermine it. Displaying a skepticism as profound as the motto of the Royal Society, although he is only an average man, an everyman more accustomed to trade than speculation, H.F. takes the word of no one. Monsters under glass? "But this I very much question the Truth of" (p. 203), he insists, and in these perilous times, he asserts his knowledge to be the equal of his scientific betters. How long might men have the seeds of contagion within them before they discover their fatal presence:

[20] Reiser, *Medicine and the Reign of Technology*, p. 74.

"I believe the most experienc'd Physicians cannot answer this Question directly, any more than I can; and something an ordinary Observer may take notice of, which may pass their Observation" (p. 197). Interrupting a "great" and "grave" debate "among our Physicians," H.F. sounds almost peevish: "I choose to give this grave Debate a quite different turn, and answer it or resolve it all by saying, *That I do not grant the Fact*" (p. 154).

Scrupulously attending to evidence, even if it kills you, H.F. refuses to give way to easy observations. Defoe the projector, although hard headed, offers clearer solutions to problems of a world in need of correction. But Defoe the writer of novels often presents a world that can only be managed through fantastic solutions that strain the most credulous readers: shipwrecked boats loaded with tools providentially provided for Crusoe's use, husbands and governesses lying in wait to rescue Moll from her misfortunes, wives turned whores turned slaves ready to care for their master/husband, the fortunate Colonel Jack. *A Journal of the Plague Year* straddles the gap between the recalcitrant materials of real life and the flexible conventions of a fiction being made up on the run. Perhaps it is because the plague year existed in history and also threatened to recur. Whether informed by Defoe's fears of the Marseilles plague, or inspired by cultural memories of London's own earlier devastation, Defoe's text emphasizes the material, unavoidable circumstances of a plague breath that kills. While scientific modes of discovery allow no truth and providential patterns cannot be extended, H.F. leaves us with these "particulars," the substance of his text.

He also leaves us with material itself. For H.F. addresses two problems in his journal, the problem of seeing past matter and the problem of being matter, mere material for the pit. By examining closely the matter that confines him to the pit, by measuring the limitations of his dull organs, the obstructions of the physical world, H.F. confronts matter that cannot be transcended or transformed. But in depicting H.F.'s struggle, Defoe exposes the form H.F. wants to exert on his stubborn materials. If body cannot be avoided or transcended, it can become nonetheless material for text, the material of spectacle, and in that process, a speaking sight after all, however qualified. In his delineation of H.F.'s struggle with his materials, Defoe finds, eventually, a way to exert form.

The urban body in the City of the Dead

The Distemper sweeping away such Multitudes, as I have observ'd, many, if not all the out Parishes were oblig'd to make new burying Grounds . . . the dead Bodies were disturb'd, abus'd, dug up again, some even before the Flesh of them

was perished from the Bones, and remov'd like Dung or Rubbish to other
Places. . .
There was a piece of Ground in *Moorfields*, by the going into the Street which is
now call'd *Old Bethlem*, which was enlarg'd much, tho' not wholly taken in on the
same occasion. N.B. The Author of this Journal, lyes buried in that very Ground,
being at his own Desire, his Sister having been buried there a few Years before.
(pp. 231–3)

The anxiety that fills H.F.'s account of the bodies blocking the way, the
sense of dislocation he exploits in telling grisly tales of bodies not only
shooting into the pit, but bodies disinterred, reflects a more general concern over the primacy of matter. All the while H.F. seeks order, he is
blocked by the bodies dying in heaps, filling the pits, "remov'd like Dung
or Rubbish." It is not just that the bodies represent fictional materials
that cannot be ordered. The bodies come to represent matter itself that
threatens to subsume reader and writer alike. We learn with some uneasiness that H.F., our narrator, also lies buried in unquiet ground, one more
dead body, not just a *memento mori*, but an irreducible material fact. Swift
would have appreciated the irony of his resting place, Bedlam, proper
ground for hack writers. That Defoe chooses such an evocative location
for H.F.'s grave, one that not only calls up threats of urban madness, but
intimates a life after death filled with disturbance, abuse, and disgrace,
indicates the great degree of fear corporeality could inspire as well as an
acute awareness of the special problems of the urban body seeking rest.
And it suggests that for Defoe, as for many of his contemporaries, the
body was presenting itself as material that could not be transformed,
could not go away, and, particularly in the city, would remain to intrude
upon civilized attempts to contain it.

   H.F.'s report of the disinterred bodies interrupts his description of
a relatively plague-free London. While the people return to a London
strangely altered, "some whole Families were so entirely swept away that
there was no Remembrance of them left" (p. 230), the bodies remain,
constantly increasing in numbers that must be dealt with. To manage the
great numbers, the authorities were obliged to create new burial grounds,
some which continued in use, and some which were converted after the
plague ended. Enumerating some of these deconsecrated grounds (one
is made into a hog yard), H.F. pays particular attention to one converted
into the foundation of Sir Robert Clayton's new house. When the ground
was opened, the bodies remained so plain to be seen "that the Womens
Sculls were distinguish'd by their long Hair, and of others, the Flesh was
not quite perished." The people "exclaim loudly" against such a sight,
fearing a return of the contagion, fearing mortality itself, and "the Bones
and Bodies, as fast as they came at them, were carried to another part of
the same Ground, and thrown all together into a deep Pit" (pp. 232–3).

The speed of the narrative reflects the unseemly haste of the procedure, and takes the reader back to H.F.'s night time visit to the great pit with its grisly account of bodies shooting promiscuously into their mass grave. This time, however, H.F.'s account is being edited by another person disturbingly anonymous, while H.F. himself has become part of the pit he was trying to comprehend.

Defoe's editorial interruption insisting upon H.F.'s own rotting state not only disturbs his reader's sense of fictional coherence, but reveals a contemporary fear of the dead body itself, particularly the urban body, and the way it could threaten the living. In the worst days of the plague, H.F. reports, people crowded into the churches "inquiring no more into who they sat near to, or far from what offensive Smells they met with, or what condition the People seemed to be in, but looking upon themselves all as so many dead corpses," huddled together "as if their Lives were of no Consequences" (p. 175). It is commonplace enough to regard the living as corpses "not yet" incorporated into providential patterns past comprehension, but in the plague year, the idea refuses to resonate with Christian, homiletic comfort. The reduction to body does not necessarily lead to heaven, save in the nervous clichés H.F. employs to gloss over the bodies at hand. Sixteen or seventeen, does it matter, bodies shoot out of the dead cart to fall naked among the rest, "but the Matter was not much to them, or the Indecency much to any one else, seeing they were all dead, and were to be huddled together into the common Grave of Mankind, as we may call it" (p. 62).

Theoretically, the fortunes of the dead body, that husk shed by a soul joyfully free of its burden, should not disturb the true Christian preparing for heaven. But in practice "the people began to exclaim loudly" against intimations of a mortality that might extend beyond the grave itself. Christian contempt for the body was giving way to a secular concern for the fate of the bodily container. It would be convenient here to expound on the many "death" studies that suggest that the eighteenth century exhibited startling, suggestive differences in its rituals of burial and mourning that point to the undeniable significance of the body itself, material that blocks transcendence, material that one attempted to order, reduce, annihilate. Both Philippe Ariès and David Stannard, for instance, point to what they consider a peculiarly English indifference to the body in the seventeenth century, a contempt they connect to a Puritan "contempt" for the body itself. This indifference, they argue, is changing by Defoe's time as the body is seen as more problematic, less easy to "shed." Robert Bolton characteristically relishes the mortification of a body we should be happy to lose:

an horrour to all that behold it; a most loathsome and abhorred spectacle . . .
Down it must into a pit of carions and confusion, covered with wormes, not able
to wag so much as a little finger, to remoove the vermine that feed and gnaw
upon its flesh, and so moulder away into rottenesse and dust . . . when the soule
departs this life, it carries nothing away with it, but grace, God's favour, and a
good conscience.

Perhaps it is the little finger not able to wag, but this passage suggests
to me a nervous denial of a body all too dear. The Puritan directives
establishing official contempt for the dead body expressed in the *Directory
for the Publique Worship of God* ordered that "when any person departeth
this life, let the dead body, upon the day of Buriall, be decently attended
from the house to the place appointed for publique Buriall and there
immediately interred without any ceremony."[21] Such indifference demonstrated towards the moldering corpse was meant to reflect a spiritual
confidence supposed to characterize Puritan reformers, who could shed
their carcasses willingly into a pit of carrion and confusion because they
could spare them. But directives enforcing austerity can also suggest an
ambivalence that must be altered, a need to apply faith rather than a state
of faith.

Even in such spare times, not every one was so sanguine. John Weever
complained bitterly of the paltry, "silent burials" conducted in the night
with "a Torch, a two penie Linke, and a Lanterne." Foreign observers
openly mocked the state of funereal affairs. "The Burials now among
the Reformed in England, are in a manner prophane," wrote Monsieur
Strange in the 1640s, "in many places the dead being throwne into the
ground like dogs, and not a word said." Pierre Muret remarked upon the
unindividuated quality of the burials: "To look at these tombs, it would
appear that the carcass of a pig or an ass was to be buried, and not a
human body." Dryden, bearing little sympathy for Puritan reformers,
suggested that the official contempt for the body disguised profane, punitive revels, "While to excess on Martyrs' tombs they drink," while another
critic complained that "among our people it makes no difference whether
we are buried in a cemetery or in the place where asses are flayed."[22]

The discourse surrounding death can never be entirely clear, and certainly never entirely rational. In his study of death in the Enlightenment,
John McManners cautions against learning "the secrets of the heart from
the more obvious external evidence. In facing death we cling to rituals,
observances, and folkways, not necessarily because we are committed to
their significance, but simply to keep despair at bay, to occupy the empty

---

[21] David Stannard, *The Puritan Way of Death*, Oxford, 1977, pp. 100–1.

[22] *Ibid.*, pp. 105–6. "Absolom and Achitophel, " *Works: Poems 1649–1680*, ed. E. N. Hooker
and H. T. Swedenberg, Berkeley and Los Angeles CA, 1961, p. 27, line 186.

and defeated mind. We set up monuments, however incongruous, because no other way is left to show our affection or pride."[23] The body, and particularly the dead body, so disturbing to all of us living, offers possibilities for interpretations that vary according to our needs. While a study of differing attitudes remains helpful, the utopian desire for a "good," "easy," or "manageable" death reveals as much about our own fears as it suggests about the nature of a comprehensible historical reality. Hamlet handling the skull of Yorick, Ben Jonson trying to come to terms with the death of his first son, Nashe attempting to order the random movements of the plague through verses that insist upon transience rather than transcendence, Milton interpreting the visit of his long dead wife, all remind us that death has never been neatly appropriated. The *Iliad* and *Antigone* demonstrate just how long the dead body has contained powerful and conflicting meaning for western culture.[24]

But in spite of cautions, some things are clearer than others, and I would like to attend to a particular aspect of the discourse on death that tells much about Defoe's and Swift's treatment of their own mortal selves. Eighteenth-century critics of the English way of death appear to be most concerned about the disorder the graveyard itself represents. Their sense of outrage is relatively new, a revulsion over a commonplace sight that has only recently become intolerable. For the graveyards had never been particularly orderly. Hamlet had no trouble finding a skull to meditate upon; parts of the body litter the graveyard, each one a potential Alexander settling into loam at last to stop up a bunghole. But in the seventeenth and eighteenth centuries the disorder of the graveyard itself becomes not just an occasion for meditations on death, but an occasion for meditations upon the uncertainty of the urban body subject to the irregular, overcrowded conditions that prevent possibilities for human dignity in life and in death.

Such cultural uneasiness can partly be explained by a growing awareness of the cost of being a body, quick or dead, in the eighteenth century. Graveyards were disorderly because graveyards, grossly overcrowded, extruding unseemly contents for the viewer's consideration, reflected an urban mass too obvious to ignore. It is appropriate that Defoe's dead bodies fill London plague pits, for in reality, Defoe's London was filling up with dead bodies. The city, growing irregularly, almost illogically, incorporated its new arrivals to feed its expansion. As the city itself expanded, its death rate notoriously exceeded its birth rate, and its cemeteries reflected the demograpic strain. In 1747, the burial yard of St.

---

[23] *Death and the Enlightenment*, Oxford, 1981, p. 2.

[24] Recent literary studies of death and its meaning include Arnold Stein, *The House of Death: Messages from the English Renaissance*, Baltimore and London, 1986 and Garrett Stewart, *Death Sentences: Styles of Dying in British Fiction*, Cambridge MA and London, 1984.

Andrews in Holborn (a parish where the death rate exceeded the birth rate), was so full of corpses "that it was difficult to dig out a grave without digging up some part of a corpse not yet decayed.'[25] The dislocation that H.F. calls up when he points to the disinterred bodies that need to be removed as fast as they are uncovered reflects the urban fear of being absorbed into material number that blocks the possibilities of both individual and communal escape. When mortal material overcrowds sacred ground, becoming matter disconnected from community, from family, from self, moving from the church yard itself into the public space, that material undercuts the chances for comfort that the church itself might once have offered.

Not just numbers, but conditions alarmed observers. In both England and France, open graves and scattered bones became matter for scandalized discourse, while conditions that had been considered typical were now deemed intolerable, "offensive to the dignity of man." Whose dignity is worth considering. To the devout, the sight of a skull should be didactically pleasing, offering one of H.F.'s speaking sights with a sermon in it. If we can discard the mortal husk on our way towards eternity, what signifies the bodily remains, of no more consequence than "the carcass of a pig or an ass." But in the eighteenth century, the dead body was seen as not just offensive to human dignity, but as dangerous to human health, waging what Voltaire called "the war of the dead against the living."[26]

Mortal warfare

When Voltaire objects to the dangerous properties of the corpse, he is articulating the modern fear of contagion that dominates eighteenth-century medical discourse. Dead bodies, viewed for centuries as natural representations of the progress of life into death, suddenly signify all

---

[25] Leslie Clarkson, *Death, Disease and Famine in Pre-Industrial England*, Dublin, 1975, p. 160. Fifty years later Thomas Pennant was still complaining about the threat of dead bodies. He reports that in the churchyard at St. Giles in the Fields, "I have observed with horror a great square pit, with many rows of coffins, piled one of the other, all exposed to sight and smell." *Of London*, London, 1790, cited in George Walker, *Gatherings from Grave Yards*, London, 1839, reprinted New York, 1977, p. 162. For discussions of the dangerously expanding city, see E. A. Wrigley, *Population and History*, London, 1969; Jack Lindsay, *The Monster City: Defoe's London, 1688–1730*, New York, 1978; M. Dorothy George, *London Life in the Eighteenth Century*, Harmondsworth, 1966, pp. 35–72; Peter Earle, *The World of Defoe*, New York, 1977; and George Rosen, "A Slaughter of Innocents: Aspects of Child Health in the Eighteenth-Century City." *Studies in Eighteenth-Century Culture*, 5 (1976), 293–316.

[26] McManners, *Death and the Enlightenment*, p. 307. See also Philippe Ariès, *The Hour of Our Death*, trans. Helen Weaver, New York, 1982, on the condition of the cemetery, pp. 315–21, 348–52. In his introduction to *Mirrors of Mortality: Studies in the Social History of Death*, New York, 1981, Joachim Whaley discusses the "problems involved in approaching Ariès' work," p. 5.

the lethal qualities of an increasingly complicated urban existence that inhibits, even prohibits, health. In 1721, the year that Defoe was writing *The Journal of the Plague Year*, Thomas Lewis argued most eloquently against the dangerous practice of churchyard burials. *Seasonable Considerations on the Indecent and Dangerous Custom of Burying in Churches and Church Yards* enumerates the ways in which the dead can pollute the living. Since every person has the "Law of Death and Power of Corruption in his Body," the danger of infection becomes greatest "when Corruption proceeds from DEAD BODIES, when the Corruption is at the highest, and fatal." The effluvia from the dead, which "naturally tend to destroy the life of others," possess a moral as well as physical quality. Infected by the effluvia, the spirit, as well as the body, "is scared, starts back, and hides itself, but strikes a Terror on the Imagination, which constantly works, and too often falls under the Burden of the Apprehension, and by fearing of the Danger falls into Danger." This is the reason that the timid fall before the bold in an epidemic, "easy prey" – because of their sensibility – "to the Contagion."

While making specific connections between body and spirit, health and disease, Lewis hints indirectly at the real reason that the dead body inspired uneasiness; it depressed a spirit all too sensitive to its presence. Lewis particularly fears the threat of the "great Numbers" of bodies "buried promiscuously of all Sorts of Distempers, and many in such Coffins as hardly hold together." His urban fear of mixture parallels H.F.'s own horror at seeing naked bodies shoot "promiscuously" into the pit, turning upon impact into heaps impossible to differentiate, yet remaining matter that will not be resolved.[27]

Lewis' fear is neither excessive nor especially "English." In his study of the French cemetery, Richard Etlin observes the shift in the eighteenth century from sacred to secular space, suggesting that urban reformers "no longer savoured the horror of putrefaction," nor sought the sanctity of church ground, but instead "betrayed a desire to banish the image of death from view rather than to live with it in the intimacy of the city." Enlightened city planners demonstrated this new sensibility when they systematically replaced old religious values with "a profound concern with public hygiene." The sacred value of cemeteries fell before more practical considerations of their contagious, infected, corrupted nature. While decomposing bodies became matter to inspire horror rather than reverence, fearful materials that could cause disease and death, death

[27] Thomas Lewis, *Seasonable Considerations on the Indecent and Dangerous Custom of Burying in Churches and Church Yards*, London, 1721, pp. 49–58. Lewis' fears prove particularly interesting in light of Mary Douglas' study of pollution and taboo, *Purity and Danger*, London, 1966; and George Bataille's *Death and Sensuality: a Study of Eroticism and the Taboo* (1962), Salem NH, 1984.

itself was seen as a threat that could sully the purity of the church. The "horrid spectacles" of coffins, decomposing corpses, and skeletons, were to be removed from sight to protect the heightened sensibilities of the viewers.[28]

Etlin's careful attention to cemetery architecture and public statements about hygiene makes a convincing argument that almost withstands the paradox of the corporeal nature of the French revolution. For all the while that the discourse on the dangers of the body advocated removal of the offensive objects, social practice demanded a more dramatic relocation of corporeal matter. The body, *because* of its fearful properties, had its uses. The architects of the revolution, far from hiding the body, exploited it as material for horrid spectacle, providing entertainment fit for a revolution founded on the most enlightened of principles. In both England and France, while the dead body offended enlightened sensibility, it remained at the same time offensively visible, a fetish of mortality.

Public executions demonstrate most sensationally the state's asserting its abstract will over corporeal matter.[29] Executions were defended for their didactic content, for they would not only "prevent the criminal from repeating his crime," but would make use of the criminal as "an example to restrain others," part of "an impressive display including every circumstance which can strike fear into the people." An estimated 40,000, including 2,000 children, crowded together at Montpellier in 1746 to witness the hanging of a Protestant pastor, while 6,000 gathered at Valence to see a smuggler broken on the wheel; "they had poured in from fifteen leagues radius all round, and paid 12 sous each for places on platforms around the square erected by enterprising householders." The *canaille*, Voltaire observed, "rush to these spectacles as they do to a sermon, because they get in without paying." Waiting sometimes for hours to watch "the drama unfold," for "the routines of the scaffold were susceptible to variations," crowds witnessing the hundreds of executions in the century bear witness to a fascination with the body on the most primitive and fundamental level.

Mass interest in tortured, mutilated, eventually motionless bodies was explained by contemporaries as the natural result of "curiosity." Just as H.F.'s "curiosity" – interpreted by the churchyard sexton as a thirst for moral instruction – drives him to the plague pit, curiosity drives the mob, the *canaille* (as well as the better sort who pay for their seats), to the scaffold. Marivaux claimed that people crowding around the wheel and the gallows were not there "to rejoice at cruelty or to mock at pain: they

---

[28] *The Architecture of Death: The Transformation of the Cemetery in Eighteenth-Century Paris*, Cambridge MA, 1984, pp. 6, 12, 17.

[29] See McManners, *Death and the Enlightenment*, pp. 368–408.

are simply in their stupid, cruel fashion, curious" to experience "the surge of powerful emotions, to weep with sympathy and tremble with alarm." The execution becomes theatre, the body becomes public property, material manipulated to engage mass sympathy. Mme. Roland, who would later experience the "curiosité secrète et sanguinaire" of the crowd, suspected that the human imagination needed to be provided with "powerful impressions" that sharpen a "keener consciousness of our existance."[30]

This idea of body made into spectacle informs English as well as French methods of punishment. Defoe notoriously managed his own exhibition, emerging from his hours in the pillory not only unscathed but covered in floral tributes to his courage. Swift, a collector of the "last words" of condemned criminals, reveals an undisguised "curiosité . . . sanguinaire" in the terrible days following the assassination attempt upon Harley. He wants the villain Guiscard to be hanged in chains, and expresses outrage that the would-be assassin died before being executed. Guiscard's public exhibition – the public could pay two pence to pass by his pickled corpse – only mildly gratified Swift's hunger for a more dramatic use of the body. But then, he lived at a time when the sight-seer could rent a telescope for pennies to stare at the heads of traitors rotting on pikes. The mad inmates at Bedlam provided a different sort of sport to a public willing to pay for its pleasures. The executions to Tyburn were free, unless the viewer purchased a copy of the "Life" of the body about to be executed.[31]

The crowds thronging around the gallows at Tyburn granted the body of the felon palpable significance, turning it into matter that reified the power of the occasion. And while the authorities exerted its will on flesh, the crowd responded to their actions by subverting official gestures to meet local needs – in rioting. In his study of the Tyburn riots against the Surgeons, Peter Linebaugh analyzes the idea behind the public occasions when the friends and relatives of the condemned met to resist the authorities claiming ownership over the dead bodies for purposes of dissection. As property of the state, the executed bodies could be claimed for the public good. Linebaugh suggests that by the eighteenth century the corpse had become a commodity with symbolic as well as economic value. As body to be dissected, it remained something to be used, material to be opened for scientific, utilitarian purposes. But in cutting up the felonious body, the Royal Surgeons were not only pursuing a disinterested scientific

---

[30] *Ibid.*, pp. 385–91. In *Crowds and Power*, trans. Carol Stewart, Harmondsworth, 1981, Elias Canetti argues that "all forms of public execution are connected with the old practice of collective killing. The real executioner is the crowd gathered round the scaffold" that approves and desires the spectacle (p. 57).

[31] *JS*, I, pp. 217, 224; Richard B. Schwartz, *Daily Life in Johnson's London*, Madison WI, 1983, p. 86.

investigation, but dishonoring the body itself and the "scum" the body represented.

Paradoxically, official dishonor sanctified the felonious public body, object of the crowd's desire for superstitious spectacle. The corpse of the hanged felon was thought capable of curing skin ailments, restoring withered limbs, reducing swellings, soothing the toothache, healing the goitre, drying up ulcers, and making sterile women fertile. At Dr. Dodd's hanging "a very decently dresed young woman went up to the gallows in order to have a Wen in her face stroked by the Doctor's hand," and as late as 1789, the traveler Meister recounts the tableau of a young woman "with an appearance of beauty all pale and trembling: submit to 'have her bosom uncovered in the presence of thousands of spectators, and the dead man's hand placed upon it." Superstition died hard in the age of Enlightenment, or perhaps it just changed course. In these ritualistic exchanges, the crowd appears to transform a place of great social dislocation into communal space. It is particularly appropriate that Dr. Dodd, author of many pamphlets on the prolongation of life, should officiate as the dispenser of his own bodily powers. As the Prussian traveler Archenholtz observed when Dodd mounted the scaffold, "the English know how to die.'[32]

The power of the corpse extended beyond the scaffold itself. The faithful collected chips from the gallows to place in a bag worn round the neck and bound pieces of the hanging halter around the temple to cure the headache. The bones themselves possessed a significance that the Royal College of Surgeons in Lincoln's Inn Fields still exploits by exhibiting Jonathan Wild's skeleton under glass. Wild, the thief taker celebrated by Defoe, Fielding and Gay, becomes another speaking sight, matter for instruction and delight. His body could be hanged, dissected and displayed because it incorporates so completely the impossibility of transcendence. Wild's skeleton announces that the thief catcher is finally fixed once and for all. This notion of apprehension dominates the public handling of the private body, material that can be elevated onto a scaffold to serve the curiosity of the crowd. In his final engraving of "The Reward of Cruelty," Hogarth captures just this sense of bodily containment. A condemned corpse, entrails spewing forth to be chewed upon by the same sort of dog the villain used to torture, starts up, aided by a pulley, appearing animated by a pain that he shouldn't be feeling. His anatomizers, his audience, seem amused by his struggle as they observe his soul

[32] Peter Linebaugh, "The Tyburn Riots Against the Surgeons," in *Albion's Fatal Tree: Crime and Society in Eighteenth-Century England*, ed. Douglas Hay, New York, 1975, pp. 65–117. See also Michel Foucault, "The Spectacle of the Scaffold," *Discipline and Punish: The Birth of the Prison*, trans. Alan Sheridan, New York, 1979, pp. 32–72. Archenholtz's praise of English stoicism is cited in W. Jackson Bate, *Samuel Johnson*, New York and London, 1977, p. 524.

straining to escape its mutilated body, a soul trapped in its corporeality. The sight is, H.F. would agree, "*very, very, very* dreadful," a speaking sight with a voice in it, and one that H.F. forces over and over on his reader.

Complicated distress

I could dwell a great while upon the Calamities of this dreadful time, and go on to describe the Objects that appear'd among us every Day, the dreadful Extravagancies which the Distraction of sick People drove them into; how the Streets began now to be fuller of frightful Objects, and Families to be made even a Terror to themselves: But after I have told you, as I have above, that One Man being tyed in his Bed, and finding no other Way to deliver himself, set the Bed on fire with his Candle, which unhappily stood within his reach, and Burnt himself in his Bed. And how another, by the insufferable Torment he bore, danced and sang naked in the Streets, not knowing one Extasie from another, I say, after I have mention'd these Things, What can be added more? What can be said to represent the Misery of these Times, more lively to the Reader, or to give him a more perfect idea of a complicated Distress?   (*JPY*, pp. 176–7)

When H.F. attempts to tell his story "to represent the Misery of these Times," when he tries to give his reader "a more perfect idea of a complicated Distress," he acknowledges his limitation – how can he see what is going on, and seeing what he does, how can he articulate perceived distress. In the course of his tale, he grows to exploit those limitations. For Defoe turns H.F.'s struggle with his materials into spectacle, creating in the process a speaking sight. Just as public executions become occasions for "feeling" and arenas for the exercising of a sympathy as dubious as it was necessary, so H.F.'s public record of the plague year exploits the possibilities for sympathy by employing sensational materials that by themselves exhaust reader and teller alike.

H.F. faces several problems in telling his tale. Blocked by bodies that impede his narrative, he must awaken sympathy for these bodies in a reader who tires quickly. Perhaps we are all only capable of so much attention to so much suffering. Defoe addresses an audience that Mandeville less politely judges hardened, one that Swift will taunt and threaten.[33] Less authoritarian, more accustomed to double-dealing in necessary disguises, Defoe entraps his reader in materials neither of them can escape. He forms in the process an indeterminate narrative that distorts chronological and logical expectations. Faced with stories that won't fit together, matter that cannot be resolved, he holds his reader in his own dilemma. And as Tyburn hangings take place in the open air, most of his own literary executions take place on the street.

The private, obsessively subjective nature of H.F.'s narrative has been

---

[33] This subject will be considered at length below in chapters 7 and 8.

often noted. But I would like to concentrate on its public nature, its insistence upon the open spectacle of the suffering at hand. Defoe denies his public's need to avoid the body by blocking the narrative itself with corporeal material that won't go away easily. The bodies usually intrude just when H.F. most delights in demonstrating the ways the plague was "managed." Just as the singularly traumatizing footprint devastates Crusoe's pleasures of enumerating the treasures of his storehold, singular bodies, individuated yet massed together, disrupt H.F.'s orderly discussion of the ways that the market place accommodated threats of contagion. Happily counting up the pots of vinegar and vials of scents the buyers and sellers employed to protect themselves from contagion and apparently in control of his narration, H.F. suddenly begins to number the innumerable "dismal Stories we heard every Day" of bodies, out of control, dropping down dead in the market place. They literally take over the narration:

These objects were so frequent in the Streets, that when the plague came to be very raging, one Side, there was scarce any passing by the Street, but that several dead Bodies would be lying here and there on the Ground . . . tho' at first the People would stop as they went along, and call to the Neighbours to come out on such an occasion . . . yet afterward, no Notice was taken of them; but that if at any Time we found a Corps lying, go across the Way, and not come near it; or if in a narrow Lane or Passage, go back again, and seek some other Way to go on the Business we were upon, and in those Cases, the Corps was always left, till the Officers had notice, to come and take them away.   (p. 79)

The bodies left for officers to take away intrude upon more formal, bureaucratic attempts at management. Officially, they are not supposed to be there at all. Thus H.F. tries to assert, as a public-spirited spokesman of the terrible times, that the streets were "kept constantly clear and free from all manner of frightful objects, dead bodies, or any such things as were indecent or unpleasant." Opening up dreadful possibilities for the sorts of horror of "indecency or unpleasantness" not included in the category of dead body, H.F. vouches for the absence of "such things." Except for the times "where any Body fell down suddenly or died in the Street, *as I have said above*, and these were generally covered with some Cloth or Blanket." Streets "constantly clear" become littered with bodies "generally" covered over, while H.F. assures his reader that "in the Day Time there was not the least Signal of the calamity to be seen or heard of, except what was to be observ'd" (p. 186). Exceptions waiting to be observed become all too commonplace, proof of recalcitrant matter that official reports attempt to contain. The general reader, hardened to cases of "complicated Distress," is likely to accept the bureaucratic attempts to manage the calamities. To counteract the hardening process, Defoe appeals to the subversive strain in the gentlest readers, setting official traps that they can spring on themselves by being attentive.

However attentive, no man, H.F. insists, can "learn all the particulars,"[34] or even more important, learn how to apply them. The problems of applying context to number become complicated by the treachery of number itself. Since the statistics H.F. uses almost always prove to be wrong, eventually his struggle with flawed materials becomes the matter of his text. When H.F. attempts to make a list of all those professionally employed who "died as I call it, in the way of their Duty," he soon discovers the impossibility for "a private Man to come at a Certainty in the Particulars." Diligently numbering "sixteen Clergy men, two Aldermen, five Physicians, thirteen surgeons," and "six and forty Constables and Head boroughs," he suddenly gives up his task, unable to "carry my List on" through the violent days of September when: "Men did then no more die by Tale and by Number, they might put out a Weekly Bill, and call them seven or eight Thousand, or what they pleas'd; 'tis certain they died by Heaps, and were buried by Heaps, that is to say without Account" (pp. 237–8). Without a proper account, H.F. makes up his own. Since some say 20,000 were buried each week, while others discount the number, H.F. prefers to "keep to the public Account" and accepts a lower number. "Seven and eight thousand *per* Week," he observes mordantly, "Is enough to make good all that I have said of the Terror of those Times." Facts themselves become figural, symbols of "the Terror." In H.F.'s account, seven or eight thousand are no better or worse than twenty or thirty thousand, dying "by heaps . . . buried by heaps," while the impossibility of accounting becomes the account itself.

Defoe not only insists upon particularity; he exploits it. Faced with too many stories that tend to burst out of a traditional narrative frame, he deflates the possibility of ever telling the truth of the plague year by suggesting that even more tales exist outside his narrative, tales he is not telling of that dismal year. As Paul Alkon notes, allusions to the "great many such Stories as these . . . true in the General, for no Man could at such a Time, learn all the Particulars," create "an oppressive density of bizarre and terrible events that readers are made to sense as having existed alongside those that are narrated."[35] Typically, after relating a

[34] G. A. Starr argues that H.F.'s scrupulous attention to the problems of verifying his tale certifies him as a trustworthy narrator taking part in an inclusive process. *Defoe and Casuistry*, Princeton, 1971, p. 52. See Starr, "Defoe's Prose Style: 1. The Language of Interpretation," *Modern Philology*, 71, 3 (February 1974); and Malinda Snow, "The Origins of Defoe's First-Person Narrative Technique: An Overlooked Aspect of the Rise of the Novel," *The Journal of Narrative Technique*, 4, 3 (1976), on the subjectivity of Defoe's style.
[35] *Defoe and Fictional Time*, Athens GA, 1979, p. 216.

chilling anecdote ("I think I hear the very sound of it") of the sudden
death of a young girl ("I think the Mother never recover'd, but died in
two or three Weeks after"), H.F. emphasizes the paradigmatic nature of
his extraordinary tale. "This was an extraordinary Case . . . but there
were innumerable such like Cases," he claims, opening up the possibility
of innumerable horrors that extend formal narration beyond the limits
of the page into the aroused imagination of the reader (pp. 55–6).

H.F. refuses to organize his material in a chronologically satisfying way.
Aimless anecdotes are repeated while suggestions of alternative anecdotes hover about the edges of the narrative frame, and discussions of
theory and practice (should the houses have been shut up; is it possible
to know the infected from the well?) appear and disappear and reappear
as mysteriously as manifestations of the plague. Defoe's avoidance of a
conventional scheme of organization locks his reader into the experience
itself; almost unwillingly, one comes to H.F.'s materials to be held there.[36]
Defoe's apparent refusal to subordinate his narrator's sensational stories,
tales that often lose their point, anecdotes doubtful to begin with, generally disclaimed in their telling, traps the reader into taking part in H.F.'s
struggle with his materials. Here, for instance, in the middle of a straight-
forward discussion of the problems he faced laying in provisions, the
particulars of his text burst out of a paragraph which looks to be designed
with quite different intentions:

I had in Family only an antient Woman, that managed the House, a Maid-Servant,
two Apprentices, and my self; and the Plague beginning to encrease about us, I
had many sad Thoughts about what Course I should take, and how I should act;
the many dismal Objects, which happened everywhere as I went about the Streets,
had fill'd my Mind with a great deal of Horror, for fear of the Distemper it self,
which was indeed, very horrible in it self, and in some more than in others, the
swellings which were generally in the Neck, or Groin, when they grew hard, and
would not break, grew so painful, that it was equal to the most exquisite Torture;
and some not able to bear the Torment, threw themselves out at Windows, or
shot themselves, or otherwise made themselves away, and I saw several dismal
Objects of that Kind: Others unable to contain themselves, vented their Pain by
incessant Roarings, and such loud and lamentable Cries were to be heard as we
walk'd along the Streets, that would Pierce the very Heart to think of, especially
when it was to be considered that the same dreadful Scourge might be expected
every Moment to seize upon our selves.   (pp. 75–6)

Readers intent upon learning the domestic circumstances of H.F.'s "Family" end up thrown back upon "our selves," ever fearful of seizure. Subjec-
tively entering into the public arena, assuming, in his imagination,

---

[36] See Tyna Orren, "True and False Accounts by Defoe," Ph.D. dissertation, University of
Minnesota, 1976, p. 210, as cited in Alkon, *Defoe and Fictional Time*, p. 222.

"exquisite Torture" impossible to be borne, H.F. also withdraws from an active consideration of suffering to report the external sights and sounds of the street, the theatre of the plague year, where victims throw themselves out of windows, shoot themselves, and vent their pain by roaring and crying through the passageways. Reporting cries that would "Pierce the very Heart to think of," he attempts to pierce the heart of a more critical reader who only wonders where this paragraph will lead to. In working at making his reader attend to his dangerous materials, Defoe violates their expectations of "form." Just as the plague body disturbs natural order in its deformation, so does its narrative. Straining against its unruly material, H.F.'s misshapen paragraph swells to burst finally into evidence as impossible to overlook as the plague buboes that so terrify H.F. When symmetry does present itself, in the formulaic tales of the unnatural cruelty of nurses, H.F. distrusts it; plague bodies are not so neatly ordered (pp. 84–5).

Spectacular suffering

Taking to the streets to observe his bodies, H.F. calls attention to the condition of urban streets Defoe knows well. His observations fix the theatricality of urban bodies jostling for a place to be seen, for in crowds of mountebanks and pickpockets and beggars, signs of suffering need to be writ large to be detected at all. Beggars were frequently accused of simulating distresses greater than their own to make their case, to "Pierce the Heart" of observers possessing eyes worn away from seeing what blocked their way. H.F.'s own narration rivals the most hyperbolic rendering of grief, rendering public the most private, particular grief:

In these walks I had many dismal Scenes before my Eyes, as particularly of Persons falling dead in the Streets, terrible Shrieks and Skreekings of Women, who in their Agonies would throw open their Chamber Windows, and cry out in a dismal Surprising Manner; it is impossible to describe the Variety of Postures, in which the Passions of the Poor People would Express themselves.   (p. 80)

The contorted "postures" of the participants in the countless "dismal Scenes" suggest the necessity of the public spectacle of private grief. Trapped in physical circumstance, the poor can only express their "Passions" through sensational acts of physical violence grossly artificial. Immediately following this paragraph, H.F. records "three frightful Skreetches," and cries of *"Oh! Death, Death, Death!"* in "inimitable"tones, which although it strikes the narrator with horror affects no other body, "for People had no Curiosity now in any Case; nor could any Body help one another." Just this insensibility becomes part of the problem Defoe addresses, for as bodily needs, bodily deformation, pushes itself into public view, it becomes boring in its tendentious regularity. If the cry *"Oh! Death, Death, Death,"* strikes the reader as melodramatic, its hackneyed quality reflects the exhaustion of all of those listening bodies that had heard such complaints all too often.

As the "Desolation" of "these terrible Times" increased, so did "the Amazement of the People," required to escalate demonstrations of their grief to be judged "very affecting." Some roar and cry and wring their Hands "along the Street," some pray out loud, behavior that impresses H.F. as being "much better, *even as it was*, than the frightful yellings and cryings that every Day, and especially in the Evenings, were heard in some Streets." The most "affecting" were the professionals. "I suppose the World has heard of the famous *Solomon Eagle* an Enthusiast," H.F. ventures, alluding to that great public figure who "sometimes quite naked" went about the City "with a Pan of burning Charcoal on his Head" to denounce the evils of the city. Even his most dramatic testimony falls short, for H.F., still curious, unlike most of the audience, could not learn "What he said or pretended" (p. 103).

Insisting as always on the incomprehensibility of necessary spectacle, in his repetitive record of grief impossible to articulate, H.F. presents the body as material moving through the streets in search of patterns that could never contain the energy he calls up. A man, almost naked, thrusts himself into public view, specifically "out of *Harrow-Alley*, a populous Conjunction or Collection of Alleys, Courts, and Passages, in the Butcher-row in *Whitechappel*." "What could be more Affecting," H.F. asks, "than to see this poor Man come out into the open Street, run Dancing and Singing, and making a thousand antick Gestures, with five or six Women and Children running after him, crying, and calling upon him, for the Lord's sake to come back" (p. 171). When H.F. watches the spectacle from his own windows, he suggests a passivity that he consistently contradicts in every strenuous foray he makes out into the pestilent street. In his frequent attempts to put unruly materials together, H.F. exerts energy that propels his story, drafting his reader into his struggle to order what cannot be seen or said.

The only thing that can be presented is the spectacle itself, as cryptic and unmanageable as the crowds thronging Tyburn, material in search of order that has disappeared. All that can be reasonably asserted is that it should not be this way. Only resistance matters in H.F.'s narration, refusal to accept the disorder as all there is. Yet by necessity, H. F. becomes bound by the disorder, bound to articulate it. For after considering the illusory community built around the threat of death, solidarity that the great "common Grave of Mankind" inspires, H.F. looks around and finds that the disparity and disunion of regular urban life has resumed. Stating flatly in his final paragraph that he can go no "farther," H.F. complains of the "Unthankfulness and Return of all manner of Wickedness among us, which I was so much an Eye-Witness of my self." Could H.F. him*self* be one of the wicked, or merely an implicated witness. His syntax evades, typically, but discloses at last the isolated self imprisoned in "a course but sincere Stanza of my own:"

> *A dreadful Plague in* London *was,*
> *In the Year Sixty Five,*
> *Which swept an Hundred Thousand Souls*
> *Away, yet I alive*! (p. 248)

The clearest solution

Yet alive, yet also dead, *N.B. in the pit,* H.F. asserts his material self to the end, a self in need of a providence "not yet to be experienced," a self subject to the material pressures being brought to bear on all victims of the plague year. Fallen into the matter of the pit, trapped in materials that cannot be transcended, he can nonetheless create coarse but sincere lines to express the spareness (and spare exuberance, for there is victory in staying *yet* alive) of the isolated self struggling against the confines of body.

Absorbing subjective narratives, erroneous measurements, false statistics, his *Journal* eventually swallows up the bodies so difficult to order. Stuffing his journal with as many kinds of materials that it can hold, exploiting the defects of his own creative process, unable to remove subjectivity from his account, H.F. insists upon it, as he incorporates his struggle into his text.

His stubborn materials imperfectly perceived take on a skewed reality. They can in effect subvert the subjective reality that they are both part of and separate from. When H.F. insists that he cannot see the Angel clothed in white waving a fiery sword over his head, even though the angel is "seen" by crowds in the street, he fills his account, nonetheless, with the angel's presence, depending upon his and his reader's capacity to see angels somewhere. For when H.F.'s visionary persuades the people into "fancying" that they see his ghost, so firmly does the "delusion" take hold that in H.F.'s own paragraph, the discounted ghost becomes for the moment a ghost in fact, and when the Bishopgate clock strikes eleven "the Ghost would seem to start; and as if he were call'd away, disappear'd on a sudden." A ghost that can "seem to start," one that can "disappear" entirely, is, for the moment, more than provisional (pp. 23-4).

Such manipulation of suspect material makes the *Journal* not just one of the first novels, but one of the most proleptic. From the start, the novel, that great pit filling up with particulars, allowed for a place for a subjective narration by its very nature suspect: lies endorsed by a lying author, a place to contain the so-called realistically circumstantial details that appeal, perhaps, to the materialists in us all.[37] Even though we know, after all, that the statistics and measurements in H.F.'s account are supplied by Daniel Defoe, sometime hosier, sometime spy, they float free from him, just as the ghost walking upon a gravestone so vigorously denied by its author takes on substance in the moment it is so concretely described.

From its beginnings, pretending authenticity, manufacturing a "real" surface of particulars, the novel depended upon a subjective reality essentially fluid, subject always to the flawed vision and the dulled sense of hearing, the impaired memory of its teller, all of those things that keep post-Lockeans from the truth. The frailty of the body itself, manifesting its weakness in the dim vision of a seer who at best becomes a broken-down recording apparatus,[38] gives us in its materiality and subjectivity as much truth as the equally frail reader can receive. Once H.F. ends his nervous accounting, in leaving behind his contradictory utterances, the uncertain renderings of an author who lies in the burial pit along with his subjects, he leaves behind a telling that hearsay or not, remains for the moment truth. In his excursions into the street to see the problems of the body made manifest, made spectacle, H.F. finally uses his defective vision to make that which can be perceived, however imperfectly, much more real to the reader. For in the end Defoe depends upon us all possessing the dull organs that he exploits in his narrative as we become in our reading part of the material so impossible to order.

[37] In "Discourse in the Novel," *The Dialogic Imagination: Four Essays by M. M. Bakhtin*, ed. M. Holquist, Austin, 1981, Mikhail Bakhtin comes closest to approaching the "bagginess" of the novel that Defoe was necessarily inventing. When he insists upon the heteroglossia that distinguishes the emerging novel, Bakhtin allows for the contradictory and often fragmentary nature of the form itself. Defoe's own reliance upon materials that naturally collapse under the weight of analysis, his construction of a qualified truth undercut always by evidence he insists upon bringing in to spoil, even deform his structure, make for a most baggy, multivarious creation.

[38] W. B. Carnochan discusses this aspect of H.F.'s passive reception of impressions in *Confinement and Flight: An Essay on English Literature in the Eighteenth Century*, Berkeley and Los Angeles, 1977, pp. 76–8.

2

The burthen in the belly

Loose Thoughts, at first, *like* subterranean *Fires*,
Burn inward, smothering, with unchast Desires;
But getting Vent, to Rage *and* Fury *turn*,
Burst in Volcano's, *and like* Aetna *burn*;
The Heat increases as the Flames aspire,
And turns the solid Hills *to* liquid Fire.
So sensual Flames, when raging in the Soul,
First vitiate all the Parts, *then fire* the Whole;
Burn up *the Bright, the Beauteous, the Sublime*,
And turn our lawful *Pleasures into* Crime.
                                        Defoe, *Conjugal Lewdness*[1]

I seek you beside me, but it seems you flee from me; and finally
the fire devouring me dissipates these illusions and brings me
to myself. By then I am so excited . . . You may not believe it,
Usbek, but it is impossible to live like this, with fire coursing
through my veins.   Montesquieu, *The Persian Letters*[2]

Two such oddly representational pieces, written only six years apart, reveal
a shared uneasiness about the physical body as material not just in the way,
but as material that when "fired," becomes impossible to manage. Their
authors confess the difficulties of reconciling desire and necessity, the
impossibility of attaining what they both call "justice" in a system of physical
economy that depends upon an injustice that can only be addressed
indirectly. While both Defoe and Montesquieu write for an audience that
supports views both patriarchal and capitalistic, their individual interpretations of the system they buttress expose its contradictions. For as they
write, problems of body are being contained, officially "forgotten," or
rationalized into systems of domestic and sexual management.[3] Schemes of

---

[1] Daniel Defoe, *Conjugal Lewdness; or Matrimonial Whoredom. A Treatise concerning the Use and Abuse of the Marriage Bed* (1727), ed. Maximillian Novak, Gainesville FL, 1967, title page.
[2] Charles Louis de Secondat, Baron de la Brede et de Montesquieu, *The Persian Letters* (1721), trans. George R. Healy, Indianapolis, 1978, p. 16.
[3] In *The History of Manners: The Civilizing Process* (1939), trans. Edmund Jephcott, 3 vols., New York, 1978, Norbert Elias considers the pains of becoming civilized, and addresses the ways in which "ought" became internalized, while "enlightened" sexuality became "increasingly removed behind the scenes of social life and enclosed in a particular enclave,

internalized repression promulgated in conduct manuals, medical tracts, novels, and sermons unsystematically attempted to replace "what is" with "what ought to be." But desire – officially repressed – only threatened all the more to "*Burst in* Volcano's," to "devour" and "dissipate" the illusions patriarchy depends upon.

The first selection introduces *Conjugal Lewdness*, Defoe's attack on "Matrimonial Whoredom," four hundred pages written against the grain of his "ill-natured" age. Defoe used his "satyr" to attack the sexual excesses of a society in need of lashing. But while setting out to scourge, "bite and tear" with the "Teeth and Talons of the Pen" (p. 382), Defoe ends up entangled in the argument he tries to make. There is in this cranky, late work, an aggressively forged prerogative to "tell" the sins of an age that implicates its teller. Threatening to publish "Black Lists, Histories of Facts, Registers of Time, with Name and Sirname" (p. 405) if his complaint is not heeded at once, Defoe seems to parody Gulliver on his worst day as he systematically lays bare all the ways the body makes impossible his program of restraint. If the body remains "what is," material impossible to transcend, its proper use becomes imperative. "Use," however, turns quickly into "Abuse" of the marriage bed, while the body remains material too often in the way. The body that Donne was able to canonize remained for Defoe "carcass,"[4] while "*the Bright, the Beauteous, the Sublime*," once ignited by physical passion, would turn into lewdness, criminal manifestations of desire.

In the second quotation, Montesquieu represents physical passion starkly and satirically as an irreconcilable condition of a maladjusted physical economy. Fatima, one of Usbek's neglected wives, reproaches her husband for the "cruelty" and "insensitivity" he demonstrated in running away from the needs of his seraglio. But at the same time, she recognizes, ironically, the reason for the fire devouring her – his absence. "My imagination is lost in its desires," she confesses, as she accuses Usbek of obtaining from her through "the mortification of [her] senses" a sexual passion that he "could not dare to gain by [his] own merit." In fact one reason for Usbek's flight is his inability to meet his wives' all consuming needs in the flesh (p. 16).

These indictments of bodily needs that can never be satisfied come from two very different writers, both men of the Enlightenment betraying less than enlightened fears of sexuality. We are accustomed to reading Defoe as a "crusty" feminist, a pragmatic Puritan more comfortable with *homo economicus* than *homo eroticus*.[5] But in his discourse on sexuality Defoe

the nuclear family," and "relations between the sexes" became "isolated, placed behind walls in consciousness" (I, p. 180).

[4] I will consider the breakdown of analogy in more detail in chapter 8.

[5] Dickens had no doubt that Defoe was "a precious dry disagreeable article himself – I mean DeFoe – not Robinson" and found Defoe's women to be "terrible dull commonplace

resembles Montesquieu in surprising ways, a father of the Enlightenment, not a dissenter, but a *philosophe*, who for all of his wit can still find no way out of one of the central dilemmas of his age, the problem of reconciling physical needs to social customs and individual desires. Both writers attend to the material natures of sexuality, exploring a sexual economy that depends upon the containment and consumption of feminine appetite. For unless desire is utilized, incorporated into the system, it threatens to "break out" of rational schemes of management. In their investigations, they uncover along the way the inequities such an economy requires.

A desperation characterizes much of the sexual discourse of the eighteenth century, suggesting an often thwarted desire to make use of the material that confines the spirit. It has been argued that erotic individualism came of age in this period. Lawrence Stone finds the eighteenth century to be a time of great emotional possibility, a time when affective individualism altered "a bleak and relatively loveless" personal landscape to one of graceful, affectionate mutuality, while Jean Hagstrum detects in the period a union of sexuality and sensibility that made possible a reconciliation of sexual and domestic needs. Roy Porter tentatively celebrates the enlightenment for its honest, lusty, apprehension of what Boswell called "the highest felicity on earth." But in spite of masculine dreams of accommodation, the corrective the body supplied to such enthusiastic schemes cannot be overlooked. The "highest felicity" was complicated by the less exalted reality of the physical intruding upon the erotic ideal.[6]

fellows without breeches." John Forster, *The Life of Charles Dickens*, 3 vols., Philadelphia, 1874, III, 135n.

[6] Lawrence Stone, *The Family, Sex and Marriage in England, 1500–1800*, London, 1977; Jean Hagstrum, *Sex and Sensibility: Ideal and Erotic Love from Milton to Mozart*, Chicago, 1980, p. 2. In "Mixed Feelings: the Enlightenment and Sexuality in Eighteenth-Century Britain," in *Sexuality in Eighteenth-Century Britain*, ed. Paul-Gabriel Boucé, Manchester and Totowa, 1982, pp. 1–27; and in *English Society in the Eighteenth Century*, Harmondsworth, 1982, pp. 278–84, Roy Porter argues for a relatively healthy sexuality that Marlene LeGates finds missing in the period. LeGates finds that: "For the most part, the man of the Enlightenment took a very unenlightened view of sex," "The Cult of Womanhood in Eighteenth-Century Thought," *Eighteenth-Century Studies* 10, 4 (1977), p. 33. John Gillis, *For Better For Worse: British Marriages 1600 to Present*, Oxford, 1985, argues persuasively that "the conjugal has always been more an illusive dream than an attainable reality," p. 5. Alan Macfarlane, *Marriage and Love in England, 1300–1840*, London, 1986, argues that the basic premises of the nuclear family go back to the thirteenth century. His chapter, "The Benefits and Costs of Children," pp. 51–78, discusses the "burdens" of sexuality in the eighteenth century. In "Spreading Carnal Knowledge or Selling Dirt Cheap? Nicolas Venette's *Tableau de l'Amour Conjugal* in Eighteenth Century England," *Journal of European Studies*, 14 (1984), pp. 233–55, Roy Porter cogently considers the problems in exploring shifting attitudes towards sexuality. Those attitudes are explored further in *Sexual Underworlds of the Enlightenment*, ed. G. S. Rousseau and Roy Porter, Chapel Hill NC, 1988. The special issue of *Eighteenth Century Life*, *Unauthorized Sexual Behavior during the Enlightenment*, ed. Robert Maccubbin, 9 (1985), offers pertinent revisionist essays on that period although the volume is lacking what its editor calls "a feminist perspective." Any recent historian of sexuality owes a debt to Michel Foucault's *History of Sexuality*, vol. I: *An Introduction*, New

Central to an uneasy discourse of enlightened sexuality is its cost, what Swift called "the *Dearness of things* Necessary to life." Characteristically deflating, Swift considers the "pleasing pain" of love in one of his riddles, "Louisa to Strephon":

> Consider, *Strephon*, what you do;
> For, should I dye for Love of you,
> I'll haunt thy Dreams, a bloodless Ghost . . .
> Thou, like *Alcides*, shalt expire
> When his envenom'd Shirt he wore,
> And Skin and Flesh in Pieces tore.
> Nor less that shirt, my Rival's Gift,
> Cut from the Piece that made her Shift,
> Shall in thy dearest Blood be dy'd,
> And make thee tear thy tainted Hyde.[7]

In this parody of amatory verse, Louisa, a louse, addresses her "patron," Strephon, promising literally to devour his body with a passion he will surely feel. While the occasion is small, the issue Swift addresses is large enough to require mock erotic reduction. Passion becomes the urge to scratch where it itches, desire a physical need to feed on one's host in a condition of perpetual consumption that can only lead to the most radical of solutions. What he explores is a condition that Swift, more extreme perhaps than gentler readers, runs away from, but his flight is imitated less explicitly by contemporaries attempting to measure not only man, but man's ability to do "justice" to schemes of sexual desire.

In pursuit of enlightened "happiness," Defoe's Moll and Roxana, and Montesquieu's Usbek take to the road to run away from the ties that bind them to the body. And more often than not, they run into themselves along the way to confront what Roxana calls "the Burthen in the Belly." Implicit in the sexual action is the sexual reaction, the childbearing and the children that follow, the disease that like childbirth can lead into death. While the family structure ideally contains and "uses" sexuality to society's advantage, in reality, what Defoe and Montesquieu (and of course Swift) recognize is the more typical abuse of the domestic system, what Defoe calls "the Thing itself, as a State of Life, grossly abused" (*CL*, vii).

While Swift embraces the rather chill compensations of celibacy to avoid the irrationalities that plague sexual activity, Defoe and Montesquieu explore alternative strategies to contain and employ the sexual body. Defoe is perhaps the most energetic projector of sexual schemes, inventing in his novels complex schemes of accommodation that require

York, 1978 and to Iwan Bloch's *A History of English Sexual Morals*, trans. William Forstern, London, 1936.
[7] "Louisa to Strephon," "Riddles," *Poems*, III, pp. 924–5.

the fantastic resilience of a Moll Flanders. Both writers eventually resort to imagining a structure of confinement that meets the irrational requirements of the age of reason in a most despotic way. Their fictional representation of the seraglio offers, at least in theory, the place where all needs, all desires, would be regulated for the good of the master, all problematic burthens in the belly subsumed into a system of rewarded confinement. Driven into extremity, both writers reveal their panic.

The following two chapters will concentrate on Defoe's and to a lesser degree Montesquieu's consideration of a sexual economy often out of balance. Clearly outlining the problems the body brings in his *Conjugal Lewdness*, Defoe develops strategies to manage physical needs in his novels, particularly in *Moll Flanders* and *Roxana*.[8] Defoe exhaustively presents in conduct manuals and tracts a strong case for domestic harmony, "mutual subordination", and an affective individualism that depends in fact upon feminine compliance to the demands of patriarchy. His *Family Instructor* particularly lays bare the strategies of suppression necessary to establish domestic peace, while depending upon an elastic domesticity that rewards compliance with stability and freedom from circumstance.[9] As he declares with questionable confidence in *Conjugal Lewdness*, matrimony, that chaste and modest scheme of living, "tis a State, not a Circumstance of Life . . . as durable as Life and bounded only by the Duration of Life" (p. 343). But matrimony in Defoe's novels is a "Circumstance of Life" reflecting the insubstantiality of comfort and the inevitability of physical needs and desires, reproducing a cacophony, as Montesquieu would say, of discontent.

Just as repentance must take place continuously in Defoe's novels, so must marriage. While he insists upon marital regularity in his didactic treatments of sexuality, in his novels he creates a world in which polygamous and polyandrous unions become necessary. The ideal of correct behavior gives way to strategies of survival, while sexuality becomes some-

---

[8] Crusoe's strategies are less apparent. Paul Hunter suggests that Crusoe's "curious unconcern about women" stems from a need to underplay the notorious adulteries of the "real" Crusoe, Timothy Cruso – "theologian, reformer, preacher and guide writer," pp. 205–6. W. B. Carnochan finds Crusoe's "buried sexuality" in his "orgies" of collection, those times he drives desire into an acquisitive fury, *Confinement*, pp. 32–3. Peter Hulme finds the relationship between the dominant Crusoe and the submissive Friday to be an erotic one inspiring Crusoe to acts of jealousy, *Colonial Encounters: Europe and the Native Caribbean, 1492–1797*, London and New York, 1986, p. 212. The most recent exploration into Crusoe's womanless interior is J. M. Coetzee's novel *Foe* (Johannesburg, 1986), in which the suppressed feminine aspect of Crusoe's – and Defoe's – version of what happened on the island is allowed to be heard.

[9] I discuss this at much greater length in "Defoe's Idea of Conduct: Ideological Fictions and Fictional Reality," in *The Ideology of Conduct*, ed. N. Armstrong and L. Tennenhouse, London and New York, 1987.

thing not to be contained so much as exploited, a means of exerting control over a reality always in flux.

Defoe's fictional representations of "reality" expose the "imaginary" roots underlying his codes of conduct. Louis Althusser argues that "all ideology represents in its necessarily imaginary distortion not the existing relations of production . . . but above all the (imaginary) relationship of individuals to the relations of production." Ideology represents "not the system of the real relations which govern the existence of individuals, but the imaginary relation of those individuals to the real relations in which they live."[10] While Defoe's manuals represent the "imaginary distortion" accompanying his behavioral demands, his novels, like Montesquieu's *Letters*, move closer to the inconsistencies that refuse to be reconciled in systems of sexual behavior always ready to "burst" open. Both Defoe and Montesquieu testify to the central confusions of their century, the contradictory desire for freedom and limitation, equality and subordination, "justice" and gratification. The physical desire that they attempt to manage propels their fictions as it mocks their failures. In their insistence that the body be acknowledged as that material that resists erotic incorporation even as it entices, in their refusal to overlook the cost of attempting to deny, and conversely, to satisfy desire, both writers speak for an age attempting to measure the cost of being both material and spirit, of living in the imagination and in the body.

"The thing itself": lewdness as an inevitable state

Conjugal Lewdness: or Matrimonial Whoredom: A Treatise concerning the Use and Abuse of the Marriage Bed begins not just as a satire, but as a feminist argument for equality,[11] what Defoe calls mutual subjection, in marriage. Women should not be yoked to an unequal partner; mutual regard rather than financial gain should determine the marriage partner. In marriage, "Justice" is required between a man and his wife, "for there is no Decency can be preserved where Justice is not done" (p. 77). The justice must be sexual as well as financial. No husband has the right to demand excessive favors from his partner. Love, "not a Passion but a Quality," should inform the ideal marriage. "Upon the whole, the Matrimonial Duty is all reciprocal; 'tis founded in Love, 'tis performed in the heighth of Affection; its most perfect Accomplishment consists not in the Union of the

[10] "Ideology and Ideological State Apparatuses (Notes Towards an Investigation)," *Lenin and Philosophy and Other Essays*, New York, 1971, pp. 164–5. From an anthropological vantage point, Mary Douglas develops the equivocations implicit in a sexual and economic system that both encourages and yet, by necessity, denies individuation – a system of sexual economy "at war with itself." *Purity and Danger*, London, 1969, pp. 140–58.

[11] See Katharine Rogers, *Feminism in Eighteenth-Century England*, Urbana, 1982, p. 63.

Sexes, but in the Union of the Souls; uniting their Desires, their Ends, and consequently their Endeavours, for compleating their mutual Felicity" (p. 27).

The ideal quickly fades as Defoe piles up too many anecdotal warnings against inappropriate partnerships. A strident weariness sets in as Defoe records marital "abuses." It has been almost thirty years, Defoe complains, since he began this piece. Emphasizing his reluctance to publish his satire, *"despairing of Amendment, grown* OLD, *and out of the reach of Scandal, and of all the Pretences to it"* (p. v), he prepares his argument by first confronting the problem he has in expressing his displeasure: "how to speak of nauseous and offensive Things, in Terms which shall not give offence, and scourge immodest Actions with an unblameable Modesty." Arguing that the beams of the sun raise not only sweet dews from the earth but vile, noxious vapours from a dunghill, Defoe decides that problems in interpretation come from "the Depravity of the Mind" of his reader, not from the mind of "the needful and just Reprover." But even as he exonerates himself, Defoe still chafes against the limitations of his language, confined as he is to "a narrow Compass of Words," when he really needs more "flagrant Examples" to tell his tale of conjugal irregularity too dark to be delineated (pp. 7–9).

While Defoe suggests greater crimes, he also alludes to greater pleasures that "would call for a Volume, not a Page, to describe" (p. 114). In his idealism, he reveals a most erotic imagination, an irritated sensibility defensively protected by the satiric mode he employs. In his study of *Sex and Sensibility*, Jean Hagstrum decided not to allow Defoe into the canon of "sensible" writers because he is "fundamentally less concerned with either erotic or ideal love than with essentially prudential relationships."[12] But *Conjugal Lewdness* reveals a Defoe obsessively erotic, far from prudent, concerned more with blowing up than cementing "prudential relationships." Probing the difficulties of sustaining both the erotic and domestic ideals so often at odds with the needs of the body, he makes a satiric exploration by turns comic and tragic bordering on farce, a record of the way the body betrays the best intentions.

Here is Defoe at his most idealistic and most erotic, discoursing upon "this great Law of Matrimony . . . by which all that which is called shamefacedness and blushing, even in the most modest and chast Virgin, is taken away":

she freely strips off her Cloths in the Room with him; and whereas she would not have shew'd him her Foot before, without her Shoe and Stocking on, she now, without the least Breach of Modesty, goes into what we call the naked Bed to him, and with him; lies in his Arms, and in his Bosom, and sleeps safely, *and with security*

---

[12] Hagstrum, *Sex and Sensibility*, p. 16.

to her Virtue with him, all the Night: And this is her Place, her Property, her Privilege, exclusive of all others, for he is her own, and she is his; he is the *covering of the Eyes to her,* and she is called in the sacred Text, the *Wife of his Bosom,* she has the only right to lodge there; it is her Retreat, the Repository of her Cares, as well as of her Delight, and of her Affection.   (p. 58)

The vision is Miltonic in its ideal of marital chastity, but Defoe sees too clearly beyond the ideal into violated conjugal beds where putative rights and privileges cannot be realized. Relentlessly enumerating the inevitable failures of such conjugal accommodation, Defoe proves even more intractable than Milton in not allowing the vision to go away easily. For unlike Milton, whom he admits to following, Defoe will not allow divorce as a way out of an impossible marital arrangement. The naked, open body becomes subject to an extraordinary number of violations as Defoe keeps attempting to accommodate body to spirit.

These violations are presented metaphorically as extrusions of a body reduced to a carcass, enslaved by its desires. Two persons mismatched in temperament or age endure the punishment of "Malefactors in *Persia, viz.* tying the living Body to a dead Corpse, till the rotting Carcass poisoned the living, and then they rotted together" (p. 216). Such partners are bound like slaves at Algiers (p. 119), "persons only bought and sold" (p. 172), no better than "two Carcasses without Souls, without assent or consent, but in meer subjection to Circumstances enter[ed] into a horrid slavery" (pp. 191–2). Marital inequalities, the diseases in marriage, fester and inflame like "so many wounds in the Body," to "mortify and be fatal," requiring at the least "a great deal of Surgery, Plaistering, and perhaps, Opening and Incision, to cure and restore them." But even when he invokes a classically satiric ideal of "healing" the body politic, Defoe repeatedly presents a vision of bodies that resist incorporation. Two persons coming together from "the promptings of the Sexes" will "nauseate one another as a sick Body that is gorged with Physick, or a consumptive Person sick of his Cordials" (pp. 106–7). "Where the spiritual part is over ruled by the fleshly," Defoe warns, "where the sensual directs the rational," and the "Order of Things is inverted; Nature is set with her Bottom upward; Heaven is out of the Mind, and Hell seems to have taken possession" (p. 271).

Trapped in their fallen materiality, conjugal partners become conjugal victims of appetite, constant reminders that the carcass rots because the body craves. Imposing as negative a vision of appetite as Swift would ever call up, Defoe presents St. Francis as the ideal manager of bodily desire: he would "fall upon his Body, with the Scourge and the Discipline. Ha! Brother Ass, says he, *that was the best Title he could give his Carcass,* do you want Correction? Is your Blood so hot still? Then he would fast forty

Hours, and all the while whip and tear himself with a Wire Scourge, till
he made the Blood come.[13] Defoe wonders about the truth of this tale, but
decides that true or not, "the Moral is good. The unmortified pampered
Carkass is the real Fund of all these raging, tyrannizing Inclinations."
Disavowing papist schemes of disciplines and fasting, Defoe "yet . . . must
tell my guilty Reader, they are absolutely necessary in the Case, to reduce
the (Carkass) Body into a due Subjection to (the Soul) Reason" (p. 314).
Since the foundation of Sodom's sins was laid in "high feeding," since
the "Varieties of Luxury . . . Wines, luscious Fruits, high Sauces, Pickles,
Preserves, Sweet-meats" and perfumes fuel the hellish fires that rage in
"the *Italians*," a people renowned for their criminal wantonness, one can
never be vigilant or abstemious enough to mortify the carcass (pp. 320–1).
For "we not only dig our Graves with our Teeth, by mingling our Diseases
with our Food, nourishing Distemper and Life together, but we even eat
our way into Eternity, and Damn our Souls with our Teeth, gnawing our
Way through the Doors of the Devil's Castle" (pp. 323–4). Defoe's horror
of appetite, his abhorrence of a body both personal and political, bloated
and vile, dominates his discourse. "Thus the Fabrick [of the body per-
sonal] sinks like a Noble opulent City swallow'd up in an Earthquake,
there it stands a sad Monument of the devouring Teeth of Crime, and a
Sacrifice to Debauchery;" thus the body politic swells prodigiously to the
extremes of Deptford and Greenwich, Bromley and Wanstead, while the
entire distempered mass is "bombarded" by "Gallipots and Glasses" of
Surgeons and Apothecaries gathered around like "Crows about the Carcase" (pp. 394–5).

When he links appetite to a physical and moral distemper, Defoe makes
an association that preoccupies many of his contemporaries. In their
attempts to regulate and rationalize the body, theorists as dissimilar as
Mandeville and Woodward, Cheyne and Swift, all perhaps following
Locke following Pythagoras, experimented with the idea of a temperance
that would cleanse the body, as well as the body politic, of its ills. Their
discourse quickly grows unruly and, like Defoe, preachers of moderation
sound radical, often cranky, as they outlaw deep drinking and high sauces
to save their nation's corporate soul. John Woodward may have been
ridiculed for his attempts to trace all civilized ills to the consumption of
rich pastries and seasoned meats and sauces, but he only exceeded slightly
the enthusiasm that Locke had earlier brought to his theoretical attempts
to effect mental and moral development by working on the body.[14] To

---

[13] Laurence Sterne refers to another saint fond of mortifying his flesh when he allows
   Walter to play with the recalcitrance of "his brother's" ass. *The Life and Opinions of Tristram
   Shandy, Gentleman*, ed. James Work, New York, 1940, pp. 583–5, VIII, chapters xxxi–ii.
[14] In *The State of Physick: and of Diseases, with an Inquiry into the Causes of the late Increase of
   Them*, London, 1718, John Woodward blames rich sauces and seasoned meats and the
   late increase in pastry shops for all civilized ills from faction and atheism to stupidity

understand better Defoe's struggle to temper the physical and sexual appetite, it is necessary to look at his contemporaries' attempts at dieting desire.

Nature is content with little

The ideal of the well-tempered body was not, by the eighteenth century, new or startling. But calls to temperance take on an urgency that suggests that in a materialistic world, eating – or, conversely, not eating – becomes part of a final state of embodiment that may well be all "that is." In attempting to modify their physical desires, therapists attending the body are at the same time reforming their ideas of self. The body they are attempting to shape becomes, left to its own desires, a site of corruption that cannot be transcended.

It is not as if we have ever enjoyed an easy relationship with our bodies. Whether it is regarded as carcass to be shed or peccant material to be pared away, it asserts in its materiality a problem to be solved. It is worth looking at the theories of two Renaissance writers more comfortable with its needs, Rabelais and Cornaro. Their acceptance of their bodily state makes more obvious the problem materialism caused their heirs.

Rabelais, perhaps the most boisterously optimistic, imagines a world of reciprocity, of desires that circulate unimpeded. In a typical story of hunger satisfied, Gargantua, waiting impatiently for supper, collects a handful of lettuces to quench his thirst. He carries along with the lettuces six pilgrims hiding in the garden. Putting the lettuces and pilgrims alike into a bowl, Gargantua "ate them with oil, vinegar, and salt . . . stuffing into his mouth at the same time five of the pilgrims."

The sixth was in the dish, hidden under a lettuce except for his pilgrim's staff, which was sticking out, and which Grandgousier saw. Whereupon he exclaimed: "That's a snail's horn, I think. Don't eat it."
"Why," asked Gargantua. "They're good all this month." And pulling at the staff, he picked up the pilgrim with it, making a good meal of him. Then he took a huge gulp of strong white wine, and they waited for the supper to be brought in.

Scrambling to keep from being swept down into the "abyss" of Gargantua's stomach, one of the pilgrims pierced a decayed tooth with his staff, causing his host great pain. To ease the pain, Gargantua probed the tooth with a pick, and dislodged the pilgrims. The pain passed, allowing

and poverty. Thomas Maresca, *Epic to Novel*, Columbus, 1974, discusses more specific connections between overeating and overproduction of sperm, pp. 43–4.

Gargantua just enough time to "piss away [his] misfortune" before eating supper.[15]

In this tale, nothing ingested is tabooed. Not pilgrims, not a snail's horn; all is "good" – at least "all this month." Pain passes, discomfort is pissed away, and always another supper awaits the omnivorous Gargantua. While Rabelais was extolling the pleasures of the belly, his contemporary, Luigi Cornaro, was, sweetly, advising temperance in his *Discourse on a Sober and Temperate Life*.[16] Notable in his narrative, however, is an optimism that brings him closer to Rabelais than to his heirs, the more frantic writers "against the spleen" attempting to battle the perils of repletion, and also places him apart from the rather grim attempts at ordering the body that preceded him. While Galen and Cicero, his most likely predecessors, approached old age with a grudging sense of obligation, Cornaro, a cozy, somewhat tepid Rabelais, argued the desirability of longevity. Writing his discourses at the ages of 83, 86, 91 and 95, Cornaro seems complacently overwhelmed at being alive to keep telling his tale, wondering over his ability to climb up hills from bottom to top, to sing with "clearer and louder pipes" than ever before (p. 84), to study, without the least fatigue, "the most important, sublime, and difficult subjects" (p. 153), and to sustain his "gay, pleasant and goodhumoured self" (pp. 69–70). At the age of 91 he writes, "O, my lord, how melodious my voice is grown! Were you to hear me chant my prayers; and that to my lyre, after the example of David, I am certain it would give you great pleasure, my voice is so musical" (pp. 166–7).

Cornaro's regimen, like Gargantua's, is "natural." He manages to make the small portions he insists upon seem the normal course of things, the only way the body can age with grace. "Nature," he assures the gentle reader, foreshadowing the bromides of Houhynhynm-struck Gulliver, "is content with little" (p. 35). At the age of 78, little was 12 ounces daily of bread, meat, the yolk of an egg, and soup, as well as fourteen ounces of wine. The meat could be veal, kid, and mutton, fish, and a partridge or thrush or two (p. 126). Reasoning that the soul is content in the body, Cornaro works on making it as comfortable as possible to attain a state of "innocent and holy sobriety."

Cornaro was understandably popular, and adopted as a model of sober inspiration.[17] But his disciples lacked his genial, easy tone. Seventeenth-

[15] François Rabelais, *The Histories of Gargantua and Pantagruel*, trans. J. M. Cohen, Harmondsworth, 1979, pp. 120–2.

[16] Luigi Cornaro, *Discourse on a Sober and Temperate Life*, 1779.

[17] The first section of the *Discourse* was published in Italian in 1558. It was translated into Latin in 1613, and into English in 1634. Joseph Addison praised Cornaro's temperance in *The Spectator*, October 13, 1711. The *Discourses* went through at least fifty editions in the eighteenth and nineteenth century in England. See Gerald Gruman's discussion of the Cornaro tradition in "Ideas about the Prolongation of Life," *Transactions of the American*

and eighteenth-century theorists extolling moderation reveal an uneasy edginess. William Harvey reported his findings on the possibility of tempering the flesh in his "Anatomical Examination of the body of Thomas Parr," who had reached the age of 152 years and nine months. The farmer owed his longevity to his "meagre diet," his freedom from care, and his situation. Breathing country air of "perfect purity," he may have lived even longer had he not visited, fatally, London, "that sink of foul air and rich and complicated foods." As a distinguished inhabitant of that fatal sink, Harvey diagnoses civilized ills that he, for one, cannot and would not escape. In much the same way Sir William Temple confesses himself "too much the libertine" to be able to follow the sober regimen Cornaro extolled. Nonetheless, Temple does admire the excellent health of the less sensually active. Poverty seems to help modify the appetite. After meeting a beggar whose necessary diet had brought him to the age of 124, Temple concludes that "health and long life are usually blessings of the poor, not of the rich, and the fruits of temperance, rather than of luxury and excess."[18] Notable in both of these reports is a necessary detachment from the ideal they examine. Harvey and Temple are men of science, men of culture, happy to observe the fruits of the meagre life, but not interested in following the regimen their subjects, by necessity, endure. Nature may be, for farmers and beggars, easily satisfied, but not for gentlemen.

John Locke emerges as more doctrinaire, more determined to mold the restless spirit into compliant matter that resists the "cravings" so perilous to physical and moral health. In him, we can see the burgeoning materialist demanding that the flesh be denied for its own good, for in a materialistic world, flesh is all that remains. Let his bed be hard, let his stool be regular, let his baths be cold, Locke insists. Above all, let his meals be spare, meagre diminutions of Cornaro's, consisting of milk, gruel, and dry bread. Looking back to the virtuous Seneca maunching on crust, Locke connects self-denial with virtue, in his attempt to "correct and master the peccant humours." It is plain to Locke "that the Principle of all Virtue and Excellency lies in a Power of denying our selves the Satisfaction of our own Desires, where Reason does not authorize them."[19] In Some Thoughts Concerning Education, Locke exhibits a confidence in regimen that will be notably missing from eighteenth-century treatises working at regularizing the "peccant" body.

In the many tracts written against "the spleen," "the English Malady," a depression of body and spirit also known as hypochondria and melancholy,

Philosophical Society, 56, 9 (1966), pp. 68–73.

[18] Gruman, "Ideas about the Prolongation of Life," pp. 72–3.

[19] Locke, Some Thoughts Concerning Education (1693), The Educational Writings of John Locke, ed. James L. Axtell, Cambridge, 1968, sections 37–38, pp. 142–3.

the flesh is not so easily modified. Writers on the eighteenth-century English Malady seem more implicated in the materials they are attempting to order. While they solemnly advise their readers to modify their desires by cutting down on flesh while replacing wine with milk, they address a problem that by its nature thwarts their finest intentions.[20] They seem stuck in the material that they attempt to modify, recording not so much cures as histories of the inevitable physical condition that envelops them. One of the most famous of these theorists is George Cheyne, a physician who repeatedly attempts to heal himself to heal his age.[21]

Cheyne addressed the problem of the English Malady obsessively and self-reflexively. In treatise after treatise he formulated the same therapies while he suffered from his own favorite disease. He discloses his own personal connection to his professional calling in his essay, "The Author's Case," a sobering history of his own battles against an all-too-corrupt flesh. He endured throughout his life the sin of repletion, growing "daily in Bulk, growing excessively *fat, short-breath'd, Lethargic* and *Listless*" (pp. 325–6). Lurching between periods of fasting and purging, taking bark and whole milk, the waters of Bath and seeds, Cheyne bears witness to the tyranny of the body. He recovers from fevers only to suffer from an appetite so insatiable that "I suck'd up and retained the *Juices* and *Chyle* of my Food like a *Sponge*" to grow plump and fat, "indeed, too fast." Ballooning at one point to over 32 Stone, he was "forced to ride from Door to Door in a Chariot even here at *Bath*; and if I had but an hundred Paces to walk, was oblig'd to have a Servant following me with a Stool to rest on" (p. 342). While dosing himself with milk and white meats, Bristol water and pints of wine, or alternately living upon vegetables and seeds, he endures extraordinary suffering that invests his "case" with an authority stemming not from his expertise as much as from his own endurance. His "*Leg, Thigh,* and *Abdomen* being *tumified, incrusted,* and *burnt* almost like the Skin of a *roasted Pig*" (p. 351), he was, he boasts, an extreme case. Maintaining "one constant Tenor of Diet," Cheyne now enjoys "as good Health; as my Time of Life (being now *Sixty*) I, or any Man can reasonably expect." Delineating his sensitivity, he seems eventually to revel in an apparently chronic condition, as he explains the different degrees of sensibility in the world. "One shall suffer more from the Prick

---

[20] I consider the theoretical implications of writers "against the spleen" at length in "Running out of Matter: the Body Exercised in Eighteenth Century Fiction," in the forthcoming volume of Clark Lectures, *Mind and Body*, ed. George Rousseau, Los Angeles and Berkeley. Writers as diverse as Bernard Mandeville, *Treatise of the Hypochondriack and Hysterick Diseases in Three Dialogues*, London, 1711 and John Wesley, *Primitive Physick: or an Easy and Natural Method of Curing Most Diseases*, London, 1747, attempted to find ways of curing both mind and body.

[21] "The Author's Case" comes from Cheynes's most well-known work, *The English Malady, or a Treatise of Nervous Diseases of All Kinds*, London, 1733.

of a *Pin*, or Needle, from the extreme *Sensibility*, than others from being run thro' the Body; and the *first* Sort seem to be of the Class of . . . Quick-Thinkers" (p. 366).

Eighteenth-century students of the body and its ills seem driven to luxuriate in excesses they are trying to wipe out. Attempting to temper their needs, they insist nonetheless upon an urgency the body presents that makes their vocation impossible, yet at the same time, imperative. The crankiness Cheyne reveals in his tracts against melancholy appears in Defoe's own work written against the perils of appetite. From *Due Preparations for the Plague* to *Conjugal Lewdness*, he demonstrates a determination to connect the decadence of the times to the fullness of the stomach. There is, however, no indication that his harsh attacks on the corruptions of the flesh will succeed or even be noticed. The frustration of his position, so far from Rabelais' joy and Cornaro's complacency, stems from a pessimistic awareness of the problems the body presents. Confronting an appetite he judges insatiable, Defoe devises projects to quell that which by its "nature" can never be controlled.

The devouring womb

Defoe's desire to control the physical appetite leads, inevitably, to more specific attempts to manage sexual desire itself, a desire more often than not labeled feminine. It was common knowledge that women, Louisa-like louses bent on pursuing self-destructive pleasures, "more amorous than Men," were more apt to consume themselves (and their partners) with their passion. While Dr. Venette warned that as "Sparrows do not live long, because they are too hot, and too susceptible of Love, so Women last less time; because they have a devouring heat, that consumes them by degrees," the more visceral Dr. Maubray isolated the "attractive Faculty" of the womb which ingests the sperm "after the same manner as a famishing stomach snatches at the victuals from the Mouth of the Eater."[22]

[22] Chapter 4 below, footnotes 7 and 8, refer to fears of the voracious womb. See also Felicity Nussbaum, *The Brink of All We Hate: English Satires on Women*, Lexington, KY, 1984; and Roger Thompson, *Unfit for Modest Ears*, Totawa NJ, 1979, for extensive discussion of the misogynist fears of voracious, volatile women. George Rousseau considers the neurological connections to desire in "Nymphomania, Bienville and the rise of erotic sensibility," in Boucé, *Sexuality*, pp. 95–119. In her study of eating disorders, Kim Chernin, *The Obsession: Reflections on the Tyranny of Slenderness*, New York, 1982, pp. 131–44, examines the threat of the women eating up men. Rabelaisian enthusiasm for the greedy, retentive nature of his Utopian women's wombs is particularly striking in light of such fears. In Book III it is noted that the Utopians bred like rabbits: "There is no need to explain how their organs of reproduction were so fertile and their women's wombs so ample, greedy, retentive, and architecturally cellulated that at the end of every ninth month seven children, at the least, male and female, were born to each marriage." Greed here becomes satisfied by children. Although less austere than Defoe, Rabelais employs just as strenuously the greedy womb for reproductive purposes. Rabelais, *Histories*, p. 289.

The perpetually hungry womb needed to be filled. As "SOLOMON says of the Grave and the Barren Womb," they are "*never satisfied*; they never say, it is enough" (p. 157). To give into bodily needs without picking up the bodily burden is to give into the "frailer part," the part that craves the "use" of a man's body without paying the price. A woman who refuses the encumbrances of children but demands sexual satisfaction can and will "have the Use of the Man, but . . . would not act the Part of the Woman; she would have him be the Husband, but she would not be a Wife, and, if you bear the blunt Stile that some People put it into, she would only keep a St—n" (pp. 133–4). The fear of being "used" like a stallion, only to fail, and then to be *said* to fail to satisfy insatiable feminine appetites generates much of the hysteria circulating throughout both *Conjugal Lewdness* and the *Persian Letters*. Both writers, while expressing common fears of their age, originate a potent harem fantasy that can employ the objects of their fears, by either filling them up with "burthens," or locking them up. But always behind such strategies, a basic fear of consumption remains contradicted by the desire to be "just."

In his tale of the "barren doe," Defoe addresses most obviously the threat of the empty womb. "One of the merry Club, called, *The Assembly of Barren Does*," a lady newly married and "ready to die with the Thoughts" of bearing a child (p. 135), asks her cousin for contraceptive advice. The cousin argues strenuously against contraception, no better than murder, for "the Difference is only here, that by this Medicine you destroy a younger Conception than you would do in the other Case . . . What Difference in Murther, whether the Person killed be a Man grown, or a little Boy?" (p. 141). When this argument fails to convince the barren doe of her duty, the cousin resorts to "art," and prescribes not a contraceptive but a placebo that sends the guilty bride into a dangerous fever. Fearful that she has murdered an unborn child (that appears to exist solely in her fevered imagination), the doe in her delirium unwisely confesses her crime to an attending nurse who in turn betrays her to a mother-in-law most eager to report her crime to a husband predictably outraged.

"Mutual subjection" and affective individualism exact not only correct behavior, but also correct thinking. The barren doe must not only be brought to recognize her duty, but must be brought to a desire to do her duty, a desire even stronger than her emotional need for physical autonomy. Thus Defoe's doe is urged not so gently into compliance by the threat of a parliamentary dissolution of her marriage that "terrified her to the last Degree; she behaved her self to him with great submission, and indeed, more than he desired" (p. 145). She is made to "wear out" above two years, "tho with many hard Struggles and frequent Reproaches from her Husband, who was extreamly soured in his Temper by it, and

did not stick to use her hardly enough about it upon all Occasions,"
until "to her particular satisfaction" she proves at last with child, "for she
earnestly desired to be with Child, to put an End to all these Dissatisfactions" (p. 150). However rigorous the reflection, however abject the submission, such companionate subjection can never, even in the case of the
fortunate doe, be absolutely sincere. For within this discourse is a fear
not only of the voracious womb, but the voracious imagination always
venting desires that must be contained by most necessary ideological fictions.

To be fair, Defoe expects a certain compliance and restraint from his
men, who pay for their sexual pleasure by taking on more mouths to
feed. A widower turned forty wants to remarry. Since a fertile woman
would produce more children to strain the fragile fortunes of his already
too large family, he is looking for a barren woman past her prime. And
after ignoring such "severe . . . very rigid" advice from a friend who
accuses him of not wanting a wife, but a woman, the widower commits
"Matrimonial Abomination" only to destroy his constitution, make a Bedlam of his house, prove an unkind father, and ruin the comfort of his
life. For to enjoy a wife "in the ordinary Way," one must "fill the House
again with a new Family," more burdens in the belly (pp. 249–50).

Conjugal Lewdness bears ironic witness to the inevitable tyranny of body
over spirit in which the most baroque strategies to cheat the demands of
the flesh fail remarkably. Most notable is the well-meaning attempt of a
rich heiress of sixty-five who, to spite her ungrateful relations, decides to
marry a little boy of nine or ten to make him her heir. Demonstrating
motives anything but lewd, she offers to put him to school and to appren-
tice him to a good trade, predicting that by the time he comes to age, she
will be dead and he will be set up for life. But it pleased God that the little
boy grew to be seventy-two years of age by the time he followed his wife's
127-year-old carcass to bury it in the churchyard. Defoe solemnly reports
that the rejuvenated bride "bred a whole new Set of Teeth, as white as
Ivory and as even as a Youth, after she was ninety years old" (p. 364).
Even as he insists that the disparity in this marriage bears "none of the
corrupt Part," Defoe's reference to the old lady's virginal teeth bears
witness to the curse of conjugal lewdness. Gnawing their way into the
devil's castle, those teeth call up unsettling images of the devouring
female, the *vagina dentata* ever ready to consume a youthful heir grown
gray. And while they remind us again of the fearful appetites women
were supposed to reveal, more terrible because they come from the womb
always demanding to be filled, they also remind us of how complicated
the problem is for Defoe to express, how impossible (and how necessary)
it is for him to explore consciously. For those unsettling teeth are, in their
way, attractive, white as ivory, while the aged bride's "extraordinary good

Temper" almost makes amends for her extenuated physical presence as carcass long overdue at the churchyard. As he suggest more graphically in *Journal of the Plague Year*, since we are all, after all, so many carcasses headed for the pit, what does physical satisfaction signify? And the answer, for Defoe, trying hard to mortify a stubborn desire, is everything.

The Persian Letters

Justice is the proper relationship actually existing between two things.   (p. 140)

Montesquieu approaches the problem of sexuality more self-consciously than Defoe, but then he protects himself by calling himself "only a translator" of letters that "accidentally" fall into place, bound "with a secret and, in some respects, hitherto unknown chain." Taking especial care to guide his reader, warning that "the nature and the design of *The Persian Letters* are so obvious that they can deceive only those who wish to deceive themselves" (pp. 3–7), Montesquieu uses his letters to make the inconsistencies of European society glaring enough to unsettle the dullest self-deceiver. Europe seen through alien eyes had become by 1720 commonplace enough in its pretensions.[23] But European sexuality measured against the traditions of the seraglio bears strange fruit. Fleeing the demands of his own harem, a refuge for "virtue" held in check by the most authoritarian of measures, Usbeck explores the states of sexual dislocation in eastern and western physical economies only to discover that neither system satisfies either culture.

Although theoretically the seraglio provides a despotic system of sexual economy that preserves order, subjugating the desires of many to satisfy the master, in reality, no matter how many strategies are employed to maintain harmony, disorder always threatens to break out. "Good God," muses one of Usbek's eunuchs – a denatured instrument of his master's pleasure – "how much must be done just to make one man happy" (p. 40). Usbek's chronic depression mocks the extremes taken to provide unattainable content. And although Montesquieu suggests in his "Serious Reflections" that "the Asiatic seraglio grows more disorderly in proportion to the length of Usbek's absence from it – that is to say, in proportion as frenzy increases and love declines" (p. 3), within the text itself the first word from his wives reminds Usbek of "the famous quarrel among your women." Confessing that every day her desire is aroused with "new violence," Zachi complains that while "Love seems to breathe in the seraglio . . . heartlessly you flee farther from it" (pp. 11–12). Such

[23] In *Letters Writ by a Turkish Spy* (1687), Giovanni Marana exposed the contrasts between oriental and occidental modes of corruption, while Antoine Galland's translation of the *Arabian Nights* (1704) alongside the travels of Jean Tavernier (1676) provoked interest in the differences between the two cultures.

anthropomorphic desire not only breathes, but crowds against Usbek himself, smothering in the process his desire. "In the crowded seraglio where I have lived, I have destroyed by the acts of loving the very love I anticipated" (pp. 14–15). Only jealousy remains, springing secretly from a fear of his wives' sexuality.

Purity can never be "too pure," not when "the slightest stain can corrupt it" (p. 48). To maintain his wives' virtue by preserving them from their own appetite, Usbek locks them up. Yet in his series of letters, even while voicing despotic solutions to problems of the flesh, he appears reasonable enough, a man embroiled in the hypocrisies his position demands, but a man also interested in the "justice" that Defoe seeks in his own work. "Justice," he somewhat tentatively claims, "is the proper relationship actually existing between two things" (p. 140). The problem is that Usbek would make such a claim while running from the claims and counter claims of his own despotic system of control that is perpetually breaking down. (He also argues, while on the road, that man should stay in one place. (p. 202)) The contextual irony of such a desire for justice does not dismiss its urgency. Montesquieu uses Usbek's compromised position to make his point. In their work Defoe and Montesquieu obsessively ask the same question: locked in the body, regardless of the formal ways physical needs are rationalized, how can men and women find satisfaction mutually acceptable to both parties. The question becomes clearer than its answer.

In examining the complications of the seraglio, Montesquieu could be accused of exaggerating the problem he cannot resolve. Confining so many women to serve the needs of one unwilling lover goes against the enlightened grain, yet precisely this disjunction points to the enlightened problem. Roy Porter argues that "naturalistic and hedonistic assumptions – that Nature had made men to follow pleasure, that sex was pleasurable, and that it was natural to follow one's sexual urges – underpinned much Enlightenment thought about sexuality." Sexuality was seen "less as a sin or vice, and more as part of the economy of Nature," something that could be intellectualized, rationalized, and enjoyed. Montesquieu's insistence upon the inequities of the seraglio makes clearer the less obvious inequalities that make "justice" impossible in Paris as well as in Ispahan. Even Porter's appreciation of the relatively healthy aspects of enlightened sexuality, that mysterious quantity that could be demystified and controlled, depends upon the compromised testimony of John Wilkes, whose famous claim that "Life can little else supply / But a few good fucks and then we die," is seriously undermined by the misogyny implicit in his *Essay on Women*. Boswell, another of Porter's enthusiastic practitioners of sexuality, glossed Wilkes's lines with the orotund assurance that there could be no "higher felicity on earth enjoyed by man than the participation of genuine reciprocal amorous affections with an amiable woman."[24] But Boswell's own attempts to find reciprocity, his farcical dealings with the equivocally accessible Louisa, and his more tragic bouts of depression, alcoholism and venereal disease discount the "healthy" aspects of the sexuality he celebrates when he is not repenting its pains.

The eighteenth-century fantasy of the seraglio suits the problems it pretends to satisfy, and in its pretense, suggests just what might have been wrong. Legend has it that in the middle of the century, Lord Baltimore kept a "real" harem in the suburbs of Kensington. One of his "Sultanas" in a probably spurious memoir describes at great length Baltimore's attempts to preserve harmony and order in his seraglio. He seems to have been particularly fond of making rules, requiring smallpox inoculations, and regular bathing. The sultanas were not allowed more than four glasses of wine after dinner, the same after supper, except for his chosen partner of the night, who was allowed eight. No toasts were permitted, but to the Bashaw's health, no public singing tolerated, and no reading was allowed in bed. While broadly outlining the gentle regimen, Sultana Watson manages to suggest confidentially that the Bashaw had trouble enough satisfying the sexual needs of one woman, let alone a collection, which might explain the eight beakers allotted to the favored bed partner. He would frequently make "a violent fit of the cholic his apology."[25]

Baltimore's fantastic menage suggests, I think, the reasons for the more general popularity the seraglio fantasy enjoyed in this period. Much of its fascination stems from the culture's passion for all things oriental and exotic, but it is also useful in providing the imaginary means to solve problems closer to home. Women, forever hungering and thirsting for pleasure, needed to be contained. Women, naturally dirty and boisterous, needed to be forced into a clean, orderly, compliant mode. Johnson, it is worth recalling, bashaw of many tea tables, confessed to a delighted Boswell that he had "often thought" that if he were to keep a seraglio, his ladies would all wear linen or cotton gowns, for while silk conceals dirt

---

[24] Porter, "Mixed Feelings," pp. 4, 6–7, *English Society in the Eighteenth Century*, p. 278. See also William B. Ober, *Boswell's Clap and Other Essays*, Carbondale IL, 1979.

[25] [Sophia Watson], *8Memoirs of the Seraglio of the Bashaw of Merryland, by a discarded Sultana* (London, 1748), pp. 9, 28. Archenhotz described an Indian nabob's harem near Soho: "He had a legal wife, but six odalisks besides, who all slept near her in separate beds. These beds stand in a circle, in order to facilitate the nightly round . . . made with his wife's consent." Iwan Bloch, *History of English Sexual Morals*, p. 133. Lady Mary Wortley Montagu's *Turkish Letters* offer a perspective on the sexual structures of her own England. She develops the paradox that "enslaved Turkish women enjoy more freedom than their English counterparts." Robert Halsband, *The Life of Mary Wortley Montagu*, Oxford, 1956, p. 68. N. M. Penzer's *The Harem: An Account of the institution as it existed in the Palace of the Turkish Sultans*, Philadelphia, 1937, provides interesting material about the seraglio. Macfarlane considers the culture's preoccupation with polygamy, *Marriage and Love in England*, pp. 218–23.

and gets very nasty before it is perceived to be so, linen "detects its own dirtiness."[26]

The greatest problem Baltimore's seraglio points to is the ultimate feminine danger − women threatening to break out of such confining roles, threatening to sing, to paint, to toast, to read, and most particularly, threatening to tell tales about men incapable of meeting their demands for satisfaction. Another bashaw, Macheath, a personal hero of Boswell's, stands "*like the* Turk" at the end of *The Beggar's Opera* not so much in triumph as in confusion, his "Passion confound[ed]" by "the different Beauties [that] subdue him by turns." "What − four Wives more! − This is too much. − Here − tell the Sheriff's Officers I am ready," he earlier cries, preferring the pains of the gallows to the dubious pleasures of the overcrowded conjugal bed.[27] In the fantasy of the seraglio, suburban, Newgate or Persian, the fear of feminine appetite promotes greater schemes of confinement that only promise greater − and more expensive − failures.[28] Defoe and Montesquieu, listening hard to the lamentations of unsatisfied wives, a "cacophony" that fills the European as well as Persian air, take considerable notice of the imbalances rife in the most rational attempts to manage physical economies.

The major problem of both eastern and western systems would appear for Montesquieu − as for Defoe − to be a feminine sexual appetite impossible to satisfy. Usbek's wife Fatima predicts that "with fire coursing through [her] veins," she will not find it possible to live without satisfaction, while Roxana, Usbek's most outwardly compliant wife, chooses to die rather than submit to the systematized suppression the seraglio imposes upon her own sexual needs. This fear of the insatiable appetite that both Defoe and Montesquieu insist upon points, I think, to a broader uneasiness about not only the nature of women, but the nature of their place in a system that used their desires. For as Roger Thompson notes in his study of Restoration pornography, women were not only considered to be voracious, but, since they were politically powerless, were by definition child-like, "naturally" irrational.[29] Usbek's wives are kept from their dangerously volatile selves by despotic methods; Defoe's good wives are kept from their appetites by being expected to be perpetually

[26] James Boswell, *Journal of a Tour to the Hebrides wth Samuel Johnson, LLD*, ed. Alan Wendt, Boston, 1965, p. 255.

[27] John Gay, *The Beggar's Opera, Dramatic Works*, 2 vols., ed. John Fuller, Oxford, 1983, II, pp. 62–3; Act III, scenes xv, xvii.

[28] The fear of impotence underlying many of the schemes of harem confinement is most notably evident in John Cleland's *Memoirs of a Woman of Pleasure*, but can also be seen in Richardson's depiction of Lovelace's fantastic daydreams of the seraglio that supplement his everyday failures with the woman Clarissa.

[29] Thompson, *Unfit for Modest Ears*, p. 97.

pregnant, but in both cases, the nature of women is something that must be filled up or locked up, but one way or other, occupied.

Usbek's fears of his wives' needs render him literally impotent. Yet even as he flees them, "devoured with grief," the seraglio renews itself. Describing a new Circassian slave, the black eunuch contemplates the pleasures that Usbek will experience when he finally returns to find "everything ravishing that Persia has to offer, and to see the graces reborn in your seraglio as fast as time and possession work to destroy them!" (p. 135). The Prophet's command to "'Visit your wives . . . because you are as necessary to them as their clothing, and they are as necessary to you as yours' . . . makes the life of a true Mussulman most arduous." Like an athlete, the good Muslim must compete only to "languish" even in victory, to find himself ultimately "buried under his own triumphs" (p. 191). Usbek reveals here the pressures he is under to perform, the cost of maintaining a system that requires one sex to subjugate – and serve – another.

When Usbek flees demands he can no longer satisfy, he runs to a French physical economy no easier to manage. His young relation Rica, a jauntier, less oppressed correspondent with a sharp eye for contrast, describes a most revealing visit to a Paris court of law. Making immediate connections between the legal, economic, and sexual systems, he notes that even to approach the court, "you must run a gauntlet of a swarm of young shopgirls, who call to you in seductive tones." The calls become more strident once the actual court cases testify to a frustrated dislocation that characterizes French sexuality. Rica does not reveal much sympathy for the feminine plaintiffs. The "modest girl" who "appears to confess the torments" of a "too-long guarded virginity," the "shameless woman" proclaiming her infidelities as reason for a legal separation, the wife accusing her husband of impotence, as well as the other women "who dare to challenge their husbands" threaten Rica's, and perhaps Montesquieu's idea of domestic order.[30] As Rica judges, "A multitude of ravished or seduced girls make the men out to be much worse than they are. This court is a cacophony of love; one only hears of irritated fathers, abused girls, faithless lovers, and aggrieved husbands" (pp. 144–5). Yet in spite of his skepticism, the grievances remain in the text itself, reinforced by Rica's additional disclosures.

Most telling of his encounters is an interview with an actress at the opera, once "the most virtuous" and now "the most miserable woman in the world," who has been seduced by a young abbé. Pregnant and unable to continue her acting career, she tells Rica that having heard of "unlimited possibilities for a good dancer in your country," she would like him

---

[30] In his chapter heading, Montesquieu seems to judge the incident as evidence of "The legal subversion of male authority in the French Courts," *Persian Letters*, p. xxix.

to take her home with him where she would be better equipped to make her fortune. Slavery in a harem would be preferable to the shame and penury she experiences in France, no place for a "free" woman on her own (p. 51).

The "freedom" of the French woman appears upon examination to be hollow, and worse still, tedious. One can bore the ladies indefinitely, Rica reasons, "provided that they are able to make you believe they have had a gay time," and in this exchange he sounds as weary of the social pretense as Usbek is weary of the physical burdens of his office. Boredom overwhelms Rica in social exchanges as he is "conducted from yawn to yawn into a lethargic sleep" that releases him from his pleasures (p. 184). The boredom sexual looseness instills bears out Rica's theory that the "tranquility" of Frenchmen – so accepting of their partners' adulteries – is based on the poor opinion they share of all women, wives and lovers alike. The fatigue of pursuing adulterous liaisons prohibits true pleasure, yet the compulsion to play must be obeyed (p. 93). As Usbek observes, "Paris is perhaps the most sensual city in the world, and its pleasures are the most refined; yet perhaps in no other city is life so arduous" (p. 177).

When Rica yawns, he testifies to the paradox at the heart of sexual discourse. In a physical economy, there is either too much or not enough. As Mandeville observes in his "Modest Defence of Public Stews," the "necessary" passion is "of such a ticklish Nature, that either too much or too little of it is equally prejudicial, and the *Medium* is so hard to hit that we are apt to fall into one of the Extremes."[31] What Defoe calls "the Sin of *Sodom*," the "Fulness of Bread,"[32] becomes ironically its own worst punishment. Attempts to balance the economy itself, to reconcile simplicity with luxury and modesty with desire, seem to fall between extremes making nobody happy.

One thing is certain in such an economy. Many work for the pleasures of the few. To feed flagging, rarefied desires, "a hundred must labor ceaselessly. A woman gets it into her head that she should appear at a ball in a certain dress, and from that moment fifty artisans can sleep no more nor find the leisure to drink and eat" (pp. 177–8). Women, as fetishes of their culture's frivolous pursuit, consume the most, cost the most, altering their physical natures to stay "in fashion." Architects (artisans plumping an economy that depends upon its luxuries) "raise, lower, and enlarge

---

[31] Bernard Mandeville, *A Modest Defence of Public Stews* (1724), ed. Richard I. Cook, Augustan Reprints, no. 162, Los Angeles, 1973, p. 28.

[32] "Whence comes all the indecent lawful Things we have been talking of, but from this Sin of *Sodom (viz) Fulness of Bread?* while the Stomach is gorged with animal Food of which no Nation in the World feeds like us; while the Blood is filled with these pungent Particles, and the Veins swelled with animal Spirits, no wonder the seminal Vessels are over full, and summon the Man to a Dismission or Evacuation, even at the Price of his Virtue, of his Conscience, and of his Reason." *CL*, p. 323.

their doors according to the exigencies of dress style" to accommodate the escalating heights of coiffures and pedestal heels. "Formerly women had figures and teeth; today they are of no importance." Their bodies become commodities, no more or less than the beauty patches that "sometimes" appear in "an immense number . . . on a face; the next day they are all gone." In such a changeable nation, "daughters are made differently from their mothers" (pp. 165–6); they are in fact made into material to be consumed in the exhausting round of pleasure.[33]

While Usbek and Rica notice with complacency that their own economy is less frenetic than the Parisian system they observe, they record irresistibly the cost that the seraglio exacts to maintain its fiction of feminine modesty.[34] Enlisting the unceasing labors of eunuchs and slaves, providing a space where it would be impossible for his wives to "fall," Usbek clothes his wives expensively in a false purity manufactured as self-consciously as the ball gowns that require the unceasing labor of fifty artisans, a purity dependent upon the attentions of denatured eunuchs and a perpetual infusion of "new graces" to add vitality to a sterile and languid seraglio. In his efforts, Usbek succeeds in building fictions that threaten to consume him.

While he never stops blaming the "women" for his trials, Usbek seems at least dimly conscious of the self-engendered trap of consumption in the last letter he writes. While "horror, darkness, and terror reign" in his artificial bower of innocence, Usbek prepares to return to restore order to his women. "A somber sadness grips me; I am sinking into a frightening depression; it seems I am annihilating myself, and I recover only when dark jealousies come to kindle and nurture fear, suspicion, hate, and regrets in my soul." But if jealousies awaken feeling, these "reflections . . . entirely inappropriate" are recognized to be products of a system that consumes individuals for an enjoyment that is itself feigned. "I shall return to shut myself behind walls more terrible to me than to the women they guard," Usbek predicts, preparing to sink at last into the material he has been strenuously keeping contained (pp. 267–8). Earlier he had blamed the decadence of his culture and the depopulation of his native land on the hunger of his women.[35]

---

[33] Laura Brown considers Pope's use of the fetish in "The Rape of the Lock," in *Alexander Pope*, London, 1985, pp. 13–14; John Sekora discusses the feminine personifications of luxury in *Luxury: The Concept in Western Thought, Eden to Smollett*, Baltimore and London, 1977, pp. 44–5.

[34] Aram Vartanian measures the strain of the sexual economy of Montesquieu's seraglio in "Eroticism and Politics in the *Lettres Persanes*," *Romanic Review*, 60, 1 (1969), pp. 23–33. Frederick M. Keener considers the cost of the seraglio in *The Chain of Becoming: The Philosophical Tale, The Novel, and a Neglected Realism of the Enlightenment*, New York, 1983, pp. 174, 178, 188.

[35] *PL*, pp. 190–2. Defoe worries about this problem in *CL*, pp. 92, 331–2.

Fearing that he will be "buried under his own triumphs," he rationalizes his "state of weakness" to be the direct result of his "great number of women, who are better able to exhaust than to satisfy us." Immured at last behind walls that lock in his own weaknesses as well as the strength of his wives, Usbek falls into materiality unredeemed by spirit. In his attempts to eroticize an artificially "simple" sexual economy, he succeeds only in confining himself to its strenuous sensual demands, as driven as any Parisian exercising his right to pursue happiness.

Although Montesquieu seems to indict both eastern and western physical economies, he allows few solutions to the problems he uncovers, and they are both fleeting and fantastic. Montesquieu offers only two possibilities for what could be called "happiness." The fortunate Anais, a character in what Rica derisively calls a "Persian Tale," finds herself in paradise, a sexual Utopia, where she controls her own harem of willing, subservient men. To aid her fellow sufferers in the seraglio, she sends down one of her willing and able angels to please them all, but after three years, even he withdraws to leave behind twelve satisfied wives and thirty-six children (pp. 238–44). More steadfast lovers, Astarte and Apheridon, sister and brother, resolve the problem of incest and overcome the burden of slavery to enjoy at last "the most amiable and pleasant society in the world." But such strategies for happiness are severely qualified, the one existing in a fictional paradise, the other violating cultural taboos that are only overcome by the "unbelieving" Guebre rites that sanctify their irregular marriage (pp. 112–19). Satisfaction can be found only in the margins between cultures, in heavenly enclaves one can only hear about in "Persian Tales." In the real world of Paris and Ispahan, satisfaction depends upon enforced slavery and universally practiced self-deception.

Such a somber awareness serves to introduce the equally complicated sexual economies of Defoe's fiction. While his characters employ strategies of accommodation to "cheat" the body, pleading "necessity" to snatch sensual pleasures, they pay for their pleasures endlessly. In order to attain some degree of self determination, like Usbek's wives, they pretend a sexuality to feed their own hungers, going as far as Roxana to play "slave" to win freedom from the demands of the material world. But in playing slave, they become enslaved to their needs, never escaping the burdens of a sexuality that becomes eventually determined by a more powerful system.

3

Consuming desires: Defoe's sexual systems

One of the greatest Reasons why so few People understand themselves, is, that most Writers are always teaching Men what they should be, and hardly ever trouble their heads with telling them what they really are. Mandeville, *The Fable of the Bees*[1]

As he runs away from the needs of his harem, Usbek demonstrates an alienation typical of his age. The eighteenth century might not have invented loneliness, but it certainly refined it. Wondering why English pornographers of the late seventeenth century were compelled to make sexuality mechanical, disgusting, and shocking, Roger Thompson considers the social and intellectual changes that were to form the period. Taking into account the growth of commercialism, the shift from communal to self interest, the rise of the nuclear family dependent upon mutuality and privacy, he suggests the strains of private, and therefore diminished, lives existing between states of connection and dislocation. While

commercialism undermined old values and relationships . . . mobility produced rootlessness. Leisure might mean emptiness, boredom and uselessness . . . Self-control raised the threshold of shame and required the repression of the body. The nuclear family could become the neurotic, claustrophobic family, demanding new commitments from its members. Privacy could become introspective loneliness.[2]

Loneliness could also become public spectacle. For at the moment that the body politic was being measured and found monstrous, the body personal was becoming, by virtue of its urban, commercial connections, an entity best studied in the street. "Home" – that place so cozily imagined in domestic discourse – Defoe's "safe Harbour," existed more often than not in the imagination. The reality which Defoe explored more rigorously in his fiction made domesticity impossible. His fictional characters live in a world of instability in which husbands wander off as if "the Ground had

[1] Bernard Mandeville, *The Fable of the Bees*, ed. Philip Harth, Harmondsworth, 1970, p. 77.
[2] Thompson, *Unfit for Modest Ears*, p. 213.

61

open'd and swallow'd them all up, and no-body had known it,"[3] lovers
turn religious and decamp, domestic havens open on to hostile public
ground, their goods "torn out," their shells "gutted," their children transformed into treacherous sources of betrayal. Acutely conscious of the
dangers implicit in political uncertainty, the cost of domesticity, the self-
doubt that undermined the scientific method, the exhilarating yet frightening aspects of geographic and social mobility, Defoe addresses obsessively the loneliness of the modern condition. And nowhere, not even on
Crusoe's island, is that loneliness more manifest than in bed.

The marital and extra-marital bed, that place where the body resists
idealization to assert its own material needs, becomes for Defoe a symbol
of dislocation so heavy that at one point it literally flattens Moll Flanders
into the street. She is attempting to relieve victims of "another Fire" of
their cumbersome possessions, committing quite casually an act of urban
anomie, one victim "biting" another lest she get "bitten" herself. Suddenly
a wench throws a feather bed out of the burning house directly on to
Moll:

It is true, the Bed being soft it broke no Bones: but as the weight was great, and
made greater by the Fall, it beat me down, and laid me dead for a while: nor did
the People concern themselves much to deliver me from it, or to recover me at
all, but I lay like one Dead and neglected a good while.[4]

To reach orgasm is to die the little death. But after the fall into matter,
when material comfort may well be all that is, determining, as Mandeville
would suggest, what people really *are*, to die is to die neglected, locked
into a physical and spiritual loneliness made ironic by its intimations of
connection. For Moll, even if the bed is soft and breaks no bones, the
weight of sexuality becomes a more palpable burden that needs to be
shed repeatedly, the burden of children, the burden of hunger itself, a
burden that can be converted again into a marketable manifestation of
desire.

Defoe can be a heavy-handed symbol maker. One footprint, upon
occasion, can fill up an entire beachfront, one feather bed spreads over
an urban street. Notably, this bed is not only symbolic, but public, part of
the physical landscape of Moll's tale. Sexuality for Defoe is almost always
openly – even sensationally – expressed, while loneliness is universalized
to become communal in its implications. He wrote, after all, four hundred
pages outlawing "private" abuses of the conjugal bed, reflecting not just
his crotchety voyeurism, but concerns his contemporaries shared. In a

[3] *Roxana: The Fortunate Mistress*, ed. Jane Jack, Oxford, 1981, p. 12.
[4] *The Fortunes and Misfortunes of the Famous Moll Flanders*, ed. G. A. Starr, Oxford and New
    York, 1981, pp. 223–4.

material world, corporeal struggles must be made darkly visible, inspiring a sexual discourse that we have not yet ended. The inspiration to rationalize the materials of the body, to organize the irrational forces of sexuality itself, suggests a deep uneasiness and a lonely need for communion and connection most difficult to fill. Speaking to an age that locates "meaning" in sensationalism, Defoe addresses nervous readers who also worry about the "sins" of "self-pollution" when they are not recoiling from the contagion of sexual connection.

The discourse was not entirely negative, but in its strategies for improving the ways of the flesh, it reveals some of the dissatisfactions that needed public address. James Graham, for instance, decrying the dreadful results of "onania," or "the heinous sin of self-pollution," turned solipsistic fears into public spectacle, by creating a lavish Temple of Venus where the public could enjoy the visual delights of nymphs like the future Emma Hamilton and for fifty pounds rent his famous Celestial Bed guaranteed to cure impotency and infertility.[5]

Graham's bed titillated the English public fifty years after Defoe wrote his attack on conjugal lewdness, but in its spectacular way, Graham's public approach to private problems reflects concerns that dominate the entire century. (The private sin of onania was first publicly attacked in 1710.) Defoe proves especially rigorous in attending to the complications of a sexuality that was fast becoming public, commercial, and "useful."[6] In his novels Defoe repeatedly turns the sexual body into spectacle, turning private consummation into public consumption. Not content merely to outlaw conjugal abuses, Defoe publishes them, presenting them as strategic alternatives in a complex world.

When he worries about containing desire, Defoe presents heterosexual dilemmas. Men may admire manliness, as Crusoe patronizes a noble savage unexpectedly good looking, but they are not threatened by their feelings, while women like Moll and Roxana may intrigue, and even seduce governesses and Quaker ladies into their service, but do not seem to fear whatever attractions they arouse. The problematic desire exists between men and women, desire certified by pregnancies and children, palpable evidence of its presence. There are strategies through it and

---

[5] Porter discusses the celestial bed in *English Society*, pp. 258–9, and in "The Sexual Politics of James Graham," *British Journal of Eighteenth Century Studies*, 5 (1982), 199–205. Guy Williams considers Graham's sexual therapies in *The Age of Agony*, pp. 188–92. Peter Wagner emphasizes the spectacle of sexuality in his study of the Old Bailey Sessions Papers, "The Pornographer in the Courtroom," in Boucé, *Sexuality in Eighteenth-century Britain*, pp. 120–40. The major and minor sins of figures wealthy enough to go to court were widely published and read in "cases" of impotence and infidelity.

[6] Roy Porter discusses the self-education sex literature that "started flooding off the presses" in " 'The Secrets of Generation Display'd': *Aristotle's Master-piece* in Eighteenth-Century England," *Unauthorized Sexual Behavior*, p. 1.

around it. One can deny it altogether to remain celibate. One can dedicate it to conjugal "use," consecrating sexual connections to its logical outcome, children. (Married seven months, asks the barren doe's cousin, "And not with Child! Why, what have you been doing all this while?" *CL*, p. 136) And one can exploit it commercially, inserting the physical body into an economic system of consumption that not only pays for its pleasures, but guarantees that the burdens of sexuality will be redistributed. Inevitably children appear and disappear as if by magic in Defoe's narratives, eased on their way by mysteriously paid nurses to free their mothers to pursue an always compromised desire.

The most radical of these strategies is celibacy. Its expression could be violent: St. Francis enthusiastically scourging his brother ass. Or it could become almost incidental: Crusoe happily setting up his self-sufficient physical economy missing ink and ale, but never, overtly, feminine companionship. For the feminist writer Mary Astell, making her *Serious Proposal to the Ladies* that they live without men in monastic retreats, celibacy was strategically necessary, freeing the soul from the temptations of the flesh. Astell argued that in celibacy, demonstrating "a sort of Bravery and Greatness of Soul," allowed to "live up to the dignity of our Natures," women could give evidence that their "Happiness depends not on so mutable a thing as this world." The celibate woman, "in a due subserviency to the Almighty, is bottom'd only on her own great Mind."[7] Defoe, less of a rationalist, sinks lower in his expectations for men and women. Although in his proposal for an "Academy for Women," he suggests somewhat facetiously that his educational structure should be surrounded by a moat to keep men out,[8] inverting Usbek's complicated system of eunuchs and dreadful walls to keep his women in, Defoe presents in his novels women bounded not by walls, but by material desires. Their appetite – and their stamina – are worth consideration, for it cannot be accidental that while his men more often than not flee desire, his women embrace it.

More than his less sexually adventurous men, Moll Flanders and Roxana expose the contradictions of their sexual system. In search of stability that they are supposed to desire, they also seem attracted to an instability that forces them to live as "artists" – sensational representations of an eroticized public imagination. Driven by desire that they need to rationalize, and driven also by cultural inequalities that force them to market those rationalized needs, both women make use of their bodies to get

[7] Astell, *A Serious Proposal to the Ladies* (1696), *The First English Feminist*, ed. Bridget Hill, New York, 1986, p. 171.

[8] *Essay on Projects*, London, 1697; reprinted Menston, 1969. A moat will "render *Intrieguing* dangerous," p. 288. "The Ladies might have all the Freedom in the world within their own Walls," p. 290.

through a complicated, compromised sexual system. Their elaborate strategies disturb readers for their unflinching recognition of the cost of things, of seeing themselves and their "patrons" as they really are. Critics sensitive to the feminist and Marxist implications of their material predicament read their subversive actions with sympathy and even exhilaration. But the costs of such independence run high.[9]

The cost, in fact, severely qualifies the triumph, while the exhilaration independence brings depends upon, in Roxana's case, the murder of a daughter. Moll triumphs, Roxana pays, in two versions of the same story. Their progress tells much about their world, a world severely confused about the domesticity it purports to value. The maternity of both Moll and Roxana is crucial here, for on the whole, they are monstrous mothers, generating life in a casual, almost Rabelaisian fashion only to deny their creations for their survival. They become, in the end, radically ambiguous figures, givers of life, yet by their own admission, murderers of the children they carry along with them. In both novels, Defoe's experiments in sexual form attempt to make the matter of the body into "speaking sights," exposing no solutions that his readers would recognize.

The door of inclination

Nothing was ever so stupid on both Sides . . . In short, if he had known me, and how easy the Trifle he aim'd at was to be had, he would have troubled his Head no farther, but have given me four or five Guineas and have lain with me the next time he had come at me.   (p. 25)

Notoriously cheapening herself, Moll recalls her fall from "Virtue" with rueful irony, dismissing that "Trifle" virginity as a wasted asset that she had undervalued. Yet whenever she approaches her sexual history, employing a reductive skepticism not entirely truthful, Moll hedges, explaining away desire in economic terms of necessity. And by reducing desire to its materiality, she remains oddly, somewhat artificially innocent, forgiven for what Defoe would surely attack in his tracts as conjugal and extra-conjugal lewdness.

Moll faces two problems in her first sexual encounter: how to get through a world of snares and cheats and how to express herself along the way. For protection is not enough. Inevitably in her episodic falls from grace, Moll opens herself up to the experience she is trying to

[9] Rogers argues that sexual experiences in Defoe's novels "frees women from inhibitions and emboldens them to deal more effectively with the world," opening up "possibilities of independence that are exhilarating even today," pp. 70–1. Lois Chaber argues that "the disbelief and the horror Moll's adaptability provoke spring . . . from expectations rooted in a sexist myth that reserves for women the 'humanity' atrophied in men competing in a vicious capitalist society." *PMLA*, 97, 2 (1982), p. 223.

control. A woman, she reasons, alone in the world, "is just like a Bag of
Money, or a Jewel dropt on the Highway, which is a Prey to the next
Comer" (p. 128). To guard her wealth, she employs her sexuality, turning
herself into a "snare," a "cheat," while giving into calculated desire. Her
discourse becomes doubled, turning on regularly invoked abhorrence of
actions that actually "fire" Moll's body and imagination. "His words I must
confess fir'd my Blood; all my Spirits flew about my Heart, and put me
into Disorder enough" (p. 22). Yet while fitting the stereotypical pattern
of the "green-sick maid," Moll corrects her passion, explaining that the
money that follows confounds her altogether. Her color comes and goes
at the sight of a purse, "with the fire of his Proposal together" (p. 29), to
reflect Moll's deliberate union of the sensual and the material. By putting
a price on herself, however low, Moll prepares the reader for future
transactions of necessity. It is not that the countless sexual exchanges are
not necessary, but that they are not *only* necessary. They are also full of
pleasure that must be "abhorred" to be rationalized.

When the young Moll loses her first love, she mourns not the loss of
his gallantry, nor his financial endowment, but the loss of his "Person,"
which "indeed I Lov'd to Distraction" (p. 42). We find the same attention
to physical person present in her last sexual episode, her dalliance at
Bartholomew Fair. What makes this final, almost nostalgic encounter
especially significant is its timing. It follows her visitation from on high,
her bare escape from being flattened dead by a falling mattress. This
accident "spoil'd [her] Market" for larceny for some time, sending her
home to her governess "very much hurt, and Bruised, and Frighted to
the last degree, and it was a good while before she could set me upon my
Feet again" (p. 224). But on her feet, wandering through the cloisters at
Bartholomew Fair, she falls in with an "extreamly well-Dress'd" gentleman, and although out of practice, allows herself to be "carried" to the
Spring Garden at Knightsbridge "where we walk'd in the Gardens, and
he Treated me very handsomely." Both the fair and the gardens offer
possibilities for sexual exchange rendered impersonal, sanctioned space
for play that Moll immediately turns into gain. Yet in returning for the
moment to her "Dead and neglected" sexuality, Moll pleases more than
her purse; she pleases her appetite.

Her words belie her actions, for while ending up almost aimlessly in "a
Room with a Bed in it," at first apparently unwilling, she yields "being
indeed willing to see the End of it, and in Hopes to make something of it
at last; as for the Bed &c., I was not much concern'd about that Part." To
explain herself, Moll takes to physical accounting, using the first opportunity to "search . . . to a Nicety" her by now unconscious "Game." Yet
while she removes his gold watch and silk purse of gold, his full bottom
periwig, silver fringed gloves, fine sword and snuff-box, she also takes

account of the physical transaction itself which she immediately deflates. Preening herself on her youthful appearance ("I did not indeed look so old as I was by ten or twelve Years"), she denounces her prey for his "absurd . . . ridiculous" vulnerability. But when she is not predicting his bad end, (for he is *like an Ox to the slaughter*") or counting his coin ("As for me, my Business was his Money"), Moll notes carefully that her victim is comely, possessing a "sober and solid Countenance, a charming beautiful Face, and everything that cou'd be agreeable" (pp. 225–7). Once she gives her gentleman the slip, she does not stop counting up his physical charms, but instead, has "a great many Thoughts" about "seeing him again" (p. 253). Although she insists upon reducing her "inclination" to its material level in vowing to "make some advantage of him," Moll spends over a year on her comely gentleman fishing somewhat languidly for a maintenance. The affair eventually runs down, leaving Moll to insist that it "added no great Store to me, only to make more Work for Repentance." But significantly, once she returns to the street to pick more pockets, she dresses up "in a very mean Habit" (p. 238), disguising most dramatically her own "Person." And although this final sexual episode can be read as yet another time that greed shapes Moll's life, this "unlook'd for" encounter seems to me bittersweet rather than tart, a time that shows us Moll trying on her sexuality one last time, "not so past the Merry part of Life, as to forget how to behave" (p. 226).

When Moll rationalizes her sexuality into something of "advantage," by reducing herself to the materials that threaten her, she protects herself from the desire, the "wicked Part" that she cannot afford. Moll does not so much whore as she "plays" or "acts" the whore, assuming a commercial hardness to cover over a physical ambivalence that must be denied. This becomes especially apparent in the Man of Bath sequence.

The episode is complicated by two problems always present in the novel, the existence of a physical desire, what Defoe the moralist would call a "lewdness," what Defoe the novelist calls "inclination," that always threatens to "burst," and contextually, the instability of a social and economic world that is always on the verge of collapse. Certainly nothing could be more irregular than Moll's condition when she wanders into Bath. Her new world husband, staple of a life that promised sober, rational advancement in an almost perversely comic version of the Oedipus story, has turned out to be her brother, while her "mother-in-law," miraculous Newgate bird able to rise up out of her ashes, is her mother-in-fact. When Moll finally gains a rather perilous freedom from her disastrous marriage and returns to England, she loses much of her financial fortune at sea. Waiting literally and metaphorically for another ship to come in, she appears suspended, "encouraged" by a landlady with "none of the best Principles" to "correspond" with a man of virtue and honor living in the same house. The financial necessity, the "cunning" landlady "pressing" Moll to make an arrangement, and the "good Humour" of the gentleman himself all prepare the reader for the inevitable seduction of a needy Moll only after "the main thing" (pp. 107–11).

The initial exchange between them reifies the financial nature of their transaction. Like a rather stolid Zeus, the gentleman compresses desire into solid coin which he showers upon a most compliant and material Danae. First he makes her fetch him all of her money, every farthing. Moll draws money out of her purse, and adds more from her "little private drawer," and throws all of her guineas onto the bed. The man of Bath inspects the coin, "Huddles" it into the drawer again, and reaching into his pocket, pulls out a key. With its attention to purses and pockets and keys, private drawers and public beds, the narrative manages to eroticize its material while making solid and substantial "good humour."

When Moll describes the transaction, she emphasizes her own amused helplessness that almost argues for her detachment from her own actions. He "made" her put her hand in the drawer, he held her "backward" hand "hard," he made her put the coins ("I knew not how much") in her lap. Moll relates her story "the more particularly" to "show the temper with which we convers'd," performing an emblematic dumb show for the reader, in which she postures sexual compliance for material gain. And the performance here is what counts, for in their conversation, "there had not pass'd the least immodest word or action between us" (pp. 112–14).

After purchasing her favors, the compleat gentleman contents himself with two years of decorous bundling, "a surprizing thing" for Moll, who was prepared to "resist" a little, but after a "little" struggle waits for the desire she resists to be filled. She is not "wholly pleas'd" with her admirer's abstaining ways, "for I own I was much wickeder than he" (pp. 115–16). And in perhaps the most curious sequence of her book, one night "warm and merry," she releases her lover from his vow of continence "for one Night and no more," violating in the process her own carefully developed case of necessity. For Moll doesn't *need* to release her partner from his self-imposed chastity; she *wants* to. The body for Moll is not the "rotting Carcass" poisoning the living, nor is it a necessary fetish of her commercial economy, but material warm and merry, material that brings pleasure – for a night.

Exchanging overnight "the Place of Friend for the unmusical harsh sounding Title of WHORE," she enters a typically equivocal position, wicked and not wicked, happy but unhappy, guilty, yet innocent, for it "was all a surprize" (pp. 117–19). Having acted the whore in the tableau of guineas, Moll being the whore retains the innocence of her early, necessitous state. And while she lectures her readers on the dangers of giving into "Inclination," for "Vice breaks in at the breaches of Decency," two pages later, she is explaining that "the Vice came in always at the Door of Necessity, not at the Door of Inclination" (pp. 126–9). For Moll to negotiate through a world of hard choices, a world in which she frequently needs to use her body to survive, she must act as if she never has a choice. Her perpetually reconstructed innocence is what gives her the resilience to carry on her life.

When Moll pleads "necessity" to justify inclination, she is entering into a discourse that measures with careful precision the cost of things. Sexual desire, officially being suppressed by Defoe the conduct manual writer, is being explored fictionally as long as it can be rationalized into a self-serving function in a consumer economy. Defoe tries to satisfy contradictory demands of desire and decorum [10] and to answer the needs of both the individual and the officially repressed society. This complicated strategy stands out in bleak relief against a more expansive insistence upon the indebtedness that Moll shrinks from, the "praise of debtors" Panurge makes in Rabelais' celebration of bodily connections. In a Rabelaisian world of perpetual debt, harmony will reign. Using the body as his microcosmic model, Panurge argues that man "with all his limbs lending, borrowing, and owing – that is to say, in his natural state," in a miraculous network of exquisite refinement must replicate his natural state in a larger world of lenders and borrowers, to be perpetuated forever.[11] Defoe tries to entertain such a vision, particularly when he waxes rhapsodic on the beauties of the capitalistic system. But Defoe was also a bankrupt, for whom indebtedness brought not glory, but rather shame and obligation. Tenaciously optimistic, he can argue that the "English Tradesman" is "a kind of Phoenix, who often rises out of his own ashes, and makes the ruin of his fortunes to be a firm foundation to build his recovery." In her own spectacular triumphs over necessity, the ever-renewed Moll exists on such a level, recuperating endlessly the losses central to her mortal condition. But the fantastic nature of her progress exists half-way between the easy, boisterous fluidity of Rabelaisian reciprocity and the hard, ungiving moral accountancy Defoe applies to Roxana's dubious success in staying

[10] Fernand Braudel considers the contradictory nature of an economy structured by needs and desire in *The Wheels of Commerce: Civilization and Capitalism, 15th–18th Century*, in *Civilization and Capitalism in the Fifteenth to Eighteenth Centuries*, 3 vols., trans. Sian Reynolds, New York, 1981–84, II, p. 461.

[11] Rabelais, *Histories*, pp. 300–1. Mikhail Bakhtin discusses the idea of indebtedness in *Rabelais and His World*, trans. Hélène Iswolsky, Bloomington, IN, 1984, pp. 324–5. John Robert Moore cites the rise of the Phoenix in *Daniel Defoe: Citizen of the Modern World*, Chicago, 1958, p. 103. David Blewett points to the instability of the phoenix's position when he notes that Defoe's characters are always faced with the threat of slipping off "the normal road of sanity, family security, natural affections to children, and so forth, not only into a world of bestial desires and ungoverned passions (as in *Robinson Crusoe*) but into a dark world of madness, incest, child murder, and suicide," *Defoe's Art of Fiction*, Toronto, 1979, p. 64.

out of debt by "eating up" her very children. "This borrowing, owing, lending world is so good," Panurge boasts, "that when this act of feeding is over, it immediately thinks of lending to those who are not yet born, by that loan perpetuating itself, if it can, and multiplying itself by means of its own replica's; that is children." In Defoe's world, just that multiplication, producing what Roxana calls "the burthen in the belly" promotes not goodness, not joyful generosity, but "murther."

"The great and main Difficulty"

Moll Flanders is notoriously adept at multiplying her burdens only to divide them. Just as the feather bed stops her dead in her tracks – until she resurrects herself for one more sally forth – her repeated childbed experiences reinforce, only to evade, the real dilemma of the body. The moral of *Conjugal Lewdness* reasserts itself each time Moll becomes pregnant, yet the dilemma itself becomes within the narrative curiously resolved. Moll appears to be both encumbered with and freed from "the great and main Difficulty," as she puts down and sometimes picks up her burden.

Her dexterous success is exhilarating, disturbing, and ultimately grotesque. Mikhail Bakhtin discusses the "unfinished" and "open body" central to images of the grotesque. "Not separated from the rest of the world," the grotesque body "transgresses its own limits" and "discloses its essence as a principle of growth which exceeds its own limits only in copulation, pregnancy, childbirth, the throes of death, eating, drinking, or defecation."[12] Bakhtin is specifically referring in his discussion to the Kerch terracotta figurines of senile, laughing, pregnant hags. Ambivalent, contradictory, the hags represent "pregnant death, a death that gives birth." Without trying to turn Defoe into an archaic creator of the grotesque, I think that it is worth thinking about his own fascination with the continuous process of begetting. For there is an excess of fertility in both Moll and Roxana. While both characters age, carefully enumerating the years and pounds they put on throughout their narratives, they retain a talent for childbearing that, if it were not serious, would become comic. Moll particularly seems to enjoy an immunity from the fruits of her miscellaneous unions. Her first two children "taken happily off of my Hands . . . and that by the way was all they got by Mrs. *Betty*" (p. 59) are not the last to be so happily redistributed. Even her most problematic of offspring, the incestuous son Humphry, nephew as well as son, proves not only tractable but recoverable and indeed proves so attractive that Moll, old enough to qualify for hag status, wishes wistfully that she could

---

[12] Bakhtin, *Rabelais and His World*, pp. 24–6.

start the world anew with him instead of remaining with the less capable Jemmy. Such uncensored desire underscores the fantastic freedom Moll enjoys, her open, unfinished sexuality generating life and death, transgressing with impunity, and points to a certain grotesque energy necessary to her progress.

Moll's paradoxical freedom becomes most apparent at the Sign of the Cradle,[13] the sexual center of the story, where babies are eased in and out of the world with uncommon dexterity. It is there that Moll commits what she calls "murther." Her action indicts her society as well as herself for acts of consumption necessary to life. Defoe's conduct code, most explicitly indicting "barren does" for their attempts to escape the implications of childbearing, become in such a setting an ideological fiction most inappropriate to Moll's "real" state.

For in her fictional reality, Moll cannot bear the cost of her child. After experiencing one of her typical reverses in her quest for stability, this time enjoying for a time a disastrously pleasant marriage to her Lancashire Jemmy, Moll arrives in London to discover that she is pregnant with his child. Not only must she arrange for her own lying in, but she must also arrange for the child's welfare. Moll is still after the main chance, this time a hapless banker in the process of divorcing his wife, a mere whore "by inclination." Since Moll cannot be courted bearing obvious evidence of her own "inclination," her personal circumstances complicate the "nice" problems that accompany extra-marital pregnancies. Ironically, once she lands her banker, she will lead her "happy Life" in her "safe Harbour" for only five years before "a sudden Blow from an almost invisible Hand blast[s] all [her] Happiness" (pp. 188–9) and turns her once more out into the world – but that's another story. At the Sign of the Cradle, Moll is thinking of the here and now.[14] Bearing a life she cannot afford, she thinks of a death that would free her only to deny the thought in a characteristic equivocation: "my Apprehensions were really

---

[13] Gaston Bachelard observes that "Before he is 'cast into the world', as claimed by certain hasty metaphysics, man is laid in the cradle of the house. And always, in our daydreams, the house is a large cradle." *The Poetics of Space*, trans. Maria Jolas, Boston, 1969, p. 7. That the Mother Midnight's establishment is named "The Sign of the Cradle" takes on a perhaps unintentional poignancy in light of the mixed quality of care found in her place of business.

[14] Keith Wrightson, *English Society, 1580–1680*, New Brunswick NJ, 1982, cites examples of the social pressure that could be applied to unmarried pregnant women, p. 86. Ruth Perry considers the perils of seventeenth-century childbirth in "The Veil of Chastity: Mary Astell's feminism," *Sexuality, in Eighteenth-Century Britain*, ed. Boucé, pp. 147–8. See also "The Veil of Chastity," *The Celebrated Mary Astell, An Early English Feminist*, Chicago, 1986. Dolores Peters discusses "Popular Medical Attitudes in the Eighteenth Century" towards childbirth in "The Pregnant Pamela," *ECS*, 14, 4 (1981), pp. 432–51. R. W. Malcomson draws on sources from the eighteenth-century provincial press and from criminal records in "Infanticide in the Eighteenth Century," *Crime in England: 1550–1800*, Princeton, 1977, pp. 187–209.

that I should Miscarry; I should not say Apprehensions, for indeed I would have been glad to miscarry, but I cou'd never be brought to entertain so much as a thought of endeavouring to Miscarry; or of taking any thing to make me Miscarry, I abhorr'd, I say, so much as the thought of it" (p. 161).

Moll abhors what is necessary to bring up. For the idea of miscarriage (and abortion) does not disappear, but hovers over the abhorrence. While Defoe insists in *Conjugal Lewdness* that his barren does lie still and do their duty bravely, in his fiction, he calculates the cost of the necessary burdens of sexuality. His equivocation colors the character of Moll's midwife, surrogate mother, governess, deliverer, a laughing hag possessing central, dangerous powers of life and death. This "Mother Midnight"[15] immediately puts "new Life and Spirit into my very Heart; my Blood began to circulate immediately, and I was quite another Body" (p. 162). Yet the midwife also "drives" a wicked trade, and is as capable of "disposing of" as delivering an "innocent lamb." While her house "nauceates" Moll, it also offers decent comforts of clean linen and tasty sweetbreads, and Moll must admit that she never saw nor believed that "there was to be seen the least indecency in the House the whole time I was there" (p. 169).

Yet in spite of the comforts, the problem, the burden in the belly remains. Before the birth, her midwife suggests that "she could help me off with my Burthen sooner, if I was willing; or in *English*, that she could give me something to make me Miscarry." Moll brandishes her abhorrence, while her nurse backs off with a "negative" before Moll can even "explain" herself. Both women depend upon an ambiguity of discourse here to protect themselves. The midwife couches her words to remain the deliverer of innocent lambs, while Moll uses her abhorrence to sustain her respectability. But the problem at hand, the "great and main Difficulty . . . must be remov'd, and that so as that it should never be possible for any one to discover it" (p. 173).

Speaking clearly now, the midwife offers to put Moll's child out to nurse, but Moll cannot even think of such a solution "without Horror." Her squeamishness comes as a surprise. Leaving children behind seemed easy enough in the past, but then this pregnancy is the first one Moll has experienced on her own, and the bastard is Jemmy's, a child of love. Pregnancy produces in the hardiest a dependence that must turn inward if it is not met outwardly, and while Moll could report blithely that her first two children were "taken happily off my hands" (p. 59), she decides

---

[15] In his discussion of "Mother Midnight," Robert Erickson, "Moll's Fate: 'Mother Midnight' and *Moll Flanders*", *Studies in Philology*, 76, 1 (1979), pp. 75–100, connects midwifery to thievery and "art." His *Mother Midnight: Birth, Sex and Fate in Eighteenth-Century Fiction*, New York, 1986, also deals with this subject.

that to give up Jemmy's child would be "to murther it, or at least starve it by Neglect and Ill-Usage" (p. 173).

At first it appears that Moll takes an unusually definite stand here. Since care is "needful to the life of Children, to neglect them is to Murther them; again to give them up to be Manag'd by those People who have none of that needful Affection plac'd by Nature in them is to Neglect them in the highest Degree . . . 'tis even an intentional Murther, whether the Child lives or dies" (p. 174). But significantly, after voicing her objections to wet nursing, she succumbs to its practical benefits. Moll's wavering scruples reflect the uneasy vacillations of a society taking into account the cost of its physical economy. Her use of a system she abhors reveals the unrealistic expense of a domesticity that only works in the middle-class fantasies promulgated in conduct codes. "I am giving an account of what was, not of what ought or ought not to be," Molls reminds her reader, pointing to the unaccountability of the "ought" she must continuously suppress to survive (p. 98).

She does not exaggerate her culture's fear of the wet nurse, nor its fascination wth the nurse's surrogate powers. In his study of eighteenth-century infant mortality, George Rosen argues that where the custom of wet nursing existed, the consequences were deadly. Children sent out to nurse in London were particularly at risk in the less salubrious section of the city "where noxious Effluvia are continually surrounding it; or in some narrow Lane or close Alley." In the expanding city, that entity that Rosen calls "the devouring Moloch," infants were said to be exposed to wet nurses "not infrequently filthy" who "suffered from skin conditions and syphilis . . . with which they infected their charges." Cadogan argued that "the ancient Custom of exposing them to Wild Beasts or drowning them would certainly be a much quicker and more humane way of despatching them," rather than commit them to slow deaths of neglect.

Such attacks may be directly related to the inhuman practices of the nurse (one drunkenly placed her charge on a fire, mistaking it for a log), but they also suggest a larger uneasiness about the dislocations of an urban life increasingly difficult to order.[16] This new way of living depends upon the close attentions of strangers, and promotes unnatural intimacy in circumstances of life and death once associated (perhaps in the imagination more than in reality) more closely to a "natural" order. Moll's acceptance of the system as necessary and ultimately beneficial suggests contradictory needs for connection and efficiency. In spite of the brutality of the nursing system, only one manifestation of a more general disorder

[16] Rosen discusses contagion and wet-nursing in "A Slaughter of Innocents." Dorothy Marshall, *The English Poor in the Eighteenth Century*, New York, 1969, cites examples of the "cruelty of nurses," pp. 98–100. The log anecdote comes from Porter's *Social History*, p. 35. The subject of wet-nursing will be discussed at length in chapter 4.

– unwanted children "over-laid," "starved at nurse," abandoned by the side of the road – Moll's own experience with her nurses (Mother Midnight offering solace for a price and her original nurse back in Colchester) remains positive.

Ironically, Moll makes her case against wet nursing to a woman who cared for her through her pregnancy as "Careful and Tender of me" as if she had been her own mother. This maternal paragon argues that the care she offers can and is duplicated by others ("they are as careful as any Mother of you all"), a commodity as palpable as a chicken roasted and hot. For "when you are gone, what are you to me" she asks Moll, "and what would it be to me if you were to be Hang'd?" Women in her position can only earn their bread by "being as careful of Children as their own Mothers can be" (pp. 174–5). The irony of this remark is not lost on Moll, a careless enough mother and a notoriously unlucky daughter. While the midwife makes her point, she strokes Moll's face: "Never be concern'd Child, *says she*, going on in her drolling way: I have no Murtherers about me." Such ominous words implying murders taking place *somewhere* accompany an appearance both maternal and macabre. Possessing a "bewitching Eloquence" – Moll calls her an old Beldam – when she is not as "silent as Death," the midwife elusively offers a solution both necessary and, in Moll's terms, deadly. Yet in spite of her callous words – "what would it be to me if you were to be Hang'd," – the midwife will later demonstrate personal loyalty to her client, standing fast behind Moll to save her from just such a fate. Within the context of such commercial comfort, Moll's final decision to resort to "murther" becomes anticlimactic. Delivering her child to its nurse, she discovers her to be "wholesome-look'd" and "likely" with good clothes and linen "and everything well about her." All the fears of murther collapse into a qualified acceptance of that which "was the most convenient for me, as my affairs then stood, of any that cou'd be thought of at that time." This solution does not "satisfy my mind," but it is all that there is. And more significantly, all that can be thought of (p. 177).

Like so many solutions in Defoe's world, it is applied a second time. Several years later, Moll looks up her midwife for additional nursing. Her faithful banker has turned out not to have been worth the bustle. Losing first his money, and then his life, he leaves her dismal, desolate, and hungry with two more children to feed. After two years of distress, of weeping and raving and wringing of hands, Moll sets out to steal for her bread. Somewhere along the way, one of her burdens disappears, for when she negotiates her new arrangements with her midwife, only one "litle Son" remains to be "taken off." Meanwhile, she is pleased to learn that Jemmy's bastard is thriving in spite of her inability to keep up her payments. His nurse proves "easie" about the matter (p. 198).

Such easy solutions to such hard problems reflect the dislocations between fiction and fact. Repeatedly Moll encounters material disasters that should overwhelm her, but just as often, she rallies, usually illicitly, to shed her burdens and move on. While Moll the moralist emphasizes the insoluble problems of the burden of the belly, Moll the unfinished, ever-renewed mother appears both encumbered with guilt yet freed from "the great and main Difficulty" that stands between her and independence. While she is guilty of incest, and what she considers "murther," Moll can still retain innocence enough to be able to reward her rich Virginia son, incestuous result of her bigamous marriage, with a stolen watch, guilty material redeemed by her action. This radical innocence converts personal experience into material to be worked for its own rewards. And it is precisely this ability to make use of the materials that block her that sets her apart from her circumscribed world. If she enjoys a triumph, it is one severely qualified not just by the cost of her own life, but by the fantastic nature of her solutions. While endowing her with grotesque qualities of renewal and freedom to transgress with not only impunity, but with the well-earned rewards of her energetic old age, Defoe uses her plight to expose a less magical, closed world of need in which debtors are not blessed but jailed.

If there is no "no" in the unconscious,[17] in her spectacularly renewed triumphs over necessity, the ever-renewed, unfinished Moll exists on just such an unconscious, grotesque level, disavowing the "ought" and the "not" that the "Family Instructor" requires. Moll's radical energy comes from her commitment to dreaming the impossible task of her culture – the union of irreconcilable objects of desire that capitalism requires. In juggling such volatile, yet corporeal materials, Defoe provides his reader with a resolution that can exist only in the imagination. For outside the world of his text, Defoe's reality – intransigent and complex – remains matter in the way.

In *Roxana*, Defoe goes further in his explorations, but without allowing the "good Humour" that Moll can depend upon. While Moll ends her adventures in a recognition scene almost sweet enough to displace the tragically ironic implications of her meeting with her own mother, Roxana is reunited with a daughter that will not fit into the material system she has constructed around her. To shed this most troublesome burden, she resorts to the "Murther" that Moll only thinks about. In this more complex treatment of sexuality, Defoe makes explicit the costs of the sexual economy Roxana and Moll attempt to master, refusing Roxana the fictional freedom over material circumstances. Unlike Moll, Roxana

[17] Sigmund Freud, "Fragment of an Analysis of a Case of Hysteria" (1905), *Dora: An Analysis of a Case of Hysteria*, ed. Philip Rieff, New York, 1963, p. 75.

remains trapped in her "carcass," forced to play over and over the "dreadful scene" of her physical need.

The dreadful scene

Then the dreadful Scene of my Life, when I was left with my five Children, &c. as I have related, represented itself again to me, and I sat considering what Measures I might take to bring myself to such a State of Desolation again, and how I shou'd act to avoid it.   (*Roxana*, p. 162)

In search of economic and sexual self-determination, Roxana exploits the dependency of women, the "slavery" of the feminine condition. She does this dramatically and publicly, turning herself into "a Roxana," contained by a harem of her own making. Stocking her seraglio with materials that will later prove tainted, her famous Turkish dress, her massive pieces of plate too large for "ordinary" use, Roxana transforms her rooms and her person, achieving "Sweet Liberty" at the cost of her self. To maintain independence, she must feign compliance and submission, sacrificing the power she is compelled to pursue. Roxana becomes imprisoned finally by the very sexual and political structures she keeps trying to control, and in the process must "murther" her own daughter, her namesake and a version of herself, to escape detection. In her struggle to escape the "Burthen in the Belly," Roxana becomes more intensely implicated in materials that she cannot overcome or transcend. By not allowing her the space to escape from either her predicament or her knowledge, Defoe forces her condition upon the reader, disallowing us his usual escape hatches of ambiguity. It is, in fact, until *Conjugal Lewdness*, his final, unusually clear word on the matter of matter, a judgment that renders inoperable the pragmatic optimism that propels Moll through her world.

Roxana elaborately presents her body as eroticized material to overcome a fundamental fear of bodily needs. Of all of Defoe's characters, she remains the most persistently hungry, even when she is wallowing in wealth. Yet from the start, she manages to undercut the need she exploits. On the first page of her story, oddly digressive (for Roxana usually sticks to the narrative point), she leaves her family history to attack the sincerity of the "miserable Objects of the poor starving Creatures" that thronged her father's door. These beggars pretend to be French refugees "fled hither . . . on Account of Conscience." Roxana, however, suspects that they are "*something else*" entirely, refugees searching for higher wages instead of religious freedom (pp. 5–6). Such skepticism towards the miserable starvation of others undermines possibilities for sympathy existing anywhere in her narrative. One of the reasons, I think, that readers detach themselves from Roxana's distress is that they follow their narrator's example.[18]

Roxana's original distress is real enough, but it is also staged. She turns herself quite consciously into a "speaking sight" of her predicament, an emblem of the deserted wife left with too many children and too many debts. "You shall judge a little of my present Distress by [its] Posture," she confides: "I was in a Parlour, sitting on the Ground, with a great Heap of old Rags, Linnen . . . and had ben crying ready to burst myself." When visitors arrive to find her in "that Posture," they enter her tableau: "when they saw me; how I look'd . . . they sat down like *Job's* three Comforters, and said not one Word to me for a great while, but both of them cry'd as fast, and as heartily as I did." Noting twice the posture, Defoe now amplifies Roxana's self-consciousness through biblical analogues. Like Job and like the "pitiful women of *Jerusalem*," Roxana is experiencing real need, but her allusion to these traditional sufferers extends that need into theatre. "The truth was, there was no Need of much Discourse in the Case, the Thing spoke it self." Yet in her own discourse, Roxana must describe just that "thing" as she sets the stage for her despair:

they saw me in Rags and Dirt, who was but a little before riding in my Coach; thin, and almost like one Starv'd, who was before fat and beautiful: The House, that was before handsomely furnish'd with Pictures and Ornaments, Cabinets, Peir-Glasses, and every thing suitable, was now stripp'd, and naked. (pp. 127–8)

Roxana is actually presenting two scenes here, one of her former affluence, one of her present "Misery and Distress." The contrast in fact *becomes* the distress. To defend herself against future devastation, Roxana will both load herself down with cumbersome possessions and clothe her nakedness with materials that will become signs of her guilt, plate that exposes her compromised career, diamonds that implicate her in the death of her jeweler-husband and, of course, her famous Turkish dress. The strategies are self-defensive. Just as her landlord "had torn the Goods out of my House like a Fury" (p. 26), Amy the maid will later "gut" his household before she and her mistress flee Paris. Material dilemmas require material solutions which are always, in Roxana's case, exaggerated.

When Roxana heightens her own distress, she justifies her actions while addressing the problem of articulating "complicated Distress" affectively enough to penetrate dull readers absorbed in their own needs. Hunger, real enough, threatens to become cannibalism. "We had eaten up almost

[18] John Richetti, *Defoe's Narratives: Situations and Structures*, Oxford, 1975, suggests that Roxana is introducing herself here as an ironist aware of two levels of reality, public and private (p. 198).

every thing, and little remain'd, unless, like one of the pitiful Women of *Jerusalem*, I should eat up my very Children themselves" (p. 18). Rather than turn cannibal, Roxana :"hardned [her] heart against [her] own Flesh and Blood" to send them away from her dilemma. Like Moll, she regards her actions with self-loathing. Parish children run the risk of "being Starv'd at Nurse" (p. 19), while parish nurses are nothing more than "She-Butchers, who take Children off of their [mother's] Hands, as 'tis call'd; that is to say, starve 'em, and in a Word, murther 'em" (p. 80). And like Moll, she sacrifices her children to "save" them, freeing herself at the same time from their needs. It is important to recognize how often Defoe presents the dilemma of superfluous "useless mouths," those hapless children of Moll and Roxana, children who might grow up to be Colonel Jack, mouths multiplied beyond computation in the dreadful plague year. Within such a context of corporate and corporeal need, only heightened distress has the chance of being felt.

But at the same time, in Roxana's case, Defoe makes us recognize its exaggerated state. For while Roxana is contemplating cannibalizing her own children, Amy, fellow sufferer and fellow actor, enters the tableau of her distress carrying "a small Breast of Mutton, and two great Bunches of Turnips, which she intended to stew for our Dinner." Ready to eat her children or be eaten by them, Roxana dines on mutton, a cheap cut, but meat nonetheless.

It is not that Roxana is merely greedy, but that she suffers from an appetite impossible to satisfy as long as the threat of deprivation exists. The dieted body retains its fat cells almost wilfully, protecting itself from the irregular regimen forced upon it by its owner trying to lose weight. Roxana acts much like that body. Once thin and ragged, she can never be too fat or possess too much heavy plate. Obsessively, she returns over and over to this "dreadful Scene of my Life." It "represents itself" to her, forcing her to consider how to "act" to prevent its recurrence.

While Roxana is exaggerating her misery, her maid Amy, "faithful to me, as the Skin to my Back" (p. 25), is transforming it. To arouse Roxana's indifferent relations to her plight, she tells a tale of woe which is strictly speaking "*something else*" than the truth. Her mistress has been turned out-of-doors, her children taken from her body, and after swooning away, Roxana has "run distracted" to be "put into a Mad-House by the Parish" (p. 22). This false story "all acted to the Life" softens hard hearts. Without Amy's lies, Roxana's relations would have stuck to their original fear of being "eaten" alive by their hungry charges. In tracing these fictional strategies, Defoe calls attention to the complications of a physical economy in which truth itself becomes a luxury. Yet he is not presenting the roguish antics of a picaro cutting a swath through the materials of necessity. He comes close, instead, to presenting a tragedy.

Irony prevents the tragic implications of Roxana's story from being fully realized. It is an irony, I would imagine, that Defoe turned on himself, for in refusing Roxana's need for complete authenticity, he undermines the rationalizations of necessity that he no doubt employed too often in his own checkered career. The problem the "real" Defoe presents is complex, for as dreamer laureate of a capitalist system that he found too hard to manage, he needs to believe what his experiences repeatedly prove false. To escape from the onerous burden of everyday life, he invokes "necessity" to explain away the more commonplace irritations that invalidate his principles. At his sternest, Defoe the apologist claims that men will steal rather than starve, and eat their neighbor if hard pressed, but Defoe's own bizarre schemes of brick making and civet-cat breeding belie these austere truths and point to a preposterous level of desire projecting schemes of predictable irregularity.[19]

When he is being most scrupulous, Defoe delineates the excessive appetite that drives his characters into their most extreme positions. All the while "necessity" is being invoked to excuse criminal actions, Moll and Roxana both reveal something beyond need in their outsized adventures. Moll attempts to haul away a trunk too heavy to manage, and steals a horse inappropriate enough to "quite confound" her usually unflappable governess, while Roxana hoards plate and jewels that weigh her down while threatening to expose her guilty past. Moll and Roxana – and Defoe – promote their baroque schemes of survival because they know that however much they accrue, they stand, "overnight," to lose what they have so painfully gained.

For the material world offers too many surprises. When Roxana's husband, "the Fool," wanders off, he vanishes as mysteriously as an apparition in a romance. Roxana knows not where he went, nor what he intended to do, "no more than if the Ground had open'd and swallow'd" him up. Her ignorance here is feigned, for, as she knows in her act of narration, he will turn up a hundred pages later in Paris, alive and well. Her heightening of his sordid departure is typical. Defoe displays a qualified commitment to the conventions of romance because in the romance, needs are idealized – starkly – to redeem actions. But the ironic qualification undercuts the necessity even as it recognizes it. Thus in keeping with the idealized mystery of her husband's disappearance, Roxana decides histrionically that she should have endured poverty rather than give up her virtue: "I had been happy, tho' I had perish'd of meer Hunger; for without question, a Woman ought rather to die, than to prostitute her Virtue and Honor, let the Temptation be what it will" (p. 29). But such dramatic stoicism becomes overwhelmed by the more mundane material circumstances of life. Prepared to perish of hunger,

[19] James Sutherland discusses Defoe's farcical dealings in civet cats, *Defoe*, p. 40.

Roxana gives up her virtue for a leg of veal and a piece of the foreribs of roasting beef.

Defoe links her taste for veal to Roxana's taste for flesh itself, an appetite both fallen and irreducible. Roasted veal awakens her inclination, while three or four glasses of wine lift up her spirits. Like her lover's words, they provide a "Cordial to [her] very Soul," and bring her "life from the Dead," bring her "from the Brink of the Grave itself" (p. 30): that same grave that, in Defoe's estimation, she is busy eating herself into with sharp, hungry teeth. The "Bounty" of her lover "surprize[s]" Roxana, for the same man "had but a little while ago been my Terror, and had torn the Goods out of my House, like a Fury" p. 26). In responding to his new "Face" of compassion and kindness, Roxana also responds to the power hidden beneath the compassion. In her submission, she uses her sexuality to propitiate both his appetite and hers.

Such tactful compliance becomes "natural" to Roxana. To contain the "Fury" and fill her belly, she yields to her landlord, confessing that the pressure of her dreadful scene, "the Memory of which lay heavy upon my Mind, and the surprizing Kindness with which he had deliver'd me" (p. 34) took away her power to deny him. Kindness is after all, only another "Face" of a fury dangerously unpredictable. Roxana's sexual strategies are designed to contain just that element of uncontrolled "Terror." For she learns in this episode that if she complies and "pleases," her fortune will be provisionally restored, her "Wilderness" will turn back into a garden (pp. 32–3). Overcome by the comforts the landlord offers her, she sits down to cry "for Joy" just as she "had formerly cry'd for Sorrow" (p. 31), connecting in her action as she always will scenes of need with scenes of plenty. In making this connection, she locks herself into a sexual system that she calls "whoring" from the start, a system that depends upon women submitting (with tearful joy) to men in power.

Her compliance is complicated by her own desire, for although Roxana insists that she "had nothing of the Vice in my Constitution; my Spirits were far from being high; my Blood had no Fire in it, to kindle the Flame of Desire" (p. 40), she is sensual enough to admit that her landlord's sexual discourse "fires" the blood (p. 36). Preferring to employ rather than own her desire, Roxana repeatedly demonstrates a sexuality made by necessity instrumental. "Reduced" to contemplation of her dreadful scene, she uses her "frailty" to attain mastery. Her incorporation of her self is so thorough that she immediately makes her condition part of a larger system that can contain "Amy's Disaster" (p. 45). Stripping her faithful maid naked, Roxana throws her into bed with her landlord-husband, not only procuring for him a "Wife of his Aversion," but marking her place as "Wife of his Affection." She is beginning to operate in a sexual system that would be familiar to Montesquieu's Usbek – the harem.

As "*Man-Woman*," denaturing herself to control her nature, Roxana plays eunuch to her own desires in an attempt to control the larger furies outside herself.

Roxana ironically uses her own body to chastise its appetite. While her meticulous inventories of her material charms betray an intense self-absorption, her self-esteem is always tempered by a more functional memory of need that both rationalizes her actions and degrades her present success. When the Prince proves "astonished" at her beauty, she alludes immediately to her dreadful scene, "the Misery I was fallen into" (p. 72), knowing too well "what this Carcass of mine had been but a few Years before; how overwhelmed with Grief, drown'd in Tears, frighted with the Prospect of Beggary, and surrounded with Rags, and Fatherless Children; that was pawning and selling the Rags that cover'd me, for a Dinner, and sat on the Ground, despairing of Help, and expecting to be starv'd." As she recalls and retells "the dirty History of my Actings upon the Stage of Life," her dreadful scene is, as always, slightly distorted. This time she misremembers that her children were snatched from her to be kept by the Parish rather than dumped upon unwilling relations. In her tale, Roxana becomes a "Whore for Bread," possessor of a "Prostituted Body," who "perhaps wou'd not have denied one of [the Prince's] Footmen but a little while before, if I cou'd have got my Bread by it." In this sudden reduction, Roxana creates a tableau of dire necessity set in her past to justify her present consumption of diamond necklaces. She debases herself, becoming fit meat for a footman's dish, but at the same time exonerates herself from her excessive greed with the plea of a necessity that can never be met (pp. 74–5). Just as Swift insists upon the "carcass" beneath the plumped flesh, the decay painted over, Roxana regards her true self as so much flesh and blood, carcass marked by a need that both devalues and rationalizes her grossest triumphs.

Even as she flails her fallen carcass, Roxana insists upon her materiality. To demonstrate that her beauty "*is the meer Work of Nature*," she calls for a cup full of hot water, asks the Prince to "feel if it was warm," and washes her face all over. In making her "undeniable Demonstration" of her physicality, Roxana transforms matter into erotic material that can be exhibited, seducing not just the Prince but herself with her sight. "I say, I was no despisable Shape," she reminds the reader. And when the Prince clasps her neck, which was "long and small," with a necklace of diamonds, catching her reflection in the mirror, Roxana goes all on fire with the sight. Having turned herself into material, she can extend herself into the "charms" artificially covering her, becoming a commercialized fetish of her own desires. In *Conjugal Lewdness*, Defoe might present the naked, eager bride as the erotic ideal, but in the real world, the unclothed carcass must be supplemented. As the Prince says, every thing must be "suitable;

a fine Gown and Petticoat; a fine lac'd Head; a fine Face and Neck, and no Necklace, would not have made the Object perfect" (p. 72–3).

Slavish freedoms: ironic structures of containment

Detaching herself from the carcass she insists upon, Roxana turns herself into an instrument of her own sexuality. In her liaison with her Dutch merchant, she demonstrates her calculation in the disposal of her body. To maintain her freedom, she resolves "at least" to "feign to be as merry as he, and that in short, if he offer'd any-thing, he shou'd have his Will easily enough" (p. 142). Roxana is generous here in one way, grudging in another, for in offering her "feigned" sexuality, she can keep her essential self intact. She can also satisfy desire, for as she adds, "we" were very merry three days and nights enjoying "unlawful Freedoms." In detaching herself from desire she nonetheless acts out, Roxana establishes a freedom most difficult to maintain. She must pretend to enjoy a sexuality that will eventually cost too much to reproduce.

By the time she encounters her merchant, Roxana has learned the cost of assigning her body to men. One husband has wandered off, one landlord has been murdered, one Prince has turned penitent. While her fool husband left her impoverished, the others left her richer financially but poorer emotionally. She almost "cry'd [herself] to Death" for the loss of her jeweler (p. 54), and confesses that the reformation of the Prince "was a Storm upon" her (p. 109). To maintain an emotional as well as financial independence, Roxana makes her infamous argument against the "slavery" that a woman must endure in marriage, a diminished condition that she considers the inevitable result of being subsumed into the life of another. Her merchant defends such dependency, arguing that since the man bears the weight of business, "the Anxiety of Living," it is fitting for the woman to do nothing but "eat the Fat, and drink the Sweet; to sit still, and look round her; be waited on and made much of; be serv'd, and lov'd, and made easie" (p. 148). She would become an object of his well-earned conspicuous consumption, as symbolic in her indolence as one of Usbek's wives locked up in his seraglio.[20] Roxana resists such easy bondage, preferring to retain her "masculine" capacity for self-direction. In her complaint against the passivity that must characterize the merchant's "Creature," she suddenly retells the "dreadful Scene" of her own married state. In trusting the exertions of a mere man, a mere wife might find herself "stripp'd to the Cloaths on her Back . . . see her Children starve; herself miserable," until she "breaks her Heart; and cries herself to Death" (p. 150). To protect herself from such dangerous dependency,

[20] Spiro Peterson discusses Defoe's ideas about the "slavery" of the matrimonial state in "The Matrimonial Theme of Defoe's *Roxana*," *PMLA*, 70 (1955), 185–6.

Roxana, speaking "*Amazonian* Language," declares that "seeing Liberty seem'd to be the Men's Property, I wou'd be a *Man-Woman*, for as I was born free, I wou'd die so" (p.171).

The context of her declaration exposes the precarious nature of her freedom. She has just delivered her merchant's bastard, the direct result of the power struggle between the two of them for "Freedom," product of Roxana's strategy to "bite" her lover rather than be "bitten" by him (p. 144). As her pregnancy suggests, the bite works both ways, leaving Roxana, not the merchant, with a burden to be dealt with. "I would willingly have given ten Thousand Pounds of my Money to have been rid of the Burthen I had in my Belly," she confides, "but it cou'd not be so" (p. 163). Roxana arranges for the merchant's bastard's welfare with icy reluctance, confessing that "I did not love the child nor love to see it." Resolving that "when it grew up, it should not be able to call me Mother" (p. 228), she "often wish'd it wou'd go quietly out of the World" (p. 263). But as her legitimate daughter Susan demonstrates, children, however burdensome, do not go quietly.

To maintain an equivocal freedom, Roxana exploits publicly and dramatically the "slavery" of unaccommodated woman by turning herself into "a Roxana,"[21] mistress to the court contained in a seraglio of her own invention. "Home," that fragile structure that can be "gutted" by furious landlords, deserted by wayward husbands, becomes a public "house" of pleasure as notorious as the Sign of the Cradle. Domestic space literally sprawls into the street "full of Coaches with Coronets, and fine Glass-Chairs," while a mob of suppliants require "a strong Party of the Guards . . . to keep the Door, for without that there had been such a promiscuous Crowd, and some of them scandalous too, that we shou'd have been all Disorder and Confusion" (p. 178). The order she maintains, like the freedom she insists upon, is illusory; the confusion underlying the glittering surface, "the dreadful Course of Calamities" (p. 329) is the reality.

Playing the slave, Roxana masquerades in the "habit of a Turkish Princess," making a spectacle out of the hunger for consumption that dominates her culture. The habit itself signifies exploitation: "A *Malthese* Man of War had . . . taken a *Turkish* Vessel travelling from *Constantinople* to *Alexandria* . . . and as the Ladies were made Slaves, so their fine Cloaths were thus expos'd" (pp. 173–4). But the fine Turkish ladies, "made Slaves," were already subordinated to the demands of the seraglio confining them. Their "expos'd . . . fine Cloaths" represent the internal slavery

---

[21] "Roxana," the rebellious wife who tries to overthrow Usbek's despotic rule in *The Persian Letters*, is also the courtesan of Alexander who killed his queen Statira in a fit of jealousy. See Blewett's (*Defoe's Art of Fiction*, pp. 123, 165) and Novak's (*Realism, Myth, and History in Defoe's Fiction*, Lincoln NE, 1983, p. 113) glosses on the name.

of the Turkish sexual economy as well as the external slavery attending
the Maltese capture of their vessel. The costume also calls up a sexuality
compromised by Roxana's own position. Her masquerade allows for a
degree of freedom that paradoxically inhibits expression of self. In the
guise of the harem, Roxana reduces herself to the confining role that
frees her to exploit her body. The costume "is not a decent Dress in this
Country," but as "costume,"[22] it turns indecencies into play. By wearing
it, Roxana, pleasing the men of the court with her suppliant posture, is
free only to please, appropriating the confined freedom of the seraglio
where women are locked up the better to display their charms.

Usbek's wives pretended a submissive sexuality that also disguised their
true nature, a nature that Montesquieu's Roxana blows up in her final
rebellion. Such compliance takes years of training. As one of "the animated instruments of men's happiness," Zelis decides to bring her seven-
year-old daughter into the confined seraglio, reasoning that it is not
enough to make women feel "natural" subordination; "we must be made
to practice submission, so that it sustains us in those critical moments
when the passions begin to arouse and encourage us to independence"
(p. 104). The passions need to be directed, "postured," and manipulated
to arouse Usbek's jaded appetite, and in the process desire becomes spectacle. When Zachi recalls "the famous quarrel among your women," she
describes a theatrical presentation of sexuality designed for Usbek's consumption:

Each of us claimed to be superior in beauty to the others: we presented ourselves
to you after exhausting our imaginations on dress and ornament . . . you mar-
veled that we had gone so far in our desire to please you. But you soon made
those borrowed charms give way to more natural graces; you destroyed all our
work; we had to remove all that ornamentation which had wearied you, and to
appear before your gaze in the simplicity of nature . . . Happy Usbek, what
charms were displayed before your eyes! . . . Your curious gaze penetrated to
the most secret places; you made us take a thousand different positions; ever
new commands brought ever new compliance. I confess, Usbek, that a passion
stronger than ambition made me hope to please.   (*Persian Letters*, p. 12)

The ironies in the presentation displace the desire being aroused. Incorporated into a larger sexual spectacle, Zachi responds erotically to those
"charms . . . displayed" before her master. The thousand different postures his wives assume mechanically reproduce an illusion of passion so
convincing that it arouses its agents. (This is not a free passion, but one
circumscribed by Usbek's eventual use of that most desirable object.

[22] Maximillian Novak connects the criminality of the Restoration Court to the excesses of
Roxana's costume in *Realism, Myth and History*, pp. 113–18.

Rivals' despair accompanies Zachi's eventual triumph.) While the members of the seraglio seduce each other as eroticized objects conscious of each other's attractions, the mental fuse of their narcissistic desire complicates the slavery. As Zelis recognizes, in her prison she has been free to taste a thousand pleasures of the imagination that Usbek could never understand. "I have lived while you have only languished," she taunts, commenting on the half-lives they both endure (p. 105). Roxana suggests this same artificially heightened awareness of the sexual power she displays when she later recalls the heady days of her masquerade. Even when her daughter Susan "tells" the story of Roxana, threatening in her discourse to disclose her mother's terrible secret, Roxana still manages to be "pleas'd and tickl'd" with "talk" of "how handsome and how fine a Lady this *Roxana* was" (p. 287).

Zelis and Zachi can achieve their severely limited "freedom" by abstracting themselves from their bodies to explore a sexuality of their own imagination. This distancing is crucial, allowing a nature not just methodized, but mutated. Just as Roxana needs to supplement her carcass with finery to please the Prince, she must posture a "Turkish" sexuality artificially constructed to please her larger audience. Her costume covers over her corporeal self with false finery better than nature itself. Her girdle is set with diamonds, "only they were not true Diamonds; but nobody knew that but myself" (p. 174). Even her famous dance is in truth a fine new figure from Paris. When rival courtesans dressed in Georgian and Armenian habits compete at Roxana's establishment with their own oriental dance, "the Novelty pleas'd, truly, but yet there was something wild and *Bizarre* in it, because they really acted to the Life the barbarous Country whence they came; but as mine had the *French* Behaviour under *Mahometan* Dress, it was every way as new, and pleas'd much better, indeed" (p. 179).

"Wild and *Bizarre*" reality must be covered over with artifice, but the true reality, the "dreadful scene" of hunger, remains just the same. As fearful of being "bitten" as she is of eating up her children, Roxana goes to great lengths to denature herself, playing both the man-woman and the Turkish slave to exert control over a nature that cannot be managed. Just as Usbek's harem depends upon systematic denaturing, turning men into eunuchs and women into imprisoned objects protected from their nature, so Roxana's own sexual economy depends upon a radical denaturing that will turn her into a "butcher" of her own flesh. When Roxana – rich and fat – tries to rationalize her situation, asking repeatedly "*Why am I a Whore now*," she attempts to repudiate desire for its own sake, justifying her "whoring" on more material grounds. Necessity debauched her, Poverty turned her whore, while excess of Avarice and Vanity continued her in the crime. "These were my Baits, these the Chains by which the Devil held me bound" (p. 202). The first link in the chain is the strongest, a hunger so strong that Roxana could eat up her own children and still not get enough to eat. For Roxana, like Moll, is bound into a chain of begetting. Sexuality leads to children leads to hunger leads to sexuality.

The burden finally becomes impossible to incorporate into Roxana's complicated sexual economy. Ironically, the eroticized costume that transformed the man-woman into compliant slave eventually gives her away. It proves so compelling that Susan, Roxana's own daughter, witness to her mother's original "dreadful Scene," can never forget its seductive power. While Roxana has been rationalizing her "debaucheries" by returning obsessively to her original hunger, Susan, the unknowing servant in "Roxana's" household, has been dwelling on the glory of her mother's apotheosis in her Turkish costume. Although the girl possesses only a "broken Account," a discourse of "broken Fragments of Stories" (p. 269), of her disrupted childhood, the material detail of Roxana's Turkish dress remains indelibly imprinted upon her memory. She describes it "so exactly," that Roxana "was surpriz'd at the Manner of her telling it; there was not a Circumstance of it left out" (p. 288).

In her account, Susan tells the hungriest part of Roxana's story, the part that forces nature to denature itself in an attempt to control material circumstances. And as her namesake, for Susan is Roxana's original name, the child bears witness to the dreadful cost of her mother's life, a cost that she, the burden in the belly, is forced to pay. Her knowledge awakens in her mother a passion most intensely felt. "I felt something shoot thro' my Blood; my Heart flutter'd; my Head flash'd, and was dizzy, and all within me, *as I thought*, turn'd about, and much ado I had, not to abandon myself to an Excess of Passion at the first Sight of her, much more when my Lips touch'd her Face; I thought I must have taken her in my Arms, and kiss'd her again a thousand times" (p. 277), Roxana recalls, expressing a passion unequalled in her erotic narrative. But feelings, we are reminded, are too expensive in a world where one eats or is eaten. Passion turns quickly to rage and repulsion, as Roxana kills her feelings for Susan, longing ultimately to "be deliver'd from her" (p. 302). Just as Roxana originally realized that if need arose, she would eat her children rather than be eaten by them, to protect herself from her own daughter's hunger for recognition that would disclose her dreadful secret, Roxana passively gives Susan over to Amy to be dispatched. And in murdering Susan, Amy breaks the natural chain of sexuality that bound Roxana to the nature she kept trying to manage.

The act of murder also ironically delivers Roxana from her "dreadful Scene," supplying new terrors that will shape her narrative. When she understands that Susan has "disappeared," after raving and crying vehemently for over an hour, she puts on "her best Looks" to deceive her husband come in from hunting. His re-entry reverses the condition of Roxana's original desolation, that time her first husband mysteriously disappeared on a hunting expedition. New dreadful scenes of Susan's suffering, her murder committed "in a hundred Shapes and Postures" (pp. 324–5), replace the old nightmare.

With the death of Susan, the narrative collapses. Roxana makes one attempt to reclaim a maternity she has been denying in visiting her other daughter, "the very Counterpart of myself" (p. 329). But after one short paragraph packed with calamities, Roxana is blasted off the page for her crime. Her failure to attain "freedom" exposes the physical system that contains her as certainly as it exposes her own "guilty" consciousness of *"the Dearness of things* necessary to life."

In killing her namesake, Roxana points to the price of surviving in a world of material and emotional cannibals, where desire, made manifest in her meeting with Susan, can only feed on itself. This world will be seen even more starkly when Defoe and Swift consider the problems of not just balancing individual needs and desires, but of feeding the only known quantity, the bodies, that refused to be idealized or incorporated into a system which depends, after all, on consumption.

Roxana's unsatisfying end emphasizes the fantastic nature of Moll's triumph. Moll escapes the strictures of patriarchy and capitalism in adventures that Defoe dreams for her, managing to succeed by denying with energetic enthusiasm the contradictions of her equivocal state. But Roxana seems to pay for Moll's holiday as she incorporates within herself the price of the contradictions of a physical economy that prohibits the "lewdness" it nonetheless insists upon. While Defoe argues in *Conjugal Lewdness* that matrimony is a state rather than a circumstance, in his fictional narratives, the circumstantial aspects of domesticity rule as arbitrarily as "the Invisible Hand" that "blasts" Moll's happiness. Subject always to the fall not into knowledge, not into experience, but into "Disorder and Confusion," "a dreadful Course of Calamities," Defoe finally stops dreaming comic solutions to tragic problems of necessity and desire as he exposes the cost of a sexual system that "murthers" its children to feed its desires.

4

Flesh and blood: Swift's sexual strategies

> For fine Ideas vanish fast,
> While all the gross and filthy last.
>
> "Strephon and Chloe," *Poems* II, 591, lines 233–4

Unlike Defoe dreaming Moll's escape from Roxana's nightmare, Swift cannot even begin to imagine women from the inside. Keeping his ironic distance, he flails and strips "the sex" to get at the truth of its loathsome condition. The knowledge he produces is always external and judgmental. For reasons cultural as well as psychological, Swift defines women according to a physicality that is gross, filthy, and lasting. Women threaten to scatter reason, waste energy, and destroy the possibility of civilization. The disorderly energies that Swift so actively invokes in his fictional explorations of women must be repressed or denied to be endured. In the end, he can only run from the engrossing feminine temptations of unreason that he has both exposed and invented.

Swift's consciousness of the absurdity of his position produces an ironic detachment that serves to protect him from the hysterical implications of his misogyny. Strephon, silly Strephon, is the cracked one, he blandly reassures his gentle reader, not me. *I* stuff rue up my nose. Indirectly, he displaces the burden of sexual detection upon the reader, so often blamed for all the filthy imaginings Swift both invents and attacks. His retreat from women is complicated even further by his need for them. He demonstrates repeatedly a fearful attraction for the nurse figure, that maternal surrogate who nourishes and punishes. Jealous of his own independence, yet hungry for the attentions of a governing yet servile feminine figure, Swift represents in his fictions a system of sexual strategies that allow repressed juvenile fantasies to be both explored and contained.

The explorer is always at risk. A central fictional situation Swift offers his reader is the paralyzing discovery of the body. Characteristically, Swiftian explorers both ferret out and run away from their knowledge. Gulliver discloses the yahoo nature he is bent on repressing when he taunts his "fellow" yahoos with his physicality. "I have reason to believe," he primly reports, "they had some Imagination that I was of their own

Species, which I often assisted myself, by stripping up my Sleeves, and shewing my naked Arms and Breast in their Sight, when my Protector was with me." On occasion, Gulliver will even strip himself stark naked beneath the lustful gaze of a young female yahoo who embraces him "after a most fulsome Manner" and quits her grasp "with the utmost Reluctancy." Mortified by her "natural Propensity to me as one of their own Species," Gulliver spends the rest of his time on the island of the Houyhnhnms trying to deny the fact that he has forced into consciousness, that he possesses the body of a species he loathes even to look at. But even his loathing seems suspect. After catching a young male of three years, he coyly supplies a "Circumstance" to vex his reader: "that while I held the odious Vermin in my Hands, it voided its filthy Excrements of a yellow liquid Substance, all over my Cloaths" (*GT*, pp. 265–7). Gulliver's shock of recognition is at best a stock response to a physical drama scripted to confirm his predictable worst suspicions.

Swift's fascinated revulsion towards the physical becomes even more axiomatic when he confronts "the Sex." It takes a female yahoo, "not . . . above Eleven Years old" (p. 267), to make it impossible for Gulliver to deny his yahoo nature. The horror of the physically known "Species," that category of creatures so like, but necessarily unlike the self, becomes the horror of the physically known woman caught inevitably in the act of being vile. Thus Strephon and Cassinus lose their wits and pride with their discovery that Celia, Celia, Celia shits, compelled as they are to seek assiduously after well-hidden secrets of the hoary deep. Spying on nature, most particularly feminine nature, they become debilitated by their own discoveries of natural acts.

Corporeal knowledge becomes particularly vexing in marriage, that dreaded state of "Repentance, Discord, Poverty, Jealousy, Sickness, Spleen, Loathing, &c." (*PW*, IV, p. 252). A "known" Chloe who farts and stinks with abandon is no more acceptable than the inaccessible Goddess exuding ambrosia. Anality might replace sublimity, but the body still gets in the way. "Love such Nicety requires," Strephon and Chloe learn: "One Blast will put out all his Fires" (lines 135–6). Swift's solution to the problem: Don't eat beans.

The advice is both serious and ludicrous, typical of Swift's radically simplified sexual discourse.

> Keep them to wholsome Food confin'd,
> Nor let them taste what causes Wind;
> ('Tis this the Sage of *Samos* means,
> Forbidding his Disciples Beans)   (lines 123–6)

The sage, Swift reminds his readers in a note, is Pythagoras, infamous for his own personal and philosophical attempts to purify the body. Such

notorious asceticism would appear to sit well with Swift, and finds its way
into the clean, bracing regimen of the Houyhnhnms, whose nature is so
very easily satisfied. But simple solutions verge on farce in the real world,
where once she "has got the Art," Miss Moll, archetypal "*Jade*," will not
be able to restrain her natural self from letting loose. "She cannot help it
for her Heart; / But, out it flies" (lines 128–31). Swift presents here a
physical nature irrepressible and gross. Inverting conduct-manual for-
mula, he suggests that maidens will need to "learn" the art of letting "it"
fly, or rather unlearn the false modesty pasted over their base nature,
but he is not implying that the natural maid is any less disgusting. Had
Strephon only been wise enough to spy on Chloe before "that fatal Day"
on her "House of Ease," he would have detected the true woman:

> In all the Postures of her Face,
> Which Nature gives in such a Case;
> Distortions, Groanings, Strainings, Heavings;
> 'Twere better you had lickt her Leavings.   (lines 239–42)

No matter how many beans incipient goddesses forebear ingesting, they
will always reveal themselves to be at bottom filthy. While blandly advising
Chloe "from the Spouse each Blemish hide, / More than from all the
World beside" (lines 253–4), Swift grimly sends out his platoons of sexual
spies in search of her nature. Inverting Platonic idealism, Swift argues
that the truly "real," the matter that is Chloe, will overcome the ideal, "For
fine ideas vanish fast, / While all the gross and filthy last." To reconcile the
demands of flesh and spirit, Strephon should shun the body altogether
and found his passion on sense and wit. Love will become friendship,
nature will be refined into "good nature," while sexuality itself will turn
into discourse.

   The ironies implicit in Swift's discourse provide a necessary distance,
for the female body threatens not only to offend, but to scatter reason
and swallow up certainty. The women themselves tend to fall apart,
revealing a dissolution that inspires terror and sometimes – in passing –
pity. Swift graphically mangles his "Beautiful Young Nymph Going to
Bed," before making a judgment that both approaches and denies his
satirical victim's need:

> But how shall I describe her Arts
> To recollect the scatter'd Parts?
> Or shew the Anguish, Toil, and Pain,
> Of gath'ring up herself again?
>   (*Poems*, II, p. 583, lines 67–70)

In spite of incipient sympathy, the narrator of the poem finally withdraws
to leave Corinna "in the Morning dizen'd," warning that "Who sees, will
spew; who smells, be poison'd" (lines 73–4). Similarly, the Celia of "The

Progress of Beauty" mechanically rots away each night to awaken to a dissolution of materials most alarming in their mutability.[1] The dissolution becomes moral as well as physical. If matter offends, scattered matter compounds the offense. The disorder which results blurs distinction and makes it difficult for Swift to find fault as precisely as he would wish. For how can he catalog chaos?[2] Chattering over their cards, roaring and railing louder than the rabble, grosser than a pack of fishwives over their gin, "Modern Ladies," each one a filthy mate, dissolve into "The Jumbling Particles of Matter" that "In Chaos made not such a Clatter" (*Poems*, II, pp. 444–53, lines 184–5). The scattered matter the women represent, "*Mopsa*, who stinks her Spouse to Death," "*Hircana* rank with sweat" (lines 156–8), threaten with a physicality that violates even the possibility of order.

When Swift rails at the disorderly nature of women, he is not only revealing personal fears of dissolution, but articulating the same uneasiness we have seen in the work of Defoe and Montesquieu. Unless they are somehow contained or occupied, women threaten to scatter vital energy that Freud would later recuperate as materials necessary to build civilization and its discontents. The sexual act, scattering material most personal, and its "necessary passion" requires, as Mandeville complained, a medium most difficult to hit.[3] While a "healthy" use of the body was encouraged, much discourse dwells on the possibility of failure, waste, or excess.[4]

By nature excessive, Swift most dramatically calls up visions of disorder that threaten to overwhelm his own plans to chastise sense. In his sermon on "The Difficulty of Knowing One's Self," Swift alludes to the problems of "collect[ing] all his scattered and roving Thoughts into some Order and Compass, that he may be able to take a clear and distinct View of

---

[1] As Felicity Nussbaum notes, "without substantial form, woman soon fades," *The Brink of All We Hate*, p. 101.

[2] In her study of Swift's "Disordered World of the Gentlewoman," Louise K. Barnett discusses Swift's catalogs implicating women as the source of earthly disorder. *Swift's Poetic Worlds*, Newark, 1981, p. 159.

[3] *A Modest Defence of Publick Stews*, p. 28.

[4] The edgy fear of emission is difficult to date. As Lawrence Stone suggests, when Tissot announces that the loss of one ounce of semen equals the loss of forty ounces of blood, he was offering a "new version of Avicenna's medieval claim that one ejaculation is more debilitating than forty bloodlettings," an old belief particularly attractive to a sexual economy dedicated to exercising their complicated iatrohydraulic sexual systems. Stone, *The Family, Sex and Marriage*, pp. 495–8. Christopher Fox discusses the "early eighteenth-century anti-masturbatory craze sparked, at least in part, by a pamphlet titled *ONANIA*, London, 1709–10" in "The Myth of Narcissus in Swift's *Travels*," *Eighteenth-Century Studies*, 20 (1986), pp. 17–33. Charles E. Rosenburg considers a later nineteenth-century concern with "control" in his discussion of repression and masturbation in "Sexuality, Class and Role," *No Other Gods: On Science and American Social Thought*, Baltimore and London, 1976, pp. 71-88.

them." The only answer is retirement from the world of sense and sensuality, "and how hard and painful a thing must it needs be to a Man of Passion and Infirmity, amidst such a Crowd of Objects that are continually striking upon the Sense, and solliciting the Affections, not to be moved and interrupted by one or other of them."[5] His solution, characteristically radical, suggests a struggle he counters with irony, for to protect his vulnerability, he insists upon the most threatening of visions made deliberately bland through a world weariness verging on parody.

Typically, he presents the terror experienced by naïve subjects enclosed within his own ironic frame. In "The Lady's Dressing Room," Strephon goes mad with the realization that *Celia, Celia, Celia* shits, but his narrator deflates this hysteria to reassure the reader that as long as he stuffs rue up his nose, Strephon should come to appreciate the sex he flees. By mocking Strephon's hysteria, Swift projects a more urbane acceptance of the gaudy tulips he purports to admire. But in one chilling couplet, Swift reveals the reason for the terror he barely contains by disowning Strephon's madness. "Should I the Queen of Love refuse," the narrator asks, "Because she rose from stinking Ooze?" (*Poems*, II, p. 530, lines 131–2). Swift alludes here to a myth of dismemberment, of scattering, and of physical devouring that calls up everything that keeps him out of conjugal beds. For in these lines, the narrator grounds Celia's being in a stinking ooze which is not just offensive, but generative at the expense of masculine sexuality. One of the variations of the myth of Venus' birth depends upon the emasculation of Uranus. In punishment for his rebellion against the gods, Uranus's testicles were ripped from his body and tossed into the sea. Venus rose out of the ooze and froth generated from his mutilation. (It is worth remembering that the Yahoos also were believed to have originated from the ooze and froth of the sea.) The way Swift negligently tosses off such volatile material complicates the terror of the emasculation, but the image remains: Venus symbolically devouring Uranus in her ascension.[6]

Swift employs images of devouring equally troubling in much of *Gulliver's Travels*. Capable of taking up twenty or thirty smaller fowl at the

---

[5] *PW*, IX, p. 356. "As soon as the Appetite is alarmed, and seizeth upon the Heart, a little Cloud gathereth about the Head, and spreadeth a kind of Darkness over the Face of the Soul, whereby it is hindered from taking a clear and distinct View of Things." IX, p. 358.

[6] Hesiod, *Theogony*, trans. Dorothea Wender, Harmondsworth, p. 29, lines 188–200. See Robert Graves, *The Greek Myths*, 2 vols., Harmondsworth, I, pp. 37–9, 49–50. Donald Greene argues that "if one wanted to be 'archetypal', one could praise Swift's awareness – in the parallel illustration of Venus, symbol of human love and warmth and the continuity of the human species, rising from the Mediterranean slime – of the great eternal facts of the human condition," and goes on to find Swift sounding "Joycean" here, "a robust Irish Molly Bloom in clerical garb." "On Swift's 'Scatological' Poems," *Sewanee Review*, 75 (1967) pp. 672–89; reprinted in *Essential Articles for the Study of Jonathan Swift's Poetry*, ed. David M. Vieth, Hamden, CT, 1984, p. 227.

end of his knife, Gulliver on Lilliput can tease his captors with his voracious ways, pretending on one occasion, penknife in hand, a readiness to eat the more impudent members of the rabble alive (p. 31). Gulliver on Brobdingnag, more obviously vulnerable, barely escapes being eaten alive by a large infant who is only pacified by "the last Remedy," a "monstrous Breast" that perfectly disgusts Gulliver (p. 91). Later an even more "horrible Spectacle," a cancerous breast "swelled to a monstrous Size, full of Holes, in two or three of which I could have easily crept, and covered my whole Body," threatens in its swollen magnitude to engulf him (pp. 112–3). But then Brobdingnag offers room for many "nauseous sights." The Queen herself, although boasting a weak stomach, "would craunch the Wing of a Lark, Bones and all, between her Teeth," while the malicious dwarf almost drowns Gulliver in a bowl of cream and manages to stuff him into a marrow bone ready to be eaten (pp. 106–8). When the dwarf plays his naughty tricks, he is turning his enemy into material for consumption, food fit for a queen. Even on Laputa, appetite interferes with the pursuit of the ideal. While their husbands keep one eye on heaven, their notorious wives keep one eye on Lagado, threatening to break out and slide down to feed on less idealistically inclined males. Even the queen appears suspicious enough to be kept confined to the island until she is past childbearing. The fate of the prime minister's lady serves as a warning. "On the Pretence of Health," she managed to slip down to Lagado to hide away in an "obscure Eating-House" where she consumed the pleasures of "an old deformed Footman, who beat her every day" (p. 166).

Overwhelmed by so many predators, Gulliver would have understood too well John Maubray's description in his *Female Physician* of the "*attractive Faculty*" of the famished womb. As Nicholas Venette warned, "The Womb of a Woman is in the Number of the insatiable things mentioned in the Scriptures . . . and I cannot tell whether there is anything in the World, its greediness may be compared unto; neither Hell fire nor the Earth being so devouring, as the Privy Parts of a Lascivious Woman."[7] For a man as (ironically) desperate for order as Swift (for "Order governs the world. The Devil is the author of confusion"[8]), the sexual act itself threatens to subsume rationality always perilous just as surely as Venus threatens to devour Uranus' manhood. Throughout his work Swift employs powerful metaphors to contain that which threatens, but at the same time, he appears compelled to explore the stinking ooze in spite of himself. For as Defoe reflects in his fiction, and as Swift demonstrates not

---

[7] Robert A. Erickson, "The Books of Generation," p. 84, and Boucé, "Some Sexual Beliefs and Myths," *Sexuality in Eighteenth-century Britain*, ed. Boucé, p. 42.

[8] *JS*, I, p. 72. See also "Doing Good: A Sermon," *PW*, IX, p. 238, for a less ironic discussion of the Devil, author of confusion, struggling against a "God of Order."

only in his literary productions but in his self-consciously acted out life, desire, even when desire leads into death, is most difficult to quell. Swift may advise us not to eat beans, but in spite of dieting, the appetite itself gets in the way.

Dieting desire

> Then *Gluttony* with greasy Paws,
> Her Napkin pinn'd up to her Jaws,
> With watry Chaps, and wagging Chin,
> Brac'd like a Drum her oily Skin;
> Wedg'd in a spacious Elbow-Chair,
> And on her Plate a treble Share,
> As if she ne'er could have enuff;
> Taught harmless Man to cram and stuff.
>   "A Panegyric on the D—N, in the Person of a
>   Lady in the North,"
>
> (*Poems*, III, pp. 894–5, lines 253–62)

We have always dreamt of having enough for all. The hierarchical structures pasted over this essential need only makes visible a yearning for a more fundamental, prelapsarian state of plenitude. Utopias rationalize this dream even as they quantify the freedom from want each of us has known, at least once, in the womb, where all needs are met. Heaven affords, for the pious, a place, always to be deferred, of plenty and rest. But as difficult as it is for any age to project even passing notions of fullness and fairness, the eighteenth century, a time of ideological strain and fractured faith, seems particularly dystopic. A frustrated idealism generated satirical responses to the disparities of a culture formed by and dedicated to a materialism that could either be rationalized or blown up. In this age of consumption, men and women began to locate themselves within the materials of their society. It became, by necessity, a time of greed, for if one is material, one can never get enough, and a time of guilt, for if one is even remotely conscious, one can see the unfairnesses implicit in the distribution of goods both physical and sexual. "We are all Adam's children," went the proverb, "But Silk makes the Difference."[9] Within such a context of desire indulged and held in check, the body becomes a site of confused attempts at ordering what gets in the way, an appetite that can never, given the conditional uneasiness of its owner, be satisfied.

Tracts on melancholy, familiar letters, fictional strategies all testify to

[9] As cited in Peter Linebaugh's forthcoming study of *The London Hanged: Crime and Civil Society in the Eighteenth Century*, Harmondsworth, 1990.

the sometimes farcical battery of purges and glisters and diets deployed against dreaded repletions and "cravings." In an attempt to achieve stability in a complex, modern world of patterns threatening to break down, theorists put their minds to material at hand, material guaranteed not to go away, the body itself. It could be crammed, purged, overfed, or starved, serving as an index for outside ills more difficult to resolve. As Lord Hervey, an "enemy" preserved in the amber of Swift's and Pope's malice, complained, all physicians "jog in one beaten track; a vomit to clear your stomach, a glister to give you a stool, laudanum to quiet the pain, and then a purge to clear your bowels, and what they call 'carry it off'."[10] It is worth wondering what "it" is. When Moll, the *Jade*, lets "it" fly, she is letting loose the same symptoms of repletion that Swift attempts to modify and displace.

"It" would appear to be a disorder of body and mind, a desire to feed a hunger which when appeased turns sour, repletion being the cause of all ills. The trouble began, according to Swift, when "*Gluttony* with greasy Paws . . . As if she ne'er could have enuff; / Taught harmless Man to cram and stuff." In the golden age, all mankind, its nature "easily satisfied,"[11] deposited freely fecal donations, sent up in "a grateful stream" to Saturn ruling the skies (line 242). Swift's vision of unconfined man freely offering that deepest, most anal part of himself inspired Norman O. Brown to celebrate Swift for his radical anticipation of Freud in his awareness of the centrality of anal erotism.[12] But Swift's vision of a bounteous goddess Cloacine confined to her cell, a vision mock-heroically contained in the light, incomplete frame of "A Panegyric on the Dean," suggests, instead, a less systematic consideration of the relationship between physical and sexual needs. For Swift, the confinement would appear to be final, the dislocation complete. There is no getting back to the fullness of "ten thousand altars smoking round." Not only Cloacine, but man – and even more, woman – is confined to a body that can never get enough. Greasy Gluttony, and her name is woman, saw to that. The only answer to the dilemma is denial.[13]

[10] Randolph Trumbach, *The Rise of the Egalitarian Family*, New York, 1978, p. 232. Examining the private histories of upper-class families, Trumbach traces patterns of loss and recovery, arguing that eighteenth-century men and women literally "ate themselves into their graves" to compensate for their emotional deprivation. See McManners' reference to Tissot's warnings against overeating, *Death and The Enlightenment*, p. 19.

[11] The phrase is Gulliver's. "No Man could more verify the Truth of these two Maxims, *That, Nature is very easily satisfied; and That, Necessity is the Mother of Invention, " GT*, pp. 232, 276.

[12] "The Excremental Vision," *Life Against Death: the Psychoanalytical Meaning of History*, London, 1970, pp. 163–81.

[13] In *Powers of Horror, An Essay on Abjection*, trans. Leon Roudiez, New York, 1982, Julia Kristeva connects the "horror" of the defiled feminine condition to more local fears of appetite. Kim Chernin connects eating disorders specifically to women in *The Hungry Self:*

Denial operates on several levels. The erotic connections between food
and sexuality operate literally and metaphorically. To chastise his unruly
desire, Swift mortifies his body, working always to "stay lean." Swift has
been described as Rabelais in a dry place; he is also Rabelais hungry, or
rather, Rabelais dieting desire. While Panurge can describe with delight
the hungry, retentive wombs his utopian women possess as signs of their
wonderful fecundity, Swift shrinks from such a vision. To temper his
unruly appetite, Swift operates "mechanically" on his spirit. His attention
to exercise and diet is obsessive, but his goals are rather typical of his
culture's response to the problems mind and body bring to an increasingly
secularized world. Swift was not alone in railing against the sins of
repletion. As we have seen, writers against the spleen were outlining
radical programs to curb desire and run out of matter. Theorists
attempted to work externally upon the spirit as well as the body by diverting and disrupting the natural tendency of the body towards depression.
Exercise was valued for "tak[ing] a Man off from close Thinking . . . for
there is nothing like Hurrying the Body, to divert the Hurry of the
Mind."[14] Riding so hard away from Vanessa's most physical reproaches
that he produced an ulcer on his thigh, running up and down hills in fine
weather, scaling staircases when it rained, Swift embraced theories of
exercise with the enthusiasm of his most ardent projectors. Even more
enthusiastically, he worked at chastising his physical appetite to cure his
soul's sickness, to "carry it off."

To "carry it off" Swift led a life abstemious enough for his major biographer and the compilers of his account books to find him "indifferent" to
its pleasures.[15] But just this resistance to food, his notorious "stinginess"
remarked upon by dinner guests at the Deanery, suggests Swift's
obsession with the cravings he attempted to correct. The urgency of correction can be glimpsed in one of his minor pieces, the "Dying Speech of
Tom Ashe." Defiantly marginal, full of "false spellings here and there, but
they must be pardoned in a dying man," "Tom Ashe" puns relentlessly
on death and diet, for: "Everything ought to put us in mind of death:

Women, Eating and Identity, New York and London, 1985.

[14] Francis Fuller, *Medicina Gymnastica: Of a Treatise Concerning the Power of Exercise*, London,
1705, pp. 162–3.

[15] Paul V. and Dorothy J. Thompson, *The Account Books of Jonathan Swift*, Newark, 1984, p.
lxxxii. Although they state that Swift was "not greatly concerned about food," they do
find that his accounts betray "a considerable fondness for fruits."

Irvin Ehrenpreis discusses Swift's preference for plain food and intense exercise in
Swift, The Man, His Works, and the Age, Vol. II, *Dr. Swift*, Cambridge, 1967, p. 557. Hope-
well Selby is the most sensitive observer of Swift's problem satisfying an appetite that
determines the corporeality he tries, ironically, to shape. I am indebted throughout this
discussion to her essay, " 'Never Finding Full Repast': Satire and Self-Extension in the
Early Eighteenth Century," *Probability, Time and Space in Eighteenth Century Literature*, ed.
Paula Backscheider, New York, 1979, pp. 217–47.

Physicians affirm that our very food breeds it in us, so that in our *dieting*, we may be said to *di eating*." Let punsters, Swift warns, "consider how hard it is to *die jesting*, when death is so hard in *digesting*" (*PW*, IV, pp. 263–6).

Gulliver carries out Swift's most thorough attack on appetite. A careful, measuring sort of man, he pays strict attention to what he ingests and digests. His needs shift drastically from the gargantuan to the pitifully small, but whether he is counting up the hogsheads necessary to quench his thirst or recalling with horror the filthy stuff his monkey nurse stuffs down his tiny throat, by the time he gets to the island of the Houyhnhnms, his needs have dwindled. Proceeding from the "Fundamental . . . that all Diseases arise from *Repletion*" (p. 253), Gulliver decides that nature is very easily satisfied by a handful of oats to grind into meal. After toasting his paste before the fire, Gulliver eats it warm with milk, and although he admits his diet to be "very insipid," it suffices (p. 232). Although his self-sufficient complacency is surely suspect, this yearning to be easily satisfied by such simple fare is shared by other physical economists attempting to regulate desire. John Locke would have applauded Gulliver's nursery diet, although he might have balked at the blandishments of warm milk. Dry bread is what Locke prescribes, "though the best Nourishment, has the least Temptation; and no Body would have a Child cram'd at Breakfast, who has any regard to his Mind or Body."[16]

Like Locke, Swift does not want to be unwittingly crammed, averse as he is to the omnivorous appetite of the odious Yahoos that "devour every thing that came in their Way, whether Herbs, Roots, Berries, corrupted Flesh of Animals, or all mingled together." Yahoos, Gulliver solemnly reports, "would eat till they were ready to burst" (pp. 261–2). Such disdain for sins of repletion reflects Swift's own aversion to being "crammed," a condition he learned about one fatal day in Richmond when he "got [his] Giddyness by eating a hundred golden pippins at a time" (*Corr*, III, p. 232).

Here Swift directly connects his own fallen condition, the giddiness that would determine his most profound attitudes of distrust towards body and spirit, to an appetite both physical and sexual. Multiplying Eve's lapse one hundred fold, he links his "bad" head to his "bad" desires, and connects a disorder which at its worst approaches madness to the irrationality he associates with sensuality. Forbidden fruit becomes for him a topic of always repressed delight. Mixing memory with desire, Swift dwells on the danger of fruit in his *Journal to Stella*. "We had peaches today," he tells Stella (p. 295), not an extraordinary confession on its own, but one that frequently turns up in the *Journal*, accompanied by moral reflections on the significance of "having" a peach. "Does Stella eat fruit,"

[16] *Some Thoughts Concerning Education*, section 15, p. 128.

he wonders, "I eat a little, but always repent, and resolve against it" (pp. 300–1). He imputes his "threatening" head to forbidden fruit, and resolves to "eat no more: not a bit of any sort," but we find him "venturing" after more, only to repent once again (pp. 314–5, 338).

Fruit appears particularly tempting to an urban Swift railing at the tedium of a summer in town. Nature methodized loses its charm in St. James's Park where the limes have already been losing their leaves "and those remaining . . . are all parched." Swift "hate[s] this season, where every thing grows worse and worse," and decides that the "only good thing of it is the fruit, and that I dare not eat. Had you any fruit at Wexford? A few cherries, and durst not eat them" (*JS*, pp. 345–6) The syntax blurs here. Who had the few cherries, Stella or Swift? And who durst not? In another entry, one week after he plaintively envies "people maunching and maunching peaches and grapes, and I not daring to eat a bit" – but one fig – he customarily resolves and relents: "Noble fruit, and I dare not eat a bit. I ate one fig to-day, and sometimes a few mulberries, but it is said, they are wholesome, and you know a good name does much" (pp. 239, 356).[17]

Like Augustine, another lover of prohibited fruits, Swift recognizes ruefully the ways that reason can work irrationally in the service of the body. We can see Swift undermining his own principles as he acts Eve to corrupt his own Adamic innocence. Daring not to eat "a bit," he eats sometimes "a few." One hundred, perhaps, or even more. As Locke notes rather petulantly, "*Fruit* makes one of the most difficult Chapters in the Government of Health, especially that of Children. Our first Parents ventur'd *Paradise* for it: and 'tis no wonder our Children cannot stand the Temptation, tho' it cost them their Health."[18]

Swift, Denis Donoghue observes, "got into the habit of modifying his desires" to "prevent as much trouble as possible."[19] But habits are made to be broken, and it is crucial to notice the lapses in modification, the palpable yearning that sometimes breaks through the self-imposed aus-

---

[17] On 11 August 1711, Swift prohibits Stella as well as himself from the delights of fruits. Forced to endure the vulgar "champing and champing" of the lord keeper relishing a present of peaches, he wishes that "Dingley had some, for poor Stella can no more eat fruit than Presto." In the same letter, less ascetic, he reports dining with "Mrs Van," mother of Vanessa. *JS*, 331–3.

[18] *Some Thoughts Concerning Education*, section 20, p. 130. Locke outlawed melons, peaches, "most sorts of *Plums*, and all sorts of *Grapes* in *England*," but allowed strawberries, cherries, gooseberries or currants, if "thorough ripe," to be safe for breakfast. Apples, he ventured, "never did any Body hurt, that I have heard, after *October*," p. 131. See J. C. Drummond and Anne Wilbraham, *The Englishman's Food: A History of Five Centuries of English Diet*, London, 1939, Drummond, on cultural fears of fruit, p. 150. In his *Treatise of the Hypochondriack and Hysterick Diseases*, London, 1730, Bernard Mandeville attributes a female attack of hysteria to the ingestion of "a great quantity of mulberries," p. 272.

[19] Denis Donoghue, *Jonathan Swift, A Critical Introduction*, Cambridge, 1969, p. 108.

terity. The desire for fruit intrudes most dramatically upon one of Swift's most physical letters to Stella, an intensely personal report of Harley's condition following Guiscard's attempt on the prime minister's life. Confessing that "it is foolish in me to be so much in pain as I am," Swift still identifies strongly with Harley's distress, taking on a "terrible pain" that remains with him for two days until he curiously breaks his shin in the Strand after falling over a tub of sand left just in the way. At first unable to stir abroad, he rouses himself to regale Stella and Bec with reports of Biddy Floyd's bout of the small pox, tales of another lady dead of the same, and descriptions graphic and vengeful of the villain Guiscard dying of his wounds. In the midst of such gory stories, nestled among notes on Guiscard's death and discussions of Harley's bloody wound, appears this starkly pastoral dream.

Oh, that we were at Laracor this fine day! the willows begin to peep and the quicks to bud. My dream's out: I was a-dreamed last night that I eat ripe cherries. – And now they being to catch the pikes, and will shortly the trouts (pox on these ministers), and I would fain know whether the floods were ever so high as to get over the holly bank of the river walk; if so then all my pikes are gone; but I hope not.

It is typical of Swift to subvert his pastoral, darkly intimating that his pikes will most likely be gone, more disappointments for a temperament accustomed to chafe, more fish that will probably get away[20] but he also hopes here, uncharacteristically, for release as he dreams of his cherries. He returns, however, to the more common materials, the blood and guts of his text, and closes with an anecdote of Sir John Percival and his lady who sits in the bed "in the forms of a lying-in woman; and coming home my sore shin itched, and I forgot what it was, rubbed off the s—b, and the blood came" (*JS*, pp. 220–2).

In his dreams of fruit, Swift employs complex metaphors to get at and disguise the truth. Just as "the s—b" cannot be fully articulated, even while the blood runs down the leg, his appetite called up must be denied, modified, rubbed away. Playing with game resolution the "perpetual . . . *Leap-Frog* between . . . *Flesh* . . . and . . . *Spirit*,"[21] Swift mythologizes his deprivation. One hundred golden pippins, reminiscent of Atalanta's race, Paris's choice, Hercules' Hesperidean booty, stuff of the drama of Eden itself, are Swift's fabulous source of his own original sin, that giddiness that threatens his head. Daring not to touch a bite while eating sometimes

[20] *Corr*, III, p. 329. "I remember when I was a little boy. I felt a great fish at the end of my line which I drew up almost on the ground, but it dropt in, and the disappointment vexeth me to the very day, and I believe it was the type of all my future disappointments."

[21] "A Discourse Concerning the Mechanical Operation of the Spirit," *Tale*, p. 280.

a few mulberries, because "it is said they are wholesome, and you know a good name does much," Swift uses his head to feed his body in jest, but also in seriousness, turning his irony at last on himself. And surely Stella understood, that fruit most forbidden. Ever vulnerable to Swift's transformation of matter, she became his most complete literary property.

Nursery tales

I dare not say nauti without dear: O, faith, you govern me . . . Faith, if I was near you, I would whip your ——   (*JS*, p. 124)

Swift's sensibility is frequently explained away by hard looks at his childhood. The story goes, of his own making, that the infant Swift was kidnapped, stolen away to England, by his overly affectionate nurse. The nurse, Swift recalled in his history of the "Family of Swift," was "so careful of him that before he returned he had learnt to spell, and by the time that he was three years old, he could read any chapter in the Bible" (*PW*, V, p. 192). Perhaps to vex the credulous, or perhaps simply to entertain friends, Swift would add to the fantastic story, giving occasion "to many ludicrous whims and extravagancies in the gaiety of his conversation. Sometimes he would declare, that he was not born in *Ireland* at all; and seem to lament his condition, that he should be looked upon as a native of that country; and would insist, that he was stolen from *England* when a child, and brought over to *Ireland* in a band-box."[22]

In their interpretations of the tale, Phyllis Greenacre and Irvin Ehrenpreis agree that however well intended, the nurse's enthusiasm proved disastrous for Swift. "If we assume a childhood to be natural when it is passed with a father and mother, in a secure family and a settled residence, Swift had to deal with shattering conditions," Ehrenpreis argues.[23] But Ehrenpreis is assuming perhaps too much here, for the "typical childhood" Swift might have missed appears to have been anything but secure and settled. Swift's early years away from his mother and from his family home may be in their dislocation more "natural" than not.

To understand better a "typical childhood of an upper-class English boy of the late seventeenth century," it is helpful to bring in for the moment an old enemy of Swift's, Robert Walpole, nine years Swift's junior. Walpole was sent out to nurse almost immediately after birth, returning home eighteen months later. At the age of six he was sent to school "where he remained, enjoying only very brief holidays, until he went to Eton, nor did he go home for all of his holidays." Until he was called

---

[22] Deane Swift, *An Essay upon the Life, Writings, and Character of Dr. Jonathan Swift* (1755), London, 1974, p. 26.

[23] Ehrenpreis, *Swift* I, p. 32. Phyllis Greenacre, *Swift and Carroll: A Psychoanalytic Study of Two Lives*, New York, 1955, pp. 88-115.

home from Cambridge upon the death of his elder brother in 1698, he was virtually estranged from his familial home in Norfolk.[24] Perhaps more of a hard-headed realist, Walpole eschewed Swift's fictional strategies to develop more material ways of countering patterns of loss, developing in the process hard forged chains of power that would alter the nation itself. This is not to say that Walpole's early years caused his self-serving career any more than we can say that Swift's early "kidnapped" years caused *Gulliver's Travels,* or even Gulliver's dalliance with so many different sized nurses, but we can say, I think, that the "typical" childhoods of both Walpole and Swift complicate our notions of what was normal for the eighteenth century, and that Swift's fantastic fictions of material loss and recovery reflect cultural concerns problematic to more than splenetic deans.

The fascination that Swift reveals in his fictional and personal strategies with the nurse figure determines much of what makes up his sexuality. In his own attempts to evade the materiality that threatens him in sexual encounters, the "filthy" part ineradicably central to "nature," he provokes desire only to transmute it into "care," or, if that strategy fails, into irritation positively lethal, for the nurse "whips" as well as caresses. And while Swift's solutions to body problems are more radical than most, his concerns are more commonplace, for as I suggested in the last chapter, Swift was not idiosyncratic in his appreciation of the power of the nurse. Nurturing but dangerous, believed to give life yet also suspected of being physically and morally contagious, the nurse became in the eighteenth century a subject of much conflicted discourse.

The practice of wet nursing itself was not new. The custom of employing wet nurses was at least 700 years old, and had been preached against since the Reformation. But by the eighteenth century, attacks on the wet nurses were becoming difficult to ignore. The rise of domesticity explains some of the hostility expressed towards the practice of wet-nursing, but I would also suggest that an ambivalence towards the complicity such a practice reinforces influenced the reformers. For it was believed that a woman's milk was in fact blood. It was also believed that a child ingested not only blood and milk, but actual personality traits from its nurse. A calm nurse would produce a calm charge, while a fretful, corrupt nurse

[24] J. H. Plumb, "The New World of Children in Eighteenth-Century England," *Past and Present,* 67, 1975, pp. 66–7. Plumb traces the formation of childhood in the eighteenth century, focusing upon Walpole's separation from his family as a typical seventeenth-century example that would be altered in the following century. Miriam Slater examines the "Fostering out of Children" in *Family Life in the Seventeenth Century: The Verneys of Claydon House,* London, 1984, pp. 133–8. In the early part of the eighteenth century, both Swift and Defoe expose a dislocation that would later provoke strategies of domestic containment as radical, and ultimately as unsatisfying, as the problem being corrected.

would spoil its little parasite.[25] Characteristically extreme, Swift plays with
this notion in one of his "polite" conversations, when he records the
notion that a man who hates women must have sucked a sow (*PW*, IV, p.
165). More urbanely secure in his assumptions about class and sexuality,
Bathurst suggests that to economize, Swift must turn off all his servants
but one "sound wholesom wench" to make his bed and warm it. "To save
all expense in House-keeping y^u must contrive some way or other that
she shou'd have milk, and I can assure y^u it is the opinion of some of the
best Phisitians that womens milk is the wholesomest food in the world."
The regimen, Bathurst promises, will "temper & cool y^r blood." Swift
suggests the same diet to Pope one day later: "My old Presbyterian House-
keeper tells me, that if you could bring your Stomach to woman's Milk,
it would be far better than Asses"[26] (*Corr*, III, pp. 454–8).

A nurse could also corrupt its child physically, transmitting diseases
like scrofula and syphilis through her milk. She could even transmit "low-
ness of character." A creature of the lower classes, the nurse naturally
exposed her charge to the corrupting impressions of one beneath its own
station. As Defoe observed with blunt irony, it was inconsistent of the
gentle class to allow their "heir to drink the blood of a slave or drudge,
the blood of a clown or a boor," but to scorn to marry that same heir
"among citizens or tradesmen . . . however furnished with wit, beauty,

---

[25] See Trumbach' discussion of nursing, *The Rise of the Egalitarian Family*, pp. 197–224; also
Stone, *The Family, Sex and Marriage*, pp. 426–32; Philippa Pullar, *Consuming Passions: A
History of English Food and Appetite*, London, 1972, pp. 155–6; Derek Jarrett, *England in
the Age of Hogarth*, London, 1976, pp. 60–1; and Jean-Louis Flandrin, *Families in Former
Times: Kinship, Household and Sexuality*, trans. Richard Southern, Cambridge, 1979, pp.
203–12. Bern. Ramazini, reasoning that milk is generated from blood and chyle, warns
that long suckling causes consumption in the wet nurse. *A Treatise on the Disease of Tradesmen, to which they are subject by their particular Callings*, trans. Dr. James, London, 1740, p.
138. L. J. Rather cites contemporary examples of the ways that anger enters the child
through its nurse's milk in *Mind and Body in Eighteenth-Century Medicine: A Study Based
on Jerome Gaub's De Regimine Mentis*, London, 1965, p. 139. Thomas Muffett, *Health's
Improvement*, 1665, reported that "what made Dr. *Cajus* in his last sickness so peevish
and so full of frets" was sucking a woman "froward of conditions and of bad diet; and
contrariwise so quiet and well, when he suckt another of contrary disposition? verily the
diversity of their milks and conditions, which being contrary one to the other, wrought
also in him that sucked them contrary effects." Cited by Drummond, pp. 148–9. R. V.
Schnucker discusses the fear of "sucking Evil from the dug" in "The English Puritans
and Pregnancy, Delivery and Breast Feeding," *History of Childhood Quarterly*, 1,4 (1974),
pp. 637–58. See also Valerie Fildes, *Breasts, Bottles and Babies: A History of Infant Feeding*,
Edinburgh, 1986.

[26] In *Seasonable Considerations on the Indecent and Dangerous Custom of Burying in Churches and
Church Yards*, London, 1721, Thomas Lewis observes the "daily experiences convinces
us" of nature's power and influence demonstrated in the way "that a more healthy and
strong Constitution may communicate Health and Strength to another that is feeble."
Lewis notes with approval the "Benefit a hail young wet Nurse has been to a consumptive
languishing Constitution," p. 49.

modesty, breeding or fortune." For as the saying went, "peasantry is a disease (like the plague) easily caught."[27]

When Defoe describes the upper-class heir literally drinking the blood of its slave, he points his criticism in two directions. First he makes explicit the exploitation of such a physical exchange, suggesting the guilt underlying much of the rhetoric of servant literature, a discourse that makes use of bodies that understandably do not want to be kept in place. But as a zealous scourge of the serving class, he also dwells on the dangers of physical and moral exposure to "boorish" ways. Locke reflects a less complicated abhorrence of the contagion nurses could spread both in his *Thoughts on Education* and in the *Essay on Human Understanding*. In his discussion of the association of ideas, Locke, as befits one of the founding fathers of the Enlightenment, speaks out against bogies in the dark, arguing that although "The *Ideas* of *Goblines* and *Sprights* have really no more to do with Darkness than Light; yet let but a foolish Maid inculcate these often on the Mind of a Child, and raise them there together, possibly he shall never be able to separate them again so long as he lives."[28] He warns even more specifically against the "indiscretion of Servants" in *Some Thoughts*, where he predicts that "*Bug-bear* thoughts . . . sink deep" into the tender minds of children to make them "Dastards when alone, and afraid of their Shadows and Darkness all their Lives after." Fifty years after Locke's warning, the anonymous author of *Some Thoughts on Moral Education* (1747) attributes such dastardly fears to Locke himself and relates the anecdote that the philosopher was unable to go to sleep at night without a candle burning by his bedside for fear of the dark.[29] The grave distrust Locke exhibits in his educational treatise towards servants might well have been personal, allying him perhaps with Swift, who asserted outrageously that they were the source of *all* misfortune.[30]

In his own *Directions to Servants* Swift considers the dangerous contagion nurses carry with them. The children's maid is suspected of telling the children "Stories of Spirits, when they offer to cry." The nurse is reserved for more heinous crimes:

If you happen to let the Child fall, and lame it, be sure never confess it; and, if it dies, all is safe.
Contrive to be with Child, as soon as you can, while you are giving Suck, that you may be ready for another Service, when the Child you nurse dies, or is weaned.
(*PW*, XIII, p. 64)

[27] See Rosen, "A Slaughter of Innocents," pp. 293–316; Trumbach, *The Rise of the Egalitarian Family*, pp. 201, 130.
[28] Locke, *Some Thoughts*, section 138, p. 242; see also section 115, p. 221.
[29] *Some Thoughts on Moral Education*, London, 1747, pp. 41–2.
[30] In "Causes of the Wretched Condition of Ireland," considering the "whole Race of Servants in the Kingdom," Swift states that "Servants are the Causes and Instruments" of "all" the "many Misfortunes that befall private Families," *PW*, IX, p. 204.

These lines come from the end of the *Directions*, the least finished part.
But they tell the most, I think, expressing succinctly the fears the wet
nurse could raise. "The woman who nurses another's child in place of
her own is a bad mother; how can she be a good nurse," Rousseau insisted
in his campaign to encourage mothers to nurse their own children. Jonah
Hanway went so far as to argue that a dead child would be "more pleasing
and more familiar to the generality of common nurses than a living one,"
and would call up as little sensibility as a common soldier would experience after experiencing a dozen bloody campaigns. Or as Benedicti put
it centuries earlier, it would be better for children "to be nourished by
some brute beast, like Cyrus or Romulus, than to be entrusted to the
mercies" of the wet nurse.[31]

It is not surprising, within such a context, to find that in the Lilliputian
utopia, the nurseries for males of noble or eminent birth do not allow
much fraternization between nurses and their charges. The boys are
dressed by men until four years of age, and the women attendants "who
are aged proportionably to ours at fifty, perform only the menial Offices."
The young males are never allowed to "converse" with servants, and are
prevented in their isolation from picking up "every bad Impression of
Folly and Vice to which our Children are subject." The young girls of
quality are also protected from corruption by being dressed "by orderly
Servants of their own Sex, but always in the presence of a Professor or
Deputy" until they learn to dress themselves at five years of age. And if
these nurses "ever presume to entertain the Girls with frightful or foolish
Stories, or the common Follies practised by Chamber-Maids among us;
they are publicly whipped thrice about the City, imprisoned for a Year,
and banished for Life to the most desolate part of the Country" (*GT*, pp.
61–2).

Such Draconian measures do not necessarily exaggerate Swift's panic
about the corrupting influence of nurses with their bugbear stories and
their debauching ways. For when he insures that nurses will not be left
alone with their charges, he is not just protecting little ears from tales,
but protecting little bodies from sexual play, "the common Follies practiced by Chamber-Maids among us." His suspicion illustrates the way that
the serving class absorbed the anxiety of their masters, but suggests even
more the powerful sexuality called up by the bodies of wet nurses, who
after all, served as maternal surrogates to free the "real" mothers to
resume their conjugal "duty." The nursery is a place where dependants
are ruled by dependants, where power can be transmitted from below as

---

[31] Jacques Derrida considers Rousseau's fears of the substituted mother in his discussion of
"suppléance," *Of Grammatology*, trans. Gayatri Spivak, Baltimore and London, 1976, p.
146. Flandrin, *Families in Former Times*, p. 207.

well as from above.[32] Particularly sensitive to the trials of being dependent, Swift dwells on the dangers as well as the delights of being subject
to the whims of the nurse in much of his work. And I would argue
that his fascination with the condition of being nursed informs his most
fundamental ideas of sexuality. The nurse "governs," but she also gives
her life's blood, becoming one of the more problematic links on the chain
of consumption. The attention she is paid to pay is attention that Swift
and many of his contemporaries actively seek. Nurturing replaces sexuality while the culture turns wives into mothers – angelic caretakers of the
body and spirit, expected most freely to care.

The god has made us April Fools

I would like to return for a moment to Defoe to extend the juvenile
dilemma that Swift perversely makes visible. Defoe is particularly pertinent here as an observer of marital strategies. Earlier I argued that *Roxana*
retells *Moll Flanders'* story, making clear through Roxana's failures the
irony of Moll's triumph. Defoe retells Moll's story another time, however,
in the saga of *Colonel Jack*, clarifying more comically the irreconcilable
strains of domesticity. Colonel Jack, Defoe's burgeoning sentimental
hero, repeatedly pleads conjugal innocence in a world of sexual corruption. Married to "four Wives, and five of them prov'd *Whores*," he finds
contentment in remarrying the most incorrigible, a veritable Moll Flanders without the luck, after she turns up as an indentured servant on his
American plantation and proves slavishly faithful to his demands. "Only
a boy," Jack eagerly puts himself under her unerring care and allows
himself at last to be "nursed," escaping the world of sexual connections
to enter a domesticity of perpetual care.[33] Jack's calculated return to a
juvenile state of innocence, free from the "postures" of whoring women,
is a flight not out of the sexual body, but rather into the nursery, a safer
place to satisfy the body.

The desire for sanctuary in both writers is usually thwarted. Defoe's
heroes and heroines, often homeless, search for settlement, "safe Har-
bours," that usually fail to remain in place. Swift's characters find themselves at home all too easily, and it is usually vile, filled with outsized
bodies excreting and swilling, pressing unruly, unseemly weight upon its
visitor. The domestic front appears nasty, brutal, and endlessly sordid to

[32] As Michel Foucault proposes in *The History of Sexuality*, vol. 1, "Power comes from below;
that is, there is no binary and all-encompassing opposition between rulers and ruled at
the root of power relations," p. 94.

[33] G. A. Starr finds Colonel Jack to be an unfinished, "essentially infantile" sentimental
hero persistently longing for the "imagined bliss of babyhood." " 'Only a Boy': Notes on
Sentimental Novels," *Genre*, 10 (1977), pp. 510–11. Defoe, *The History and Remarkable Life
of the Truly Honourable Col. Jacque*, ed. Samuel Monk, Oxford, 1965.

the peeping eye taking in its squalor. But in one particular poem, almost entirely free from the usually self-protective ironic structures, Swift gives vent to his most basic yearnings for domesticity, for his place in the nursery where he can be cared for by a self-sacrificing creature who will become the angel in the house.

In a complimentary poem to the Cope family, "The First of April," Swift sets up an April Fool's joke fit for the gods. The context of the poem could be important, for if, as his editors suspect, it was written in 1723, it marks the terrible time when Vanessa was dying and Stella was in retreat at Wood Park.[34] Self-exiled from the two women who both depended upon his own fearful strategies to contain dependency, Swift creates a most revealing fictional situation that seems to work out needs impossible to realize in life. Apollo sends forth his muses, all nine, to enter the Cope household and take charge of its children. They set out with "due Submission," but are puzzled by his whim. Thalia decides that it's all a "Bubble," and warrants that the mother of the household is "some flaunting Dame" who deserves to be spied upon. But when the muses stand unseen, "T'observe her Management within," they confront not the usual Swiftian scene of sordid disarray, but a vision of harmonious order:

> They peep'd, and saw a Lady there
> Pinning on Coifs and combing Hair;
> Soft'ning with Songs to Son or Daughter,
> The persecution of cold Water.
> Still pleas'd with the *good-natur'd Noise*,
> And *Harmless Frolicks* of her *Boys*;
> *Equal* to all in *Care* and *Love*,
> Which all *deserve* and all *improve*.
> To *Kitchin, Parlour, Nurs'ry* flies,
> And seems all *Feet*, and *Hands*, and *Eyes*.
> No thought of her's does ever *roam*,
> But for her 'Squire when he's *from home*;
> And scarce a *Day*, can spare a *Minute*
> From *Husband, Children, Wheel* or *Spinnet*.
>
> *(Poems*, I, pp. 321–2, lines 29–42)

The muses spy upon a child's view of the domestic ideal. The squire might be on mother's mind, but in the poem itself, he's "from home," freeing the lady to go about her rounds unencumbered by conjugal duties. All "*Feet*, and *Hands*, and *Eyes*," the mother figure, and in this case, since she is a "proper" mother, the nurse figure, fills the domestic landscape as efficiently as any Brobdingnagian giant, managing to fly from kitchen to parlor to nursery all at once, without a minute for herself. Not only does

---

[34] Both Harold Williams and Pat Rogers, editor of *Jonathan Swift: The Complete Poems*, New Haven and London, 1983, agree that it is likely that Swift wrote the poem in 1723; Rogers, p. 730.

she transcend the demands of time and space, but she keeps herself and her children clean, painlessly, softening Lockean doses of cold water with songs and fulfilling in the process both of Swift's demands from his first love, Varina, that she possess cleanliness and competency (*Corr*, I, p. 36).

The lady's efforts overwhelm the less cherished offerings of the muses. "Can *we* do more than what *she* does," they mutter, as they beat a hasty retreat back to Parnassus to answer the invocations of more needy "bawling" poets. Their retreat seems significant, as does Thalia's wager that they are all victims of an April Fool's prank. Art possesses meaning when it can order a world in disarray, but when all is well, it serves no purpose. Nowhere does Swift's notion of a corrective art take on such urgency, for here his art itself is obsolete, a superfluous trick not up to the more exalted sphere of the nursery song itself. Swift's art supplements loss that, within the space of the poem, seems rectified. Just as the Houyhnhnms have no need of any formal culture, so the Cope family transcends the need for arts beyond the domestic sphere. The lowly spinnet and the bathtub lyrics are enough. And one wonders, within such a frame of reference, just who is the April Fool, Thalia, the displaced muse, or Swift, the displaced poet?

Displacement for Swift turns out to be as farcical as it is tragic, and just as he places solemn Gulliver in his sweet-smelling stable to preserve him from the stink of Yahoo while subjecting him to the fragrant ordure of horse, so in his flight from the sex Swift still plays relentlessly and recklessly at games of a most equivocally sexual nature. Bondage is a particular favorite. Whether he is being tied down to Lilliputian sands by slender ligatures, tethered to his filthy kennel to play at being a hound abject enough to satisfy Antonio of *Venice Preserved* in his most cringing desires, or whether he is being diddled by gigantic maids of honor, "crammed" by an ape driven to kidnap and nurse him, or led about on cumbersome leading strings by a nine year old giantess nurse, Gulliver reflects a fearful, almost furtive penchant for the nursery, where he is both monarch and subject. Calling attention to the darker side of the nursery games, Swift insists upon exposing the dangers of the domesticity which always eludes him.[35]

For the nursery is not necessarily safe. Childhood for Swift is at best an

---

[35] John Traugott connects Gulliver's "Pleasure of Being the Cause" (the phrase is Piaget's) to Swift's own "range of . . . attitudes from playfulness to idealism, from an anarchic impulse figuring human 'purpose' in games of no purpose to a repressive impulse figuring human purpose in a rationalism that acknowledges the idea as obvious and sanctions a simple-minded collectivism." Traugott argues that Swift's impulse to kill the world to make it better is "not so different" from the child's desire to assimilate the world "to a game of mimicry that suits his own notions of a proper order." "The Yahoo in the Doll's House: *Gulliver's Travels* the Children's Classic," *The Yearbook of English Studies*, 14 (1984) pp. 148–9.

uneasy state where one must always be on guard. Blessed with a ridiculously pliable frame, Gulliver learns that his body will, given the opportunity, invariably betray. Like a child, Gulliver becomes hostage to the irrational world of larger, indifferent demands where apples are ready to bludgeon him to death while minuscule queens can ask for his eyes in recompense for his untimely showers of urine.

Always at risk, Gulliver depends upon the good hearts or the blind eyes of others. From his first hours on Lilliput, he gives in to the demands of his tiny captors; they must surely, every one so grown up, every one at least six inches high, know best. W. B. Carnochan argues persuasively that Gulliver's first moments on Lilliput parallel those that a new-born infant would experience.[36] He literally enters a world of buzzing confusion, and must make sense of the pain, thirst, hunger, and need to excrete he would never have known before. Perhaps most importantly, Gulliver washes up on his new-born shore ignorant of the language. Swift repeatedly plunges Gulliver into a state of incomprehension, and even though he vaunts his creature's linguistic abilities, after four journeys, the adjustment has taken its toll. Gulliver as bound baby, Gulliver as diminutive doll whose shins and brains are endangered by the merest acorn, Gulliver maunching finally on his nursery oats, adjusts and readjusts as willingly as any child. The tantrums he tends to throw at the gentle reader's expense testify to the cost of his compliance.

Although the nursery has its perils, they are familiar ones. The nurse's breast might be monstrous, but as an object of indulgence it serves a function that the equally gargantuan maids of honor cannot perform. The maids are just out for play, outsized play, and far from offering suck, they use little Gulliver "without any manner of ceremony, like a creature who had no sort of consequence." Gulliver turned dildo mocks his own pretension, for on Brobdingnag, he possesses no sort of consequence worth owning. Swift's own demands for self importance, demands expressed quite clearly in his *Journal to Stella* and his letters to Vanessa, as well as his determination to retain an intact sensibility while reaping the rewards of the nursery, are in comparison, much more complicated.

The extent of the complications can be seen in the following letter written to Stella on 3 April 1711:

I called at Mr. secretary's, to see what the D— ailed him on Sunday; I made him a very proper speech, told him I observed he was much out of temper; that I did not expect he would tell me the cause, but would be glad to see he was in better; and one thing I warned him of, Never to appear cold to me, for I would not be

---

[36] W. B. Carnochan, *Lemuel Gulliver's Mirror for Man*, Berkeley and Los Angeles, 1968, pp. 133–5.

treated like a school-boy; that I had felt too much of that in my life already
(meaning from sir William Temple).   (*JS*, p. 230)

Swift's outburst seems all the more poignant in light of Temple's own
summation of "human existence" as a child's business:

When all is done, human life is, at the greatest and the best, but like a froward
child, that must be played with and humoured a little to keep it quiet till it falls
asleep, and then the care is over.[37]

Whatever his philosophical position, it would seem that Temple didn't
humor Swift near enough, and far from keeping him quiet, goaded him
through negligent, gentlemanly play, to break out "like [the] school boy"
he was determined to outgrow. And in the very letter he sends to Stella,
both pupil and nurse, the recipient of his most self-indulgent and self-
denying emotions, Swift reveals his most needy self, chafing to be the
"cause" of Harley's, the "cause" of Stella's, and surely the "cause" of "sir"
William Temple's discomfort in his attempts to break into and out of the
nursery.

It is appropriate that he write to Stella this way, intimately, petulantly,
yet at the same time keeping her at a distance, for he writes from London,
far from Ireland. Even Stella, ever compliant, possesses "little teeth,"
and remains part of a larger threatening world.[38] Women, individually,
separate from that large category of "beasts in petticoats," just might
surprize Swift with their nurturing pliability, but then again, they might
turn out to be giants, possessing gargantuan appetites and making out-
landish and outsized demands on a diminutive Swift, "a small man," only
a dean writ small. The following chapter will look at Swift's literary and
personal relationships with the two women most visibly important to him,
Stella and Vanessa, strained friendships that reflect Swift's struggle to be
free from demands, yet to be free to make demands, to write the rules of
a game in which nobody ultimately wins.

---

[37] Temple cited by Ronald Paulson, *Theme and Structure in Swift's 'Tale of a Tub'*, New Haven,
1960, p. 178.
[38] *JS*, "Morrow sirrahs, I will rise, spight of your little teeth," I, pp. 247–8.

5

The ladies: d—ned, insolent, proud, unmannerly sluts

For, what was ever understood
By Human Kind, but Flesh and Blood?
"A Receipt to Restore Stella's Youth," (*Poems*, II,
pp. 758–60, lines 35–6)

It could have been his dripping nose, "the first time I ever got a new cold before the old one was going," or it could have been the more pressing uncertainties of the Tory ministry, but in spite of Christmas, Swift sounds less than charitable in his estimation of post-partum joys:

I was to see lady ——, who is just up after lying-in; and the ugliest sight I have seen, pale, dead, old and yellow for want of her paint. She has turned my stomach. But she will soon be painted, and a beauty again.   (*JS*, p. 443)

Lady —— might possibly be Lady Pembroke, around forty-three years of age, but her situation more than her identity is the issue, for her bare corporeality offends. Paint, Swift suggests, can cover over her flaws, turning her into a "beauty" once again, but beauty so restored reveals itself to be rotten, the (dead) body beneath the varnish always retaining a certain stench.

Notable here is the neutrality, the flatness of the description. Swift is perfectly capable of lashing feminine offenders for any number of vices he longs to root out. Irish wives, for instance, who "under their present Corruptions seem to be a kind of animal suffered for our sins to be sent into the world for the Destruction of Familyes, Societyes, and Kingdoms," spend the revenue of a "moderate family to adorn a nauseous unwholesom living Carcase" (*PW*, XII, p. 80). But here, we find no direct attack on the morals of Lady ——. She is accused neither of playing cards "severall hours after midnight," nor of revelling upon "Indian poisons." She doesn't even demand to ride about in soft cushioned chairs. She is merely observed – "just up after lying in" – and gazed upon, one more "living Carcase," she turns Swift's stomach.

This uncompromising anatomy is meant for a very special reader, his own MD, "My Dears" – Esther Johnson, better known as Stella, and her companion and duenna, Rebecca Dingley. They are childless women, gentlewomen, presumably virginal women who wait patiently back in Ireland for news from their Dean, their "Presto," who writes to his dears daily with news of his political and social triumphs. Swift covers many topics in his *Journal*, offering up a document rich in historical and personal detail, but of all his topics, perhaps the most telling is the subject of the body itself, that material always ready to betray. Noses drip, shins break, women breed, while carcasses inevitably grow "pale, dead, old and yellow." The only way out is to break out of the process altogether, to retain what Swift calls the "lustre of virgins,"[1] while sublimating sexuality into witty foreplay.

Sexuality unchecked can end in death. One of his favorite ladies, "that poor dear Lady Ashburnham," dies in her twenty-third year. "The poor creature was with Child," Swift laments, and "in excessive Concern for her Loss," he confesses hating life to think it "exposd to such Accidents." To see "so many thousand wretches burthening the Earth while such as her dye," makes him think that "God did never intend Life for a Blessing." Small wonder that when Lady —— comes to town to have her child, he prays automatically that God grant her a good time. "Her death would be a terrible thing" (*JS*, pp. 594–5).

One way Swift can contain fears impossible to resolve is through a preposterous style of irony. To assuage his personal grief over Lady Ashburnham's death, he impersonally condemns the "many thousand wretches burthening the Earth" with their unwelcome bodies. His excess is characteristic. Similarly, just as he disposes of the vexing problem of the bodies of the poor by turning them into fantastic sides of bacon, Swift reduces his worry over childbirth by turning it into a long running joke at poor Goody Walls' expense. Mrs Dorothy Walls, wife to the Archdeacon of Achonry and a personal friend, is about to give birth in Ireland, while Swift, teasing his MD from London, is already supposing her misfortunate issue dead and gone:

No truly, I will not be godfather to goody Walls this bout, and I hope she'll have no more. There will be no quiet nor cards for this child. I hope it will die the day after the christening.   (*JS*, p. 129)

In the next Walls entry, Swift archly reports that the unfortunate lady has been "brought to-bed of a girl, who died two days after it was christened; and betwixt you and me, she is not very sorry" (p. 156). The game continues almost under the breath. "A girl, hmm; and died in a

[1] *Corr*, I, p. 46.

week, hmmm, and was poor Stella forced to stand for godmother?" (p. 166).

In the real world of flesh and blood, Swift is outraged to find that "Mrs. Walls' business" is not even "over yet." He had hoped that she was up and well, "the child dead before this time" (p. 186). Swift won't let go of the subject, and in his next entry supposes the child not dead, but a girl, almost as bad, supposes that poor Mrs. Walls has had a hard time of it, not to mention the Archdeacon who looks positively simple when he learns the sex of the newest issue. Swift plays a game that even he recognizes to be "plaguy silly" (pp. 202–3), but he keeps at it, offering once again his fantasy of the child dying the next day after it was born, only to correct silly Presto for his error; "it is a fine girl, likely to live." Even now the information is wrong, for the baby, not dead, is also not a girl at all (p. 208). Swift submits at last to be the baby's godfather; "let his Christian name be Harley," he demands, "in honour of my friend, now lying stabbed and doubtful of his life" (p. 213). Even in triumph, scenes of birth settle uncomfortably close to scenes of death.

One wonders what they made of it, the two dears anxiously waiting for news of both Mrs Walls and faithful Pdfr. Did they preen themselves on their own lustrous virginity, their exemption from the perils of active sexuality? Swift for one seemed to enjoy reminding MD of the vulgar aspects of the married state. In his final letter to MD, written in haste from Chester, he still finds the time to remind Stella of an old suitor, one Swift himself ran off. Slyly informing his correspondent that the wife of William Tisdall is "very big, ready to ly down," he brings up the cause of her pains. "Her husband is a puppy. Do his feet stink still" (p. 671). Juxtaposing stinking feet to big bellies, Swift reduces that which threatens while reinforcing Stella's virginal worth. In his own territorial letter chasing off the puppy Tisdall, Swift had long before defined Stella's essence, arguing that while it might be held "so necessary and convenient a thing for ladies to marry," in his own eyes, time would not dull "the lustre of virgins" (*Corr*, I, p. 46).

Time is crucial here, that agent which turns spirit into carcass. Swift's own riddle on "Time" is most pertinent here:

> Ever eating, never cloying,
> All devouring, all destroying,
> Never finding full Repast,
> Till I eat the World at last.[2]

To engage in the chain of begetting is to enter into the realm of all devouring, all destroying time itself, to depend upon its vagaries, to risk

[2] *Poems*, III, p. 930. Pat Rogers omits this particular riddle in his edition of Swift's poetry, *Complete Poems*, pp. 757–58.

exposure to the "accidents" of nature that make one think that "God did never intend Life for a Blessing." Swift's commitment to celibacy is self-protective, his way of defending himself and those he loves against the body that will always betray. But he still insists throughout his life and letters upon calling up a sexuality he is bent on denying. This chapter will focus upon his most desperate strategies deployed at the expense of more than one spirit.

To protect himself from a sexual knowledge – and appetite – that both fascinates and horrifies, Swift creates his own creatures, safe creatures that he can control, both goddesses and sluts. The equivocal nature of the word "slut" makes it worth glossing. Typically a slut is a woman of dirty, slovenly or untidy habits, a kitchen maid, perhaps even a nurse maid, a drudge and, more infrequently, a troublesome, awkward creature. She might also reveal herself, under the surface dirt, to be a woman of low character, perhaps even a bold or impudent jade. The dirt that encases these meanings becomes both moral and physical as the word itself floats free, presumably, from its derogatory connotations when it is used in play. You saucy slut they say in such moments, impugning so broadly the object of subtly affectionate derision.

Swift defined the word in an exchange with Laetitia Pilkington, a writer often maligned for her own sluttish ways.

The Dean set about making the Coffee; but the Fire scorching his Hand, he called to me to reach him his Glove, and changing the Coffee-pot to his Left-hand, held out his Right one, ordered me to put the Glove on it, which accordingly I did; when taking up Part of his Gown to fan himself with, and acting in Character of a prudish Lady, he said, 'Well, I do not know what to think; Women may be honest that do such Things, but, for my Part, I never could bear to touch any Man's Flesh – except my Husband's whom perhaps, says he, she wished at the Devil.'
'Mr. P—n, says he, you would not tell me your Wife's Faults; but I have found her out to be a d—nd, insolent, proud, unmannerly Slut:' I looked confounded, not knowing what Offence I had committed.[3]

Aside from providing the astonishing delights of watching Swift play prudish lady, this anecdote offers helpful instruction on what "offends." It is, it would appear, sluttish to touch a man's flesh. Swift manages to insinuate two contradictory positions here as he dramatizes a hypocritical punctilio which he undermines by suggesting that Mrs. Pilkington should, nevertheless, guard her person more carefully. Swift in these exchanges

[3] Laetitia Pilkington, *Memoirs With Anecdotes of Dean Swift, 1748–54*, Dublin, vol. 1, *Swiftiana*, 17, New York, 1975, pp. 58–9.

gets it both ways, while his tutorial victims get it no way. And it also turns out to be sluttish not to battle over the honors of making "the coffee." Since the making of coffee (and the spilling of coffee) become significant in his dealings with Vanessa, it is fascinating to watch Swift busy at work making up his own rules to confound his guest's peace while keeping her nonetheless in the game. Never appearing entirely comfortable in any Swiftian exchange, little Mrs. Pilkington reports herself only "modestly contented" to escape further censure. Apter pupils like Vanessa and Stella were more willing to wrestle with Swift's equivocal imputations, to fight for their place in his "Sluttery," where he could invest the world with nervously ambiguous meaning as the word became flesh, at least for the moment. Swift transforms flesh through language, acknowledging in each verbal transaction a body that cannot, on its own, be borne.

Stella was his earliest and most successful creation, a product of his imagination from the time he tutored her at Moor Park. She was eight or nine then, while Swift, in his twenties, served and chafed as secretary to Sir William Temple. Imprinting his student's mind with the systems of Plato and Epicurus, the "errors of Hobbes" (*PW*, V, p. 231), the contingency of wit and the shape of his very own handwriting, Swift informed the mind and soul of Esther Johnson, for that, we must remind ourselves, is her real name, from the start, and left her body to heaven. Stella serves two purposes, as a model of Swiftian virtues, a "softer Swift" possessing the rigor of his mind, and as a link to the nursery itself, where sexuality, with all of its looseness and dirt, its rouzers and stinks, can be more easily handled. And in his *Journal*, Swift explores that world with great pains, tracing the convolutions of desire through assorted mazes.[4]

Vanessa proved not to be so malleable, but then she was probably twenty or so when she entered the game, although even then Esther Vanhomrigh, the little Misessy, or Hessy, sometimes Skinage, still played the child. Apparently more than willing to allow her mother the privilege of playing merry widow, Vanessa stayed quite cozy in the nursery, waiting for Swift to invade her privacy. Her world of puppies and pouts, the place Swift calls affectionately the sluttery, and finds to be "the most agreeable chamber in the world," a place to meet over a pot of coffee which Vanessa might spill, provides an arena both provocative and innocent.

Combining lists of spelling faults and extracts of heroic actions, Swift offered his pupils formal methods of containing the physical world of error. "I will have you spell right, let the world go how it will," he instructs Stella (*JS*, p. 393). Implicit in such correction is a sense of license, for it could be said that Swift teaches spelling to emphasize the liberties he takes

---

[4] I have discussed the "softening" of Swift's martial, manly women at length in " 'A Softer Man': Pope's, Swift's, and Farquhar's Feminine Ideal," *South Atlantic Quarterly*, 84 (1985), pp. 51–62.

in his nauti nauti nursery language. How will the pliant pupil recognize the implications of his libertine badinage unless *she* can discern the limitations of his form? As the tutor turns his charges into sauci doxies and sluttakins in sore need of correction, Swift turns the tutorial process into a seductive game that he controls, while he remains always ready to end up the most cossetted figure of all in the nursery.

Such liberties move close to libertinism itself, and as much as he abhorred the likes of Wharton and Walpole, Swift played at being a rake. At Holyhead he dreamt that Lord Bolingbroke, notorious for "drinking like a fish, and —— like a stoat" (*JS*, p. 164), preached in his own St. Patrick's Cathedral. Missing his surplice, forced to squeeze amongst the rabble, for his own stall was "all broken," Swift uncomfortably observes my Lord mount *his* pulpit and quote Mr. Wycherley by name, "and his Plays," in a most unorthodox sermon.[5] (*PW*, V, pp. 205–6).

The dream reference to Wycherley and his plays proves particularly revealing, for in his most famous production, *The Country Wife*, the master debaucher, Horner, exerts power because he radically disavows his potency. Certified as eunuch, he relinquishes a reputed sexuality to exert clandestine sexual control over the virtuous gang. He is used in the process, for his women always crave more china than he can manufacture, just as Swift's Vanessa craves more coffee, and Stella more Presto, than they can obtain.

In spite of the equivocal nature of Horner's triumph, in a world of cuckolds, the self-professed eunuch rules. Swift's own assumption of sexual power resembles Horner's most in this sense of marginality. Just as Horner as eunuch resists being categorized, so Swift, not the gravest of divines, shocking the ladies of the court with his bawdy *Tale of a Tub*, exerts control precisely because he seems to exist outside of sexual boundaries. He is, he teases Vanessa, "only a dean." In his "Answer" to her "Rebus," a riddle in which she compares him to "the *Patriarch* in *Egypt*," Swift counters coyly that "a *Dean*'s but a *Parson*." Vanessa, on the other hand, is a "great Witt," too much for the likes of the "small Man" the dean represents. A small man enamoured, nonetheless, with a power he plays at withholding (*Poems*, II, pp. 715–16).

Disavowals of power prove merely tactical. While provoking a flirtatious epistolary relationship with a "Toast of the Kit Kat," one Mistress Anne Long,[6] he complains to Stella of one of Long's letters "that has quite

---

[5] See Swift's identification with Bolingbroke, Hagstrum, *Sex and Sensibility*, pp. 149–50. Ehrenpreis calls Bolingbroke Swift's super-Id, "a person who combined precocity and talents which the late-arriving Swift envied with the vices he never let himself contemplate" (*Swift*, II, p. 457).

[6] "A Decree for Concluding the Treaty between Dr. Swift and Mrs. Long" affords a glimpse of Swift in his most coyly autocratic mode, cited in *Vanessa and her Correspondence with Jonathan Swift*, ed. A. Martin Freeman, London, 1921, pp. 183–5.

turned my stomach against her: no less than two nasty jests in it with dashes to suppose them" (*JS*, pp. 118–19). Mrs. Long's nasty dashes violate the sexual boundaries Swift creates in order to define his world, for without rules that only he can break, his own transgressions lose significance. This is at the heart, I suspect, of the little language itself, and the private references to "coffee" in his letters to Vanessa. When Swift makes up the rules, he declares even smudges suspect, suggesting a significance that makes our little language "ourrichar gangridge." Thus in one letter he smears the word "clap," adding a disclaimer that merely insinuates deeper, richer meaning. "I don't care to write that Word plain," he explains, inspiring Harold Williams to suggest that the smudge resulted from "motives of delicacy" (p. 519). But surely the word "clap" so smeared becomes even more indelicate when it becomes illegible, making the reader strain all the harder with poor "abused" eyes to decode the play while implicating herself in the process.

This process of self-implication is crucial. Just as Horner ends his drama surrounded by cuckolds dancing to pay him homage, so Swift dominates the rhetorical center of his verbal world, the better to enjoy the pleasures of being the cause of its pains. "Aboozing" his fine "radyes" with nasty smudges and dashes (p. 565), he places them into a rhetorical sluttery, a marginal space of looseness and dirt which only he can enter. And in the process, forming strategies to contain the body while capturing the mind, Swift plays transformational games with the sexuality of a Vanessa or a Stella, contriving and controlling his nauti nauti girls of his own invention. To remain players, they must remain malleable, content to be softer versions of a ticklish Swift who teases them with possibilities he just as playfully snuffs out. His erotic strategies parallel his satiric strategies, for in both games, playing for high stakes, he arouses a desire for certainty he refuses to satisfy, promising a truth he consistently deflates. Just as Vanessa and Stella become implicated in constructs of erotic desire, so Swift's readers become trapped in constructs of utopian desire that always fall flat. And it is always for our own good.

Esther Vanhomrigh

Swift begins his epistolary relationship with Esther Vanhomrigh, the little Misessy, in a clandestine letter written for her own "good" to draw her into a correspondence illicit from the start. In typically triangular fashion,[7] he writes Mrs. Long apparently innocent lines indirectly praising (there is not better girl upon the earth) and blaming Esther for her sluttish ways. "I have writ three or four lyes in as many Lines," he candidly

---

[7] Ehrenpreis describes Swift's epistolary indirection, *Swift*, III, p. 64.

confesses, as he instructs Hessy to read his enclosed letter to Mrs. Long before sealing up the paper with an "outside starched Letter." The trickery clanks and clatters from the start, and Swift delights in it: "See what art people must use, tho they mean ever so well," he sighs, bending meaning. He may "mean well" enough, but his secret letter can be read not only as a subtle admonition, but as an even subtler way into his pupil's heart. For didactically, ingenuously, he has insinuated himself into his lady's bedchamber, where he imagines his packet lying "two hours till you awake." Even now, he can see "you and Puppy lying at your ease, without dreaming any thing of all of this" (*Corr*, I, pp. 275–6).

Swift would like to enter his lady's dreams as well. "If you cannot guess who is the writer," he teases Esther's mother, in a letter designed to intrigue the daughter, "consult your pillow, and the first gentleman you dream of is the man"[8] (*Corr*, II, pp. 365–7). He is playing another game, and this time the letter itself displeases Hessy, who counts up the number of textual references to sister Moll and to herself, and decides that even if the number balances out, the tone varies, for "you talk to Moll, and only say, Now Hessy grumbles" (*Corr*, II, p. 368).

Throughout her letters, Vanessa suggests a formidable intelligence and a sharp talent for closely reading Swift's managing ways. He doesn't grant her much room to maneuver, for when he writes "Hessy grumbles," he casts her in a role that only he can alter while promising possibilities of change, if only "she" will be better. He comes close only to hide, turning intermediaries like Mrs. Vanhomrigh, Mrs. Long, and ailing sister Moll, "poor Malkin," into screens, but also into competitors to make Hessy grumble even louder. Swift goes so far as to write poor Malkin while commanding her "not to shew [Vanessa], because it is a Love-Letter." Enclosing provocative verses praising his Hessy while wondering "who could such a Nymph forsake / Except a Blockhead or a Rake," Swift insinuates significance somewhere, if only Vanessa can decode it (*Corr*, II, pp. 349–51).

Handwriting helps to obscure the matter. "What this letter wants in length it will have in difficulty, for I believe you cannot read it . . . I hold a wager there are some lines in this letter you will not understand tho you can read them" (*Corr*, II, p. 351). But then Swift is an old hand at writing badly when need arises. As he confides to MD, a bad scrawl is so snug (*JS*, p. 79).

Enraged by his evasions, Vanessa demands clarity, but Swift counters with more code which allows everything and nothing to its recipient. "A stroke thus – signifies everything that may be said to Cad – at beginning

---

[8] Freeman considers this a letter written to Mrs. Vanhomrigh, *Vanessa*, p. 83; Williams cites it as a letter to Esther addressed to Madam Van.

or conclusion," he informs his "Skinage," and closes this letter with five "nasty dashes"[9] (*Corr*, II, pp. 353–4).

Swift plays a deep game here, costing "a great many thoughts to make [his] Letters difficult," even while he threatens to "be in a huff that anything written to Cad – should be difficult to Skinage." Dashes extend a degree of freedom to his correspondent, but a freedom essentially solipsistic, for Swift's demands for obscurity make reciprocity impossible. Although he promises "all she would have me *say*," Swift dodges even verbal performance in offering spaces he refuses to fill (*Corr*, II, pp. 352–4).

Although she appears to receive the dashes with an enthusiasm painful to read, Vanessa's responses fail to please Swift. She lacks the cryptic touch. "I thought the last letter I wrote you was obscure and constrained enough," she complains; "I took pains to write it after that manner" (*Corr*, II, p. 354). But Vanessa can never match Swift's indirection. All the while he keeps her in the sluttery, that place of looseness and dirt where he can play "the chapter of hide and whisper," he keeps offering flirtatiously formal confirmation of their arrangement, the clarity Vanessa keeps after. "What would you give to have the history of Cad – and – exactly written through all its steps, from the beginning to this time," he writes, promising chapters on the spilling of coffee and the drinking of coffee, chapters of "the lost Key; of the Strain; of the joyfull return two hundred Chapters of madness . . . a hundred whole Books of my self and so low" (*Corr*, II, p. 356). More dashes, seven in one line, accompany a letter of unkept promises with his wishes to walk fifty times about her garden and then – drink your coffee, – so adieu ——" (*Corr*, II. p. 361).

But the promises prove as impossible to keep as the physicality Swift found impossible to express. Sheridan suggested that for Swift, marriage could only end up in talk. Once Swift substitutes language for sexuality, performing verbal feats so skillfully that Horace Walpole for one entirely accepted the word coffee as a code name for sexual intercourse, he needed to guard against language itself. The dashes extend a degree of freedom, but they also offer a comforting space between him and the object of his affection.[10]

When Swift is not obscuring the meaning he nevertheless insists upon, he is making very clear demands. Misessy must become Vanessa, heroic,

[9] Freeman publishes five dashes following 4 Aug, *Vanessa*, p. 118.

[10] Thomas Sheridan, *The Life of the Rev. Dr. Jonathan Swift*, 1784, *Swiftiana*, 15, New York and London, 1974, cites a letter Swift wrote to John Kendall in which he described his "conjured spirit . . . that would do Mischief if I would not give it employment." This humor "makes [Swift] so busy . . . and since it commonly ends in talk, whether it be love, or conversation, it is all alike," pp. 285–7. J. H. Bernard records Walpole's speculation in his introduction to the *Correspondence of Jonathan Swift, D.D.*, 6 vols., ed. F. Elrington Ball, London, 1910, I, p. xxv.

hardy, "more like a man of this world," more like Swift himself, content to spend her energies at reading the right works, exercising the right sort of body, and checking her romantic tendencies to become a "softer man." Early in their friendship, Swift had been attracted to Vanessa's masculine traits, praising them so vigorously that Mrs. Long writes in bewilderment that "my poor cousin is taken for an hermaphrodite." Superior to all other women, who are in comparison mere "beasts in petticoats," Vanessa possesses virtues "For manly Bosoms chiefly fit."[11] In the world of "Cadenus and Vanessa," the poem Swift wrote to explain or explain away their relationship, feminine virtues become by nature impossible: a woman's worth is measured by the circumference of her hoop and the banality of her banter (*Poems*, II, pp. 686–714, lines 364–403). In such a world, Vanessa's studious, sober ways subject her to public scorn and waspish considerations of her sartorial poverty. Cadenus alone possesses the sense to love his pupil for her putative virtues, virtues coincidentally his own, for as Vanessa argues, her love for Cadenus reflects their mutual self-love. "His virtues she might call her own" (line 681). Her vices also match Swift's. Perhaps what most separated the two was a mutually splenetic and critical intelligence not easily satisfied.

In defending the purity of his love for Vanessa, Cadenus renders it platonic, refining away sexuality as he concentrates upon his delight in her pedagogical progress. If he is guilty, he argues, he is only as guilty as the school master hugging his "secret Joy / In School to hear the finest Boy" (lines 552–3). In other words, Swift is loving "only a boy," an innocent enough pursuit satisfying his own need to stay free of the complications of the chain of begetting that accompanies a more complicated form of sexuality. School masters, however, harbored love for their finest pupils not entirely separate from the flesh. Writers as diverse as Dryden and Smollett, Pope and Rochester, Fielding and Swift bear witness to a system of education where the birch not only reinforced discipline but expressed desire.

When he responds to the "finest boy" in Vanessa, Swift is expressing a "platonic" sort of love as sexual as the love Socrates explores in Plato's *Symposium*, a love both ideal and physical, a love of the forms and a love of the flesh. In his own tutorial relationships with Vanessa, Stella, and later with Lady Acheson, he offers repeatedly the strange mixture of the ideal and the real, as he approaches sexual knowledge of the other, only to withdraw at the end into a narcissistically ironic appreciation of a self transmuted through instruction into a "softer" version of Swift. To avoid the body that threatens, the pale, dead old yellow carcass that cannot be

---

[11] *Corr*, I, p. 275; *Corr*, II, p. 326: "Quelles bestes en juppes sont les plus excellentes de celles que je vois semeès dans le monde au prix de vous." "Cadenus and Vanessa," *Poems*, II, pp. 686–714, line 204.

covered over, Swift splits his creatures right up the middle, and dwelling on their heroism and their manly, scholarly ways (even if they do lapse in the spelling of philosophically knotty words), he turns his pupils into softer men, finer boys. The homoerotic elements of this strategy cannot be divorced from the devaluation of women that Swift's culture endorses. While the feminine aspects of their nature must be expunged or "reformed," their masculine virtues sanitize and redeem them from their naturally filthy ways, and ultimately keep them safely free of the chain of begetting that leads into death. The pains of his radical cure are as fatal as the problem he purports to solve.[12] And the ones bearing the largest share are those creatures he cannot do with or without, the ladies, damnable sluts.

Esther Johnson

————See how far I am forced to stand from Stella, because I am afraid she thinks poor Presto has not been careful about her little things.   (JS, p. 149)

In Esther Johnson Swift found a most compliant pupil, one grateful for so little that "we really wonder how she lives" (Poems, II, p. 735, line 30). While Vanessa's chiding letters delineate her struggle to separate herself from Swift's all-conforming imagination, any letters Stella wrote to Swift have disappeared. Only two of her poems remain, one so resembling Swift's in subject and style that he felt compelled to advertise her authorship, and one other, less noble, addressed to jealousy, suggesting that the unreconstructed part of Stella chafed most bitterly at the "little" she got. Swift's own letters and poems to Stella determine the way he meant her to be read.

As Jean Hagstrum notes, nauti Stella of the Journal is an "Agreeable Bitch," while in the poetry, she becomes a "noble generous Mind." And the two phrases "pretty well measure the difference between the two art forms in which Swift chose to embody his 'love'. "[13] The nauti nauti sluttakins of the Journal becomes heroic nurse and androgynous redeemer in the poems, a softer man possessing the "safe" virtues of charitable self-denial.

When Hagstrum refers to the two art forms Swift employs, he takes

---

[12] Nora Crowe Jaffe suggests that Swift characteristically turned his feminine pupils into masculine versions of himself as a defense against their sexuality. "Swift and the 'agreeable young Lady, but extremely lean'," in Contemporary Studies of Swift's Poetry, eds. John Fischer and Donald Mell, Newark, 1981, p. 154. Ellen Pollak, The Poetics of Sexual Myth: Gender and Ideology in the Verse of Swift and Pope, Chicago and London, 1985, argues that Swift uses "Cadenus and Vanessa" to urge a redefinition of the concept of propriety, pp. 129–30.

[13] Hagstrum, Sex and Sensibility, p. 156.

into account the most significant aspect of the relationship between Swift and Stella: its literary density. For Swift encloses Esther Johnson in language as he changes her into a Stella subject to his own verbal maneuvers. Just as his first nurse, the kidnapping nurse overwhelmed with affection for her charge, taught Swift his letters, Swift in turn teaches his own more pliant nurses how to read him, painstakingly drawing up spelling and book lists for all of his female charges, from Vanessa to Lady Acheson. The language learned at the breast becomes a weapon to defend against further displacement. Living and dying in language itself, Swift locks those dearest to him in its bonds, replacing chains of begetting with chains of irony. And it is all as permanent as the paper on which it is written, material for the butchers and the close-stools, just as suitable to the wrapping of pies as it is to the containment of emotion.

Nauti nurse

Swift wrote his *Journal* to Stella over the months turned into years that he spent in London from September 1710 to June 1713. At the time he began the journal, Esther Johnson was twenty-nine years old, Swift's friend and pupil for twenty-one years, a woman of allegedly great charm possessing a spirit of independence, but a woman dependent nonetheless upon the overseeing of a companion, Rebecca Dingley, and even more dependent upon the strictures of Swift. Legends of secret marriages and sobbing Stellas notwithstanding (most recently David Nokes comes out for the marriage, J. A. Downie against it),[14] we can have no idea of the actual circumstances of their domestic situation save public reports that both Swift and Stella observed "an almost exaggerated propriety." Swift wrote to Tickell that he had only seen Stella once or twice in a morning for at least a dozen years (*JS*, p. xxix), and it is a well-known "fact" that the dean and his friend had never once been seen alone together. Yet however scrupulously Swift observed the proprieties in real life, displaying the habits of a self-protective nature even in the days Stella was dying (for she couldn't draw her last breath in the deanery), in his *Journal* the diffident dean becomes bold, irrepressible, a boisterous child bent on provoking his nauti nurse. Protected by distance, shielded by duenna Rebecca Dingley's presence, the safe half of MD, Swift used his *Journal* to invade Stella's mornings, to insinuate himself into her chamber, into

[14] David Nokes, *Jonathan Swift, a Hypocrite Reversed: A Critical Biography*, Oxford, 1985, "favours the notion of the secret marriage in 1716," p. 342. J. A. Downie, *Jonathan Swift, Political Writer*, London, 1984, argues that because "the God-fearing Stella . . . signed her name" as "Spinster" in her will, she could not have been married. "Would Jonathan Swift, Dean of St Patrick's, Dublin, have let her describe herself as a spinster in a legal transaction in which he was concerned? I think not," p. 342.

her bed, as he embodied his and her letters with a nature so physical that it can only exist on paper.

Swift speaks to Stella in many modes, employing a colloquial style flexible enough to hint of both state secrets and domestic irregularities, but he is perhaps most revealed when most disguised. "Ourrichar gangridge," the "riddle gangridge," proves richer by far than the worn-out words that can be detected by meddling messengers in a hostile world. Swift's heady baby talk testifies to his love of word play for its own sake, but just as strongly bears witness to an inveterate love of nursery secrecy, the game "of hide and whisper." The little language provides an ambiguous medium for play. Its equivocal marginality allows Swift to enter a dream state where, verging on the edge of sleep, free from public responsibilities, Swift can give vent to his most private and irresponsible needs.[15] While addressing, however ironically, posterity,[16] Swift also smudges and distorts private words to go further than he should, freed always by semantic difficulties he creates to retreat at will. "Are you good Huswifes, & Readers, are you walkers," he chides, "I know you are Gamesters; Are you drinkers? Are you – O Rold, I must go no further fear of aboozing fine Radyes" (*JS*, p. 565). Not only does he abuse his fine ladies with imputations of deep drinking, but he ends his ruminations on their boozing with a nasty dash, the kind that delights Vanessa and turns Swift's stomach. Dashes flow easily from Presto's pen, for he is aboozing Radyes, not ladies. His "MD you must know are not women" (p. 90) but rather "nauti nauti nauti girls," "sirrahs," or "sollahs," or even "dollahs," "deelest richar logues," fellow players eager for their sport.

The game begins in bed. "For you must always write to your MDs in bed, that's a maxim. Mr. White and Mr. Red, Write to MD when abed; Mr. Black and Mr. Brown, Write to MD when you're down; Mr. Oak and Mr. Willow, Write to MD on your pillow. – What's this? faith I smell fire" (p. 139). "I am writing in my bed like a tyger," Swift reports, as he opens up a world of emendations. Writing or writhing, wonders his editor Forster, or could the word "tyger" be a "mistake of Deane Swift or of the compositor" (*JS*, p. 99). Swift could very well be writhing, for he takes pains to make his physicality known, whether he is holding water in his mouth just so (p. 89) or pursing his lips "just for all the world as if I were talking in our own little language to MD" (p. 261). Swift dreams "confusedly" of Stella and smears tobacco over the page: "Is that tobacco

[15] Felicity Nussbaum discusses marginality in the *Journal* in her paper "Smoking Swift's *Journal to Stella*," given at the Western Society for Eighteenth-Century Studies, Huntington Library, March, 1984.

[16] Ehrenpreis suggests that the *Journal* was written for public as well as private reasons, Swift's way of setting down historical notions of what would later pass for fact. *Swift*, II, pp. 653–4.

at the top of the paper or what? I don't remember I slobbered. Lord, I dreamt of Stella &c, so confusedly last night" (p. 56).

To slobber over the letter is to slobber over Stella herself, for embodied in the journal, "you are just here upon this little paper, and therefore I see and talk with you every evening constantly and sometimes in the morning, but not always in the morning, because that is not so modest to young ladies" (p. 232). Swift might work at preserving Stella's morning modesty, but when he gets hold of Stella's letter in bed, he turns it into a most compromised fetish:

Come out, letter, come out from between the sheets: here it is underneath, and it won't come out. Come out again, I say: so there. Here it is. What says Presto to me, pray? says it. Come, and let me answer for you to your ladies. Hold up your head then like a good letter. There. Pray, how have you got up with Presto? madam Stella. (pp. 146–7)

As he folds his own smudged letter so carefully in the dark, "and make what you can of this," he promises his "wheedling slut" to "come again to-night in a fine clean sheet of paper" (p. 154). The sheets cover over his letter and his body as he piles up masturbatory *double entendres*. Checked from familiarity at home, on paper Swift can wish that his cold hands were in the warmest part of his MD (p. 184). On a hot night, he reports that he is sitting before his letter wearing "nothing but my nightgown," and follows this disclosure to promise Ppt that she shall have at last "a great Bible" (p. 549). Not until Richardson would a didactic writer mix piety with prurience so easily. As Swift confesses, he is "a Beast for ever after the order of Melchisedec" (p. 154).

"A subject fit for me"

The intimacy of the *Journal* depends upon the geographical space between Swift and Stella. From London, Swift allows himself to see in his mind's eye Stella "shewing a white leg, and putting it into the slipper" (p. 410), but back in the Deanery, he seems compelled to avoid morning visits altogether, and waits, in fact, six years after writing the journal to address Esther Johnson publicly in the first of what would become a series of birthday poems. And in these poems, he treats his subject with a firm sense of proprietorial right as he controls her physical nature with a language of substitution and containment.

Swift begins his birthday tributes by insisting upon Stella's temporal existence even as he goes about altering it. Hailing her thirty-fourth year (she's in reality thirty-eight), he refuses to "dispute a Year or more"

(*Poems*, II, pp. 721–2), all the while he not only pares off four from her age but doubles her physical size. No Petrarchan conceit, she appears to live in a real world of flesh and blood, but it is nonetheless always a verbal one of Swift's own making.[17] From the start, taking liberties with her vital statistics, he invests his goddess with fat and gristle she may not have ever possessed. We only know about Stella's fat from Swift himself; pictures of Esther Johnson, if they are authentic, belie his estimation of her weight.[18] And we know for certain that Swift "saw" Stella, the brightest virgin on the green, at least seven years before the time he specifies in his nostalgic paean. But double rhymes with trouble, reason enough to plump Stella's frame even as Swift makes the paradoxical point that her true "Form" can never be altered (save in verse). Introducing the notion of Platonic form only to undercut it, Swift cleaves Stella in two, and turns her corporeality into matter for jesting.[19]

In his poems to Stella, Swift exerts control over her body by accommodating himself – relentlessly – to the inevitable decay of her flesh. He waits until she is thirty-eight years old before he can "safely" sing her virtues, for at that age, long past the time that younger nymphs lose their noses and poets lose their muses, Stella's physicality no longer threatens. Her virtues "on no Accidents depend," but are grounded in friendship.[20]

This is not to say that the friendship was without strain, and one senses in the poetry that Swift is trying through his language to compensate for the sexuality he has worked so hard to contain. The "Agreeable Bitch" must have possessed a sharp enough tongue to provoke even in her final illness at least one prayer in which Swift asks God to "Forgive every rash and inconsiderate Expression, which her Anguish may at any Time force from her Tongue" (*PW*, IX, p. 254). The poem written "To Stella, Who Collected and Transcribed his Poems," reveals some of their struggle. The poem itself is one that Stella would copy out, and in the lines written in her own hand, so like Swift's, she would receive a pointed lesson in mortification. For the Stella addressed in the poem possesses an unruly

---

[17] Both Hagstrum, *Sex and Sensibility*, p. 153 and Nussbaum, *Brink*, p. 115, emphasize the materiality of Stella.

[18] Swift cannot be relied upon when he measures "the ladies' " size or appetites. "Mrs. Johnson eats an ounce a week, which frights me from dining with her," he reports, *Corr*, II, p. 450. Later he tells Charles Ford that Mrs. Johnson grows leaner, "eats about two ounces a week, and even drinks less than she did," *Corr*, III, p. 47, revising this dire picture a few months later with the news that "she eats now but a mouthfull a day," *Corr*, III, p. 52. In his study of the portraits of Stella, Henry Mangan cannot call any of them authentic. "Here, indeed, are faces, but the serious eyes keep their secrets, the closed lips tell no tales; their identities we may but guess." *JS*, II, p. 702.

[19] John Fischer, *On Swift's Poetry*, Gainesville FL, 1978, discusses the way Swift "splits" Stella up the middle, p. 133.

[20] *Poems*, II, pp. 727–32, lines 79–80.

temper as fierce as "*Aetna*'s Fires" (line 105), one that must be checked. Worse still, she defends her outbursts, arguing that

> . . . this Turbulence of Blood
> from stagnating preserves the Flood;
> Which thus fermenting, by Degrees
> Exults the Spirits, sinks the Lees.
>
> (*Poems*, II, pp. 727–32, lines 127–30)

Swift objects to her reasoning and warns that nothing but acid can come from her rage. Far from sublimating her passion into cleansing anger, she is only turning it into peevishness. Passion should be sublimated more safely into wit. But when he offers this advice, Swift avoids the truth of his own work on sublimation, the iatrohydraulic principles he so devastatingly sends up in *Mechanical Operations of the Spirit* and *Tale of a Tub*. Ignoring his own truism that passion will out somehow as a fistula on a king's anus or as a conscripted army marching across continents, in his poems to Stella, Swift expects his goddess to contradict nature and sublimate her passion "safely" into a wit softened by her love. This exemplary behavior separates her from the rest of "Human Kind," turning her into a goddess holding "true Contempt for Things below."[21]

She is also a true nurse, serving Swift on his "sickly couch," running to answer his "unmanly" laments. In his verses "To Stella, Visiting me in my Sickness," Swift approaches the domestic idyll celebrating the idealized Mrs. Cope, mother and nurse soothing her children with soft songs:

> Then *Stella* ran to my Relief
> With chearful Face, and inward Grief;
> And, though by Heaven's severe Decree
> She suffers hourly more than me,
> No cruel Master could require
> From Slaves employed for daily Hire,
> What *Stella*, by her Friendship warm'd,
> With Vigour and Delight perform'd.
>
> (*Poems*, II, p. 726, lines 101–8)

"Soft . . . silent . . . unheard," Stella moves about Swift's bed the better to serve his needs. By playing, seriously, the role of child, Swift receives, greedily, perhaps even sadistically, all the care the nursery provides: the cheer, the grace, the suffering borne "with Vigour and Delight."

Even as he emphasizes his juvenile dependency, Swift, child enough to make his nurse first "taste each nauseous Draught" (lines 111–13) before him, seems finally embarrassed over the inverted roles he insists upon. He escapes this problem by pushing them both – nurse and patient –

---

[21] *Poems*, II, pp. 727–32, 724, line 44; p. 765, line 68.

slave and master – into their eventual "safe" states of "ruin" and decay, warning:

> If, while your Tenderness secures
> My Life, it must endanger yours.
> For such a Fool was never found,
> Who pull'd a Palace to the Ground,
> Only to have the Ruins made
> Materials for a House decay'd.   (lines 119–24)

Within the constraints of their arrangement, in applauding Stella's commitment to his decaying "materials," Swift insures that noble Stella play the fool, victim of another bubble played on mortals by jesting gods. As always, Swift reserves the freedom to retain the dual roles of trickster and victim, the agent of her suffering ("No cruel Master could require" more "From Slaves employ'd for daily Hire,") and the suffering victim supine and impatient "on my sickly couch."

Stella is not only nurse, but hero, blessed by Pallas Athena with manly virtues. Just as Vanessa possessed the brave metal of the finest boy, Stella owns a "manly Soul . . . molded . . . with Female Clay" (lines 85–90), that burns all the brighter for her bravery.[22] And as a softer Swift, she must, to conform to her heroic frame, exhibit not just contempt and "Indignation in her Mind / Against Enslavers of Mankind!" but "true Contempt for Things below" (lines 61–2).

The lines referring to "Things below" come from his final and most touching poem to Stella written when she is surely dying, literally passing from the physical world:

> Believe me *Stella*, when you show
> That true contempt for Things below
> Nor prize your Life for other Ends
> Than merely to oblige your Friends;
> Your former Actions claim their Part,
> And join to fortify your Heart.
>   (*Poems*, II, pp. 763–6, lines 67–72)

---

[22] *Poems*, II, pp. 722–7, In his memorial to Stella, "On the Death of Mrs. Johnson," Swift praises her heroism. "With all the softness of temper that became a lady, she had the personal courage of a hero. She and her friend having removed their lodgings to a new house, which stood solitary, a parcel of rogues, armed, attempted the house, where there was only one boy: She was then about four and twenty: And having been warned to apprehend some such attempt, she learned the management of a pistol; and the other women and servants being half-dead with fear, she stole softly to her dining-room window, put on a black hood, to prevent being seen, primed the pistol fresh, gently lifted up the sash; and, taking aim with the utmost presence of mind, discharged the pistol loaden with the bullets, into the body of one villain, who stood the fairest mark. The fellow, mortally wounded, was carried off by the rest, and died the next morning, but his companions could not be found." *PW*, V, pp. 229–30.

"Not the gravest of Divines" is offering "for once some serious Lines" (lines 13–14), but even in this final tribute Swift can't stop punning away his gravity and sinking grave thoughts into "mortifying Stuff" (line 8), more decayed material. His reference to "Things below," alludes unexpectedly to a poetic world outside the ostensible boundaries of this final poem to Esther Johnson, for it recalls another martial virgin, the more worldly Goddess Belinda, not subject – yet – to the "Grief, Sickness, Poverty, and Age" (line 32) of a dying Stella, but subjected to the vexations of a more volatile sexuality. Like Stella, Belinda is initially charged to remain in a state of sexual innocence, exhorted to "Hear and believe! thy own Importance know, / Nor bound thy narrow Views to Things below."[23] But just as Swift insisted in the *Tale* and *Mechanical Operation*, that "Things below" will out in the end, Pope demonstrates comically in his poem the way in which denied sexuality can fester. Thwarted desire howls through his Cave of the Spleen while maids turned bottles call aloud for corks.

In his treatment of sexuality in "The Rape of the Lock," Pope appears to be of two minds about the nature of Belinda. Both girl and goddess, she is chastised by the more sententious Clarissa, who sounds a lot like Swift tutoring Stella when she holds forth on the virtues of "Good Humour." Yet, even while she is criticized for her coquetry, Belinda still manages to transcend Clarissa's commonplace advice to add "new Glory" to the heavens with her lock. With his "quick Poetic Eyes," Pope invests her lock with supernal radiance, making immortal the very sign of Belinda's mortality. By recalling at such a critical time Pope's complex tribute to Belinda and the temptations of regressive virginity, Swift also invokes Pope's ambivalence toward his "moral." Unlike Clarissa, urging Belinda to enter the world of the flesh, Swift demands from Stella a contempt for "Things below" that calls up the other side of "The Rape of the Lock," the canker of virginity and the waste of good humor turned to spleen. For Stella is no stranger to the spleen, subject to his warning that her passion not turned to wit will turn to acid: "From Passion you may then be freed, / When Peevishness and Spleen succeed" (*Poems*, II, p. 731, lines 135–6). And all the while, almost ironically, she is dying of a most exquisite good humor.

In this equivocal treatment of Stella's chastity, Swift attempts to plumb her nature even as he defines it. While he insists that Stella check and sublimate her passions, he recognizes that ultimately she cannot transcend her bodily self, not when things below are dragging her into death. He confronts the problem in contradictory ways, first insisting upon pla-

---

[23] "Rape of the Lock," *The Poems of Alexander Pope*, ed. John Butt, New Haven, 1963, pp. 217–42, lines 35–6.

tonic form, but then paradoxically exploiting the trap of the flesh, as he
offers up his own physical frailty to compensate for Stella's.

The birthday poem written on the "Angel-Inn" considers the platonic
implications of "Stella's Case in Fact" (*Poems*, II, pp. 734–6). Embodying
an angel's mind, her face, the sign of the angel, remains "a little crack't"
(lines 15–16). But the face itself signifies nothing, for the true Stella, the
form of Stella, remains whole, unmarred by the "Cracks and Wrinckles"
(line 56) of a lesser mind. Swift dwells on the decay itself, those cracks
marring the surface, since we live after all so much on the surface of
things past knowing. To accommodate Stella's decline, Swift resorts to his
own, and offers his failing eyesight to compensate for Stella's decay. In a
later birthday poem, refusing to believe evil reports of locks turning grey,
Swift gives thanks that his own eyes have "somewhat dimmish grown,"
admirably adapted to her "Decays" (*Poems*, II, p. 757, lines 42–4). Insisting
upon the failings of both bodies, Swift manages (in his poetry if not in his
life) to circumvent the trap of the body – "For Nature" is "always in the
Right" – by exploiting its inevitable betrayal. The price is high, the "real"
sight of Stella herself. Looking through worn-away eyes, Swift trades the
sight of the real for the sound of the ideal, Stella's sense and wit. But
always sensitive to the cost of life and the cost Stella herself so freely pays,
so little getting for what she gives, "We really wonder how she lives"
(*Poems*, II, p. 735, line 30), Swift demands the price from them both.

In his "Receipt to Restore Stella's Youth," Swift further accentuates
Stella's physicality and sets her flesh free in the process. To restore not
just her youth, but her health, Stella has been sent down to Quilca to
"graze." Just as famished cows put on fresh flesh over the summer, Stella
should gain new pieces of herself. When the starving cow puts on fresh
flesh, she "Grows plump and round, and full of Mettle, / As rising from
Medea's Kettle" (*Poems*, II, pp. 758–60, lines 17–18). This allusion to
Medea calls up not only her successful rejuvenation of Aeson, but
reminds the reader of the more unfortunate King Pelias, an old man
slaughtered by his well-meaning daughters, tossed mangled and bleeding
into Medea's boiling kettle in his desperate attempt to cheat time itself.[24]
(Even the Struldbruggs, in comparison, possess more dignity and arouse
more sympathy.) Although Stella might not boil away entirely, she might
lose her "self" as she gains new flesh. Old veins will be flooded with
"sprightly blood," sagging skin will be plumped fresh and firm, while
Stella herself disappears. Only the name will remain, her nominal
essence, for "if your Flesh and Blood be new, / You'll be no more your
former *You*" (lines 37–8).

Reducing Stella to essential flesh and blood, the only thing intelligible

---

[24] See Ovid, *The Metamorphoses*, Harmondsworth, pp. 161–4, Book VII, lines 251–94;
    Graves, *The Greek Myths*, II, pp. 250–3.

("For, what was ever understood / By human Kind, but Flesh and Blood?"), Swift paradoxically insists upon her infirmities as part of her true self. Just as he was only able to string his harp "safely" when she was "no longer young" (*Poems*, II, p. 728, lines 9–10, 79–80), Swift seems here unable to contemplate a truly healthy Stella, without imagining her gone entirely. But he just as stubbornly returns to the flesh that binds, and promises to make firm the new Stella with beef and claret, more matter. Beginning his poem by comparing Stella to the starving cow, Swift ends filling up her failing flesh with the matter of the cow itself.

In his final poem to Stella, Swift embodies her virtues one last time, turning them into the nutriment that feeds the mind. Reversing the reduction of his "Receipt," Swift argues that as the body thrives on food ingested twenty years before, so then should the mind thrive on good actions committed twenty years past. In this final reworking of the problems the body presents, the last public word to pass between Esther Johnson and Jonathan Swift, most painfully evident is a rueful awareness of the physical strain, the impatient suffering that by now makes up much of a dying friend's existence. Swift is trying to appease not just any "difficult" woman, but a woman he has *made* difficult. With great uncertainty, he entreats her to look at her life with an acquiescence and a satisfaction that he tries to invoke for one last time through language. "Say, *Stella* . . . Believe me *Stella* . . . Me, surely me, you ought to spare."[25]

Swift resorts finally to himself, the center of the poetic world he has built around his subject, the center of the nursery. Even though he asserts that "human Kind" can understand little else but "Flesh and Blood," he insists once and for all that Stella not relapse into body, but remain apart to temper her passions into wit, flesh into mind. In his poem "To Stella: Written on the Day of her Birth, but not on the Subject, when I was sick in bed" (*Poems*, II, pp. 754–5), taking into account Stella's humble slavery, her ability to "feel my pains alone," he promises, once he is "out of pain," to "be good again" (lines 17, 33–4), a promise immediately contradicted by his wish that they "long continue thus, / Admiring you, you pitying us" (lines 37–8). For the partnership to work, Swift must remain if not bad, at least not good enough for the long-suffering Stella to stop nursing. It is fitting, therefore, in this last poem, that the poet calls attention for one more time to "Me, surely me," and that he once again pleads for pity on a pitying friend. He asks finally that her "Ills affect" not her mind, but that she prove capable of transcending the demands of the flesh without giving into the peevishness of the spleen. And he resorts for the last time, to *his* own needs, while praising "You, to whose Care so oft I owe, / That

[25] Richard Feingold is particularly sensitive to the modulation of tone in this poem in "Swift in His Poems: The Range of his Positive Rhetoric," *The Character of Swift's Satire*, ed. Claude Rawson, Newark, 1983, p. 194.

I'm alive to tell you so" (*Poems* II, pp. 763–66, lines 81, 87–8). It becomes clear in this poem just how very much Swift depended upon Stella's ability to adapt to Swift's version of herself, her willingness to live in his language. Sauci doxi, generous noble mind, through it all, she is invoked through his word made incarnate, yet only to the extent he can bear. And through it all, she remains Swift's.

This proprietorial sense, this assumption of "Me, surely me," colors one of his most curious relationships with women, his patronage of a "seraglio" of poor women. We are back in the harem, that necessary structure of containment of desire always threatening to break out. Delany bristles with indignation at Orrery's indelicate suggestion that Swift was surrounded by a "constant seraglio of very virtuous women" who could not have attended him more ardently had he been the "Grand SEIGNIOR himself." In Swift's defense, Delany enumerates the "professed nominal mistresses" the dean tended to keep. "Truth obliges me to own, that he also visited some of them even in by-alleys, and under arches; (places of long suspected fame.)" Swift's benevolence here appears unimpeachable; he patronizes one mistress wanting an eye, another a nose, a third an arm, a fourth a foot, a fifth possessing all the attractions of Agna's pollipus, "and a sixth, more than all those of Aesop's hump." The objects of charity have names, "for distinctions sake, and partly for humour; Cancerina, Stumpa-Nympha, Pullagowna, Fritterilla, Flora, Stumpantha." Flora, one imagines, was the ugliest.[26]

Deflating pastoral expectations as he so often does, to insist upon a world of flesh and blood where all too frail nymphs can lose their noses with the waning of the moon, Swift plays an old game as he indulges himself in one last transformation of the flesh. Just as Esther Vanhomrigh must play at being Vanessa, the saucy slut or the softer man, and Stella must lurch between her position as nauti girl and noble nurse, so these final members of Swift's seraglio give up their identities to Swift in exchange for his patronage. It could be said that they're not losing that much, these decrepit sellers of plums and hobnails and gingerbread. Their name is legion and they stand on every corner. But it could be said that they give up their souls. Swift refers to one of his ladies in a letter to Sheridan in which he reports that "No soul has broke his Neck, or is Hanged, or Married; only *Cancerina* is dead, and I let her go to her Grave without a Coffin and without Fees" (*Corr*, IV, p. 130).

The irony here is too complex to suggest that Swift is being "Turkish" about his nymph by denying her a soul. He is writing a peevish letter to an old friend filled with splenetic reminders of his own old body's ills, a page covered in the hundreds of "blunders" that irk him so. Can a soul

---

[26] Patrick Delany, *Observations upon Lord Orrery's Remarks on the Life and Writings of Dr. Jonathan Swift*, London, 1754, *Swiftiana*, 12, New York, 1974, pp. 128–33.

break its neck at all, Swift nervously jokes, as he plays as always with the doubleness of language.

Cancerina, a soul demographically if not metaphysically, is part of the world Swift holds at bay through language that also allows him to come as close as he can to the problem the body presents. By treating her cancerous rotting state mock-heroically, he contains it, exerting verbal power over flesh and blood. Just as he controls the sexuality of Stella and Vanessa, changing their identities with his titles, for they are two Esthers, Johnson and Vanhomrigh, not goddesses at all, by naming the members of his "seraglio," he keeps off, for the moment, the mortality threatened by one cancer-ridden corpse. It is all done with "the assistance of Artificial *Mediums*, false Lights, refracted Angles, Varnish, and Tinsel" (*Tale*, p. 172), that bagatelle that Swift deflates yet depends upon, those words properly spelled learned from a nurse long dead. The process of transformation depends upon a verbal dexterity more supple than the material resistance called up against it, a play of mind that can savor "grave Matters" even into death, and can find pleasure in a mock heroic pastoral sending up such fragile, decadent material that Cancerina offers. And that in the end, is all a word, however spelled, can do.

6

Chains of consumption: the bodies of the poor

A Mountebank in Leicester-fields *had drawn a huge Assembly about him. Among the rest, a fat unwieldy Fellow, half stifled in the Press, would be every fit crying out, Lord! what a filthy Crowd is here: pray good People, give way a little. Bless me! what a Devil has rak'd this Rabble together: Z—ds! what squeezing is this! Honest Friend, remove your Elbow. At last a* Weaver *that stood next him, could hold no longer. A Plague confound you* (said he,) *for an overgrown Sloven; and who (in the Devil's name) I wonder, helps to make up the Crowd half so much as yourself? Don't you consider (with Pox,) that you take up more room with that Carkass than any five here? Is not the Place as free for us as for you? Bring your own Guts to a reasonable Compass (and be d—n'd) and then I'll engage we shall have room enough for us all.* Tale of a Tub, *p. 46*

As I said before, the good Management of the Lord Mayor and Justices did much to prevent the Rage and Desperation of the People from breaking out in Rabbles and Tumults, and in short, from the Poor plundering the Rich; I say, tho' they did much, the Dead Carts did more. *Journal of the Plague Year*, p. 129

When the "fat unwieldy Fellow" makes his notorious complaint against the filthy crowd, he is reacting to the literal press of bodies always on display in the urban arena. His own discomfort becomes absorbed in the larger mass come together to observe the spectacle at hand – the mountebank selling his wares to a sick, bloated – yet wasted – society. Swift removes himself from this particular crowd by assuming an ironic detachment that allows him to regard the scene of "poxed" carcasses jostling for "room enough." But although he defuses the complaint with a "reasonable" prescription impossible to fill, the problem he observes remains. Both Swift and Defoe confront in their fiction and in their tracts the body politic, its swollen carcass five times greater than it should be. If one body blocking transcendence becomes cumbersome, one city filled with bodies, particularly the bodies of the poor, becomes hell itself, "It being," Swift reminds us, "as hard to get quit of Number as of Hell" (*Tale*, p. 55). In their strategies to come to terms with corporeality on such a large scale, both writers consider rational solutions – badging beggars and projecting schemes of forced labor and institutionalized charity, filling schools and hospitals and mad-houses – but in the end, both also devise reductive schemes of radical annihilation to end the problem they are compelled to explore. "The Lord Mayor and Justices did much," H. F. observes, to prevent the people from breaking out "in Rabbles and Tumults," but "the Dead Carts did more."

While purporting to examine ways to "manage" the plague, Defoe also represents the plague's purgative quality, its ability to empty a teeming city of "useless mouths," the bodies of the poor. Swift offers an even more radical solution to the problem of a swollen corporate body in his *Modest Proposal* where he devises satiric schemes to consume the superfluous bodies of the poor, pickled or fricaseed. Both invent fictions of consumption to "solve" the problem the poor made visible. Each turns to the figure of the cannibal to represent the failures of a society that "devours" its poor to maintain its consumptive growth.

These next two chapters will consider the way both writers confronted the body writ large dominating an urban life becoming increasingly difficult to order. In treating the problem of the body, particularly the urban body, they pursue strategies desperate and painful, calculated to prod the reader into consciousness. Considering the operation of the political unconscious, Fredric Jameson observes that "history is what hurts, it is what refuses desire," that "ground and untranscendable horizon" which "needs no particular theoretical justification."[1] Defoe and Swift, certainly not politically *un*conscious, coming up against that "ground and untranscendable horizon," expose the historical necessity of their complex economy through remarkably similar images. In their consumptive fictions, mothers "butcher" and "murther" their babies lest they be consumed by their needs, while the slaughterhouse itself, "the shambles," moves into the center of society to dispatch – more efficiently and more visibly – bodies meant for consumption. While the consumption they delineate is a commercial result of civilization, the behavior of the consumers reveals its "savage" origins. The revelation seems within the logic of the writers' texts inevitable, yet indirectly it is both contained and avoided. In their treatment of the savage within and without, the yahoo nature that demands incorporation, Defoe and Swift confront a problem that they finally run from. Their final schemes of annihilation reveal the limitations of consciousness as it confronts a history that "refuses desire." But since we live in a society still unable to manage the problems that Defoe and Swift exposed, their attempts to cure a sick body should not be dismissed as shortsighted. They did not need Marx to tell them their history. It stopped them dead on the street every day of their urban lives.

[1] Fredric Jameson, *The Political Unconscious: Narrative as a Socially Symbolic Act*, Ithaca NY, 1981, p. 102.

I would first like to consider Defoe's use of the plague as purge, a killing cure for the city's ailments. Within that discussion, I will pay particular attention to the tale of the three men from Wapping that H.F. keeps trying to tell. The problems his men face negotiating their way through hostile, threatening territory reflect the "real" condition of the poor that Defoe cannot help observing. A consideration of the significance of the cannibal figure in both Defoe's and Swift's fiction will make up the following chapter. While Defoe uses the cannibal to explore the inequities of the consumer economy that devours the poor to feed its need for luxury, Swift uses the cannibal more aggressively, not only implicating his reader in the consumption, but forcing the reader to turn cannibal and "eat" the need it depends upon.

"A Little Room"

So are the Joys which Nature yields
Inverted in May-Fair;
In painted Cloth we look for Fields,
And step in Booths for Air.
    " 'In Pity to the empty'ng Town' "
                            (*Poems*, I, p. 122, lines 9–12)

When H.F.'s three men from Wapping arrive on the outskirts of Epping, they are leading a rag-tag band of fugitives running away from the plague. Their needs, they argue, are simple. "They only desir'd a little Room to breathe" (p. 143). Such a modest request for fresh air seems reasonable enough when it is made in the out-of-doors, but coming from the bodies of the London poor, such a request becomes outrageous. "Room to breathe" had become a luxury. Swift would lightly satirize civilized discontents in his poem "In pity to the Emptying Town," a celebration of an urban taste so "corrupted" that in May Fair, nature yields joys "inverted": "In painted Cloth we look for Fields, / and step in Booths for Air." More trenchant examinations of the problems of a city not "emptying," but filling up, would suggest that the booths had become overrun with customers.

Londoners in 1722, Defoe's own plague year, breathed "in their own steams." Dr. Arbuthnot worked out a most Swiftian calculation to prove this point:

The perspiration of a man is about 1/34 of an inch in 24 hours, consequently one inch in 34 days. The surface of the skin of a middle sized man is about 15 square feet; consequently the surface of the skin of 2904 such men would cover an acre of ground, and the perspir'd matter would cover an acre of ground one inch deep in 34 days, which rarefied into air, would make over that acre an atmosphere of the steams of their bodies near 71 foot high.[2]

Arbuthnot is writing a serious treatise here on the benefits of "fresh air," but he is also engaging in a calculated form of hysteria. By magnifying the perspiration issuing from just one body, he literalizes the abstract, making visible the invisible "steams" which fill up as if by magic an area one acre wide, seventy feet high. He creates in the process an urban space filling itself up with stale, used air that presses down on bodies guilty only of breathing.

The problem of finding a "little Room" – Swift would say "room enough" – became particularly daunting in London, the locus of material anxiety, a place that could never be brought to a "reasonable compass." Its size had become *un*reasonable, swelling from some 200,000 inhabitants in 1600 to 675,000 in 1750. Defoe made a wild stab at estimating the million and a half people he imagined filling the "monster city," the "great and inexhaustible maw," the "great God Moloch" that consumed its children, that "prodigious thing" so difficult to order.[3]

The hyperbolic tags denote the wonderful threat London's size and energy called up. The city was monstrous, the dropsical head too big for its body, the wen leaching nourishment from the larger political and organic entity that was England. An organic deformity, it sprawled in a "most straggling, confus'd Manner, out of all shape."[4] As early as 1598 John Stow complained of the ramshackle suburbs overflowing with "filthy cottages" that "pestered" and "blemished" the city limits with "unsavoury and unseemly" entrances into its center.[5] Augusta, the urban body politic, had become debauched, a place where complexity suggested corruption. Observing the "great irregularity" of the physical body of London, Henry Fielding observed that the "immense numbers of lanes, alleys, courts and bye-places" appeared to be designed "for the very purpose of conceal-ment."[6] What was being concealed was the corruption that the city both inspired and depended upon. The sprawl had become moral, a reflection of an urban knowledge that by its illicit nature required official sup-pression.

---

[2] John Arbuthnot, *The Effect of Air on Human Bodies*, London, 1733, pp. 11, 17, cited in Charles Creighton, *A History of Epidemics in Britain*, 2 vols., New York, 1891, reprinted 1965, II, pp. 84–5.

[3] See chapter 1, note 25, for references to the monster city.

[4] Max Byrd, *London Transformed*, pp. 13–17 and Louis Landa, "London Observed: The Progress of a Simile," *Essays in Eighteenth-Century English Literature*, Princeton, 1980, pp. 218–31 discuss the development of this metaphor at length.

[5] Stow's Survey of London, "Suburbs Without the Walls," cited in Creighton, *A History of Epidemics*, p. 85.

[6] Raymond Williams, *The Country and the City*, p. 145.

Unnatural in shape, the city, naturally "barren," seemed to cut its citizens off from a more "natural" order of life. John Graunt, one of the first English statisticians, calculated the disparity between the relative fertility rates of urban and rural areas to argue that "the minds of men in London are more thoughtfull and full of business than in the Country." This meant "that their attention was necessarily diverted from the more necessary labour of reproduction."[7] Country imports were required to infuse fresh blood into a body politic living on stale air and running out of physical energy.

The city also strained spiritual and communal connections. Treatises written against the rising tide of both luxury and melancholy look back nostalgically to a purer, less complicated physical economy that predated the city, an unmixed state off prelapsarian innocence that is labeled "English." Advocates of temperance railed against the strange mixtures urban living inspired, the "new Dishes, new Modes of Cookery, brought amongst us by the Foreigners that have come over, in so great Numbers," establishing a national tendency towards gluttony "owing [to] the late great Multiplication of Pastry-Cooks" as well as gin sellers servicing the bloated, yet sterile, body politic.[8] Not only pastries, but urban dislocation served to sever man from God. As Keith Thomas notes, it was suspected that cities needed more sermons, so that "their inhabitants, who . . . see for the most part but the works of men, may daily hear God Speaking unto them; whereas such as are conversant in the fields and woods continually contemplate the works of God."[9] When he does want a word with his urban children, God tends to strike them down with a plague, filling up churches that will inevitably empty once he relents. The communal space itself had shifted from the church and family into the street, public arena for the drama of the plague year.

Within such a denatured yet organic urban context, Defoe's "plague year" represents the moral and social imperative of his own time. He attacks his culture's excesses with an urgency so deeply felt that he presents his urban prognosis twice, publishing in the same year not only *A Journal of the Plague Year*, but also *Due Preparations for the Plague, as well for Soul as Body*.[10] *Due Preparations* particularly addresses the problems of

---

[7] Clayton D. Lein, "Jonathan Swift and the Population of Ireland," *ECS* 4 (1975), p. 446.

[8] John Woodward, *The State of Physick: And Of Diseases; with an Inquiry into the Causes of the late Increase of them*, London, 1718, pp. 194–6. In a similar vein, George Cheyne blamed the "mixing and compounding of *Sauces* with foreign *Spices* and Provocatives," French cookery and eastern pickles for the corruption of body and spirit in England: *The English Malady, or a Treatise of Nervous Diseases of all Kinds*, London, 1733, p. 51. See discussion in chapters 2 and 4 of appetite and temperance.

[9] Thomas, *Religion*, p. 664.

[10] *Due Preparation for the Plague as well for Soul as Body, Works*, 16 vols., ed. George Aitken, London, 1905, XV, hereafter cited as *DP* within the text.

the London of 1720, a city Defoe judges to be morally and physically unprepared to meet the threat of the plague then raging in and around Marseilles. The French plague provided the occasion for Defoe's attack, but the London condition provided the reason.[11]

In *Due Preparations*, Defoe argues that the people of London have created an infection that stems from their own corruption. Much has already been said, Defoe reminds his reader impatiently, of the need "for paving and cleansing the streets, that no noisome, offensive stench may rise from the dirtiness and heaps that are usually found there," for closing up the tide-ditches, "loathsome by-places" full of carrion, "from whence such filthy unsufferable smells are sensibly perceived, as make people loth to pass by them." Like Arbuthnot, he complains of "notorious fountains of stench, enough to corrupt the very air, and to make people sick and faint as they pass by" (pp. 27–8). His criticism would be repeated throughout the century. In 1741, Johnson put into the mouth of Lord Tyrconnel a complaint against the "heaps of filth, as a savage would look on with amazement," alluding darkly to unexpected chasms, and offensive mountains of filth blocking the public way.[12] Ten years later, John Gwynn was still listing "nuisances" in an *Essay on Improvements*: ordure and rubbish, broken pavements, ruined houses, the driving of bullocks through the streets, the prevalence of mad dogs, and most notably the swarms of beggars – and the deluge of profanity – in the way. Defoe wonders at *any* freedom from disease, considering the "stinks and nastiness" infecting the town.

His argument quickly turns moral as he indicts victims of corruption for their own appetites. The people "ought to turn their thoughts to cleansing a worse jakes than that of the tide-ditches in Southwark or Fleet Ditch, &c." The bodies and the minds of the rich and poor alike should be purged of ill habits and gross distempers to deliver "Nature from all the burthens she was loaded with before" (pp. 31–2). Revealing his radical distrust of appetite so central to *Conjugal Lewdness*, Defoe predicts that crammed with "high feeders" and "deep drinkers," the London of 1720 would fall even faster to the plague that ravished the London of 1665. Driven by vitiated appetites, rich and poor alike eat flesh so grossly that:

[11] McManners discusses the Marseilles plague, *Death and the Enlightenment*, pp. 43–5. See also Manuel Schonhorn, "Defoe's *Journal of the Plague Year*: Topography and Intention," *Review of English Studies*, n.s. 19 (1968), pp. 387–402; F. Bastian, "Defoe's *A Journal of the Plague Year* Reconsidered," *RES*, n.s. 16 (1965), pp. 151–73; Maximillian Novak, "Defoe and the Disordered City," *PMLA*, 92, 2 (1977), pp. 241–52.

[12] Carole Fabricant is particularly good on the "heaps of filth" in urban streets in "Excremental Vision vs. Excremental Reality," *Swift's Landscape*, Baltimore and London, 1982, pp. 24–42. Richard Schwartz discusses Johnson's "imitation" of Lord Tyrconnel in *Daily Life in Johnson's London*, Madison WI, 1983, pp. 20–1. Walter Besant, *London in the Eighteenth Century*, London, 1903, pp. 89–90, cites John Gwynn's report on the dangerous conditions of the street.

"If we were but to be seen by the people of any other country," we would be taken for "if not cannibals, yet a sort of people that have a canine apetite." Comparing English consumers to the Tartars, "who eat their horse-flesh raw," Defoe has heard it said that "we devour our meat, but do not eat it, viz., devour it as the beasts of prey do their meat with the blood running between their teeth" (p. 37). This connection between cannibalism and consumption will inform much of Defoe's fictional discourse on the consumer economy. Here it is used didactically. "We" are guilty savages – cannibals, Tartars – bent on satisfying a Hobbesian appetite. "We" can, must, reform.

When Defoe considers his subjects consumers, Tartars who eat their horseflesh raw, but also reduces them to carrion, flesh to be preyed upon by a natural or supernatural avenger of mortal appetite, he locates most equivocally the problem of the body in his discourse. Envisioning a plague that will carry off bodies, he must also envision in his apocalyptic schemes all manners of bodies, rich and poor, bloated and pinched, that clog the public arteries. A fear of appetite, which would logically seem to be confined to attacks on those rich enough to indulge in their taste for flesh, extends into a more complicated fear of *all* bodies taking up room, for poor bodies, however "pinched," will swell, given the chance. There is, in both Defoe's and Swift's treatment of poor bodies, a sympathy undercut by a deep distrust of need which, if met would only produce more consumers guilty of a fatal indulgence. Desire threatens to compromise the most austere demonstrations of necessity. Moral and physical frailty is, within such a tangled context, excused, and yet punished. The English, therefore, when most pressed, still remain guilty of excess. Defoe reckons that "the *English* labouring people eat and drink, but especially the latter three times as much in value as any sort of forreigners of the same dimensions in the world."[13]

Ranting against the excessive drink going down the corporate gullet, Defoe speaks for his age. Everyone knew that the idle poor were especially given to drink. Drink offered a cheap route out of more pressing matters, causing an insensibility that was conventionally regarded with horror. Sir John Gonson observed with cold distaste the fallen state of the drunken poor beholding their rags and nakedness "with a stupid Indolence, and either in senceless Laughter or in low and insipid Jests, to banter all Prudence and Frugality, drowning [their] pinching cares and losing with [their] Reason all anxious reflections."[14] Hogarth captures this kinetic

[13] "Giving Alms No Charity, And Employing the Poor, a Grievance to the Nation," London, 1724, p. 31, from a *Select Collection of Scarce and Valuable Economic Tracts*, ed. John R. McCulloch, London, 1859, p. 57.
[14] Marshall, *The English Poor*, pp. 34–5; See M. Dorothy George, *London Life in the Eighteenth Century*, Harmondsworth, 1966, pp. 41–55; Thomas, *Religion*, p. 17; Rudé, "Mother Gin and the London Riots of 1736, *Paris and London in the Eighteenth Century*, London, 1974,

insensibility in *Gin Lane*, conflating in his study of urban need the compassion and exasperation Defoe demonstrates towards the poor. In the foreground, a drunken madonna slouches against a banister to pinch some snuff while her infant, grasping on to her nipple with his feet, plummets inevitably to the ground. She is so unconscious that her bared breast does not even appear to register the shift in weight. To her left, the gin seller, more skeleton than flesh, lounges, while behind her, two bottle companions pour spirits down the throat of a third as they wheel him off in a barrow, a diminished plague cart. Dominating the background, piling up under the sign of the undertaker, bodies slump against heaps of matter, more material to be stuffed into coffins. Just as Defoe's own plague victims either sprawl senseless or run up and down the streets "in the height of their Fever, Delerious and Distracted," the gin drinkers are either stupified into deathly stillness or propelled into feral action. While a frenzied dwarf shares a bone with a bear, another sodden mother pours gin down her baby's throat. "As a mad Dog runs on and bites every one he meets" (p. 162), the citizens of Gin Lane become objects of contempt exempt – because mad – from their sins, yet guilty – because mad – of a need impossible to relieve. They become because of their complicated distress emblems of Defoe's – and Swift's – work.

However complicated his response to corporate need, Defoe is clear in his radical desires to rid himself of the material problem. The bodies, pathetic yet offensive, needed to be removed from the streets. In *Due Preparations*, Defoe considers at length the vulnerability of the poor bodies lacking mobility, that depend upon a faltering economy. He offers various ways of "reasonabl[y] encourag[ing]" their departure. Workhouses could be emptied, debtor's prisons shut up, persons without a "legal settlement" sent "home" to their original parishes. Whatever the method, "no beggars, vagabonds, or loose people" are "to be suffered in the streets" (p. 21). Typically compulsive, Defoe does not stop clearing out the poor bodies, but rids the streets of *everything* in the way: "dogs, cats, monkeys, parrots," "and any creatures that eat flesh . . . especially all the weasels, rats, and mice," extending his projections until there is not a "swine, hog, or sow left alive . . . no, nor a horse" (p. 26).

The compulsion to cleanse the corporate body of the mixture that sickens it expressed in *Due Preparations* becomes reified in *A Journal of the Plague Year*, where "useless mouths" (p. 198) are not ordered through

pp. 201–21; Lindsay, *The Monster City*, p. 39, Maximillian Novak, *Economics and the Fiction of Daniel Defoe*, New York, 1976, pp. 73–4. John Walter and Keith Wrightson, "Dearth and the Social Order," *Past and Present*, 71 (1978), discuss the connections made between dearth and drunkenness, pp. 28–9; Peter Clark, "The Alehouse and the Alternative Society," *Puritans and Revolution: Essays in Seventeenth-Century History*, ed. D. Pennington and K. Thomas, Oxford, 1978. See also John Bender, *Imagining The Penitentiary*, Chicago, 1987, p. 83.

thirteen "measures" out of town, but are "carried off" by the plague. For all the while Defoe is committed to saving lives, to reforming his high-feeding, deep-drinking reader, he is also in search of peace, a stillness that can accompany the emptied space the plague provides. In a series of conversations between his doubting son and devout mother, Defoe uses his *Due Preparations* to explore the most reductive margins of his desire for order. His "true, affectionate mother" (p. 95) seems to yearn for a period of national humiliation to bring the wicked city of London to its knees. To be cured, the misshapen monster must be brought down, its shops, ships and ports emptied of the bustle and confusion that "feeds" its "wickedness." "Oh that I could see such a sight in London," she muses, "indeed it ought to be" (p. 102).[15]

The devout mother's dreams of devastation close down an abstraction – wicked London. But the plague works on real bodies, not symbols of "high feeding." In his depiction of the "complicated distress" of his plague victims, the plague poor, Defoe creates a dialectic in which the poor bodies are present and absent, guilty yet innocent, all too pressing in their need and just as easily carried off by the thousands to a mass grave where they will no longer offend "poor unhappy gentlewomen" with their bodily presence. When they are seen en masse, they are just as easily distributed en masse. Their very number displaces their individual distress on to the threatening infectious mass they become. Once infected, the poor body victimized by the problem *becomes* the problem. En masse, the poor burst out of alleyways, break out of confinement, and pester the streets. Yet in the *Journal* H.F. also personalizes their dilemma. His poor become victims of the corruption the author of *Due Preparations* rails against. They are members of what John Graunt called "the consumptive trades." How few, Graunt observed, "are employed in raising and working for necessary Food and covering."[16] How many, H.F. noticed, were trapped in plague-ridden London as appendages to a "youthful and gay Court." No less than one hundred thousand ribbon weavers alone lived in and about the city when the plague struck. While the court flees to pursue safer pleasures, their weavers stay behind to pay for such expensive gaiety (p. 19).

Ribbon weavers, footmen, serving maids, bakers, sail makers and carpenters all become by circumstance idle but able bodies in search of settlement. When H.F. considers their dislocation, he contemplates the problems of relieving a class deserving yet hardened. For just as the victims of *Gin Lane* are guilty and not guilty of their condition, the plague year poor are both needy and a nuisance.

[15] Byrd, *London Transformed*, p. 41.
[16] Landa, "London Observed," *Essays*, p. 222.

"Ignorant and stupid in their reflections, brutishly wicked and thought-less" (p. 29), the poor seem to rush mindlessly into danger. "It was imposs-ible to beat anything into the[ir] Heads" (p. 209), H.F. decides, but as Defoe repeatedly demonstrates, H.F. is also driven into danger by a curi-osity that almost proves fatal. Their predilection for risk connects to their need, for guilty of their own hunger, they "push" into the most dangerous businesses as nurses, grave-diggers and watchmen (p. 169). (Not poor, H.F. is able to avoid such onerous duties.) While H.F. pities the poor, he suspects that even when easy, the poor would still betray a lavish extravagance. "Fool-hardy and obstinate . . . Thoughtless for tomor-row," they lack even "one jot of better Husbandry" (p. 210). When fruit floods the market, "madly careless of themselves," the poor gorge them-selves into attacks of "the griping of the Guts" which helps to "precipitate" them into the plague they richly deserve (p. 272).

Although Defoe's poor are victims, their vulnerability is in itself dangerous. Not only is there no disease as contagious as poverty, but there is no strength so compelling as weakness. Babies sent out to nurse could and did spread city contagion on to the countryside,[17] while crimi-nals suffering from prison fever would infect juries with their moral and physical corruption. In the calico riots, the main threat of the rioting workers became their physical presence, their bodily power to infect their public.[18]

H.F., while extending sympathy, goes so far as to contemplate the "Wickedness" of plague victims, probing in his consideration the mutu-ality of innocence and guilt that binds its urban victims together. However weak they appear, the poor threaten a violence bred of desperation. "In hot tempers," driven by drink, they might let "loose the Tongue to all the Indecencies and Rudeness of the most Provoking Language, as well as the most hellish Oaths and Curses, and which is frequently followed by Quarrels and Fightings, and sometimes hath been the cause of Murder."[19]

---

[17] Walter Harris, *De Morbis acutis infantum*, London, 1689, illustrated the contagion of the city when he reported: "The Rector of a Parish twelve miles from London with great grief of mind told me that his Parish which was not small either in its Bounds or Number of Inhabitants and was situated in a very Wholesome Air was, when he first came to it, filled with sucking Infants, and yet in the space of one Year that he had buried them all, except two and one of his own whom being weak he had happily committed to my care from his very Birth, and that the same Number of Infants being soon twice supplied, according to the usual Custom of hireling Nurses, from the very great and almost inexhaustible City, he had committed them all to their parent Earth in the very same Year." Cited in Williams, *The Age of Agony*, pp. 54–5.

[18] Creighton gives examples of the dangers of infection, *A History of Epidemics*, pp. 90–8, 63–7. Novak, "Defoe and the Disordered City," *PMLA* (1977), p. 246, reminds us that Defoe defended calico rioters; Clarkson discusses the threat of jail fever, *Death, Disease and Famine*, p. 46; Guy Williams cites examples of the fears of jail fever, *Age of Agony*, p. 82.

[19] Gonson, as cited in Marshall, *The English Poor*, p. 35.

Plague victims similarly run amok, "running out of their own Government, raving and distracted, and often times laying violent Hands upon themselves, throwing themselves out at their windows, shooting themselves, &c." (p. 81). No story of H.F.'s is more terrible than his tale of the "poor unhappy Gentlewoman" molested by "one of those terrible creatures," a plague victim who kisses her into the grave (p. 160).[20]

Her attacker is described in various ways. He is a "Creature," he is "raving mad to be sure, and singing," he might be drunk, he might have the plague, he is "only a rude Fellow," and finally, he is "but weak." His mastery over the gentlewoman appears accidental. "Unhappily, she being so near," he manages to pull her down to his level. His greatest crime appears to be disclosure, for "worst of all, when he had done, [he] told her he had the Plague." The creature's rude weakness defuses the violence he inflicts upon his victim while her distress compels the reader to fix categories to contain such agents of infection. For there is within us all a deep yearning to be safe from such arbitrary attacks, but perhaps even stronger, a desire to be safe from the *knowledge* of such arbitrary conditions. In spite of his weakness, the creature is guilty of "murthering" his victim, yet the ambiguity of his and her condition (did he have the plague, it seems so, did she have the plague, I never heard) blurs the guilt, spreading it over the plague year itself. It belongs ultimately to a condition rather than to an individual.

Perhaps it is because the guilt can be attributed to a condition rather than to an individual that Defoe is able, within a paragraph, to dispatch the corporate body that so unwittingly offends. H.F. reports a most "melancholy article," which he calls a "deliverance in its kind." In the worst days of the plague, thirty or forty thousand poor bodies, "which had they been left, would certainly have been an unsufferable Burden by their Poverty," are carried off. Since the city could not have supported the cost of their live bodies, they would have been driven in time to plunder the city and the adjacent country for subsistence. Their deaths ironically "Deliver" the city from their burdensome presence (p. 98).[21] Ultimately, faced with the problem the poor bodies represent, H.F. recognizes the reasonable efficacy of such a final solution, for although the Lord Mayor and Justices "did much, the Dead Carts did more." The poor creatures, "with great difficulty kept from running out into the Fields and Towns, and tearing all in pieces where-ever they came," become contained and

---

[20] Austin Flanders cites this encounter as an example of the irrational aggression and subsequent state of urban anomie that Defoe represents in "Defoe's *A Journal of the Plague Year* and the Modern Urban Experience," *Daniel Defoe: A Collection of Essays*, ed. Max Byrd, Englewood Cliffs NJ, 1976, p. 156.

[21] See Nicholas Rogers, "Popular Protest in Early Hanoverian London," *Past and Present*, 79 (1978), pp. 70–100, and Wrightson, *English Society*, pp. 177–9, for discussions of food riots and roving bands of needy migrants.

controlled: "They rather went to the Grave by Thousands than into the Fields in Mobs by Thousands" (pp. 128–9). In resorting to such words of dire expediency, Defoe, a reformer who supported the calico rioters, points to the real problem the poor bodies represent. His solution radically cleanses the corporate body of its disease-laden numbers. Burdens are carried off, lest they turn, by necessity, into the thousands driven, by necessity, into the fields in mobs. In his general consideration, H.F. contemplates the mass deaths of thousands, but in his tale of the three men of Wapping, he presents the personal fortunes of singular victims made needy by their circumstances. In that tale, we can see even more clearly the difficulties facing the individual poor body searching for a "little Room to breathe."

The three men of Wapping

The three men of Wapping, although of "mean Condition," are neither idle nor poor. One, a soldier wounded in the late wars, bakes biscuits; his brother, a former seaman, "hurt of one Leg," makes sails; while the third, the ingenious joiner, is a carpenter with no wealth but his basket of tools (p. 58). In spite of their individual efforts to make a living wage, and in spite of their sacrifice to a military machine that has consumed part of one leg and the strength of one other body, the three men become squeezed by circumstance. If the plague comes to Wapping, they will be turned out of doors: "People are so afraid of one another *now*," that they will have nowhere else to go. In his portrayal of their individual attempts to find settlement in a society that reinforces their dislocation, Defoe demonstrates his sympathy for their situation even as he reveals his doubts of finding a solution to their dilemma.

The tale is generally appreciated as a welcome celebration of stalwart, dogged virtues. Establishing "with their skills a community of survival,"[22] and offering in their pastoral retreat an alternative to loneliness and exploitation of economic individualism, they promise "a Moral in every Part" of their tale, "a Pattern for all poor Men to follow, or Women either, if ever such a Time comes again" (p. 122). But as so frequently happens in Defoe's didactic structures, patterns dissolve as the moral dwindles under scrutiny that Defoe will not forbear applying to his story.

H.F.'s reluctance to tell the tale undermines the usefulness of its moral. He begins with vigor, only to trail off, "having yet for the present much more to say before I quit my own Part." Leaving his three men stranded in their preface, driven by a fearful curiosity to look into the plague pit at Aldgate, H.F. will not return to his tale for over sixty pages. When he

[22] Richetti, *Defoe's Narratives*, p. 238.

does return, breaking into a series of "dismal Stories,' he touches upon their plight only to leave them once again to consider the wisdom of fleeing the plague and to enumerate the number of dogs and cats – forty thousand dogs and five times as many cats – sacrificed in the plague year. Catching himself in his acts of narrative evasion, H.F. "comes back" to "my three Men" at last, promising a moral in every part "whether my Account be exactly according or not" (p. 122). The history so difficult to tell turns out after all to be not "exactly according to fact."

In finally giving up his tale, H.F. presents three men trapped in their material circumstances. In a debate over staying or leaving their home, John the Baker urges immediate action, for "*if we stay here we are sure to die.*" His brother clings to home, for "*Here we were born and here we must die,*" suggesting that if they even set down the road they will risk being sent back to "*their last legal Settlement*" as vagrants. John continues to argue that

"*the whole Kingdom is my Native Country as well as this Town. You may as well say, I must not go out of my House if it is on Fire, as that I must not go out of the Town I was born in, when it is infected with the Plague. I was born in* England, *and have a Right to live in it if I can.*"   (p. 124)

These are important words. John the Baker appeals here to national rather than parochial rights, demanding a broader distribution of public responsibility than the Act of Settlement allowed. His unhappiness with the present system is well founded.

The Act of Settlement, first instituted by the Parliament of 1662, "the pivot around which the administration of poor relief was destined to swing for nearly two centuries," granted Parish overseers the right to remove any person coming "to settle themselves" who could not show proof of possessing the yearly value of ten pounds. Persons unable to prove their ten pound worth, deemed "likely to be chargeable to the Parish," were to be removed to their "home" parish , the place where they were last legally settled. The ten-pound rule tended to bring the majority of the laboring poor under its power, since the average rural laborer never paid more than three pounds for a cottage. The constant threat, therefore, of parish removals exacerbated the sense of uncertainty that marked life at subsistence level, making it even more difficult for the working poor to take to the open road. Faced with the threat of whippings, brandings and transportation for moving out of place, the poor tended to stay put. Just as the three men from Wapping worry considerably about procuring certificates of health allowing them safe passage between towns, a poor person on the move in the eighteenth century needed to secure the proper certificate from his home parish and then worry about getting it accepted by the overseers at his destination. Movement was painfully uncertain. As Keith Wrightson ruefully notes, the poor often found their "final settlement" as dead bodies found in barns and under hedges.[23]

Fearful of starving between hostile towns, the three men of Wapping experience what Dorothy George calls the "uncertainty and insecurity"[24] of the single individual attempting to subsist in an alien, often dangerous environment. No sooner do they set off than they are stopped by the checkpoint at Bow Bridge where the watch is on guard against travellers from London. To get past the checkpoint, the men resort to what H.F. calls "a little Fraud" (p. 129). They must negotiate a certificate of good health not quite right swearing that they had not been at London at all. Such an oath is, they decide, under the circumstances, "literally true," since Wapping is not exactly part of either the City or the Liberty of London. As J. S. Taylor suggests, the Act of Settlement tended to hone the sensibilities of the poor by rewarding intelligence, provoking initiative, and demanding "a little fraud" (pp. 56–60).[25]

The "little fraud" seems to me very significant. Traditionally the poor were suspected for manufacturing their distress, for pretending disease and deformation in order to live off the labor of others. Jacques Donzelot suggests that a "whole array of spectacular tricks" were believed to be employed by beggars – "false infirmities, lying spiels, and even deliberate mutilations."[26] Beggars needed to be badged to be properly certified in an attempt to protect the public from their fraudulent activity. More, I suspect, the public needed to believe in the frauds themselves as one way of protecting itself from need. We can see an example of the conventional

---

[23] *English Society*, p. 142. Peter Clark discusses the "members of the lower classes who did take to the road" and "ran the risk of running foul not just of the settlement laws but of the vagrancy statutes as well." "Migration in England During the Late Seventeenth and Early Eighteenth Century," *Past and Present*, 83 (1979), p.84; Marshall, *The English Poor*, pp. 225–45, and James S. Taylor, "The Impact of Pauper Settlement, 1691–1834," *Past and Present*, 73 (1976), pp. 52, 60–1, illustrate the failure of the act of settlement with examples of the extremity of removals. The classic analysis of the Act is Sidney and Beatrice Webb's *The English Poor Law History*, Part I, *The Old Poor Law*, London, 1927. Gertrude Himmelfarb defends the act of settlement for reaffirming the "principle of public responsibility for the poor," *The Idea of Poverty: England in the Early Industrial Age*, New York, 1984, pp. 26–7, 40–1. Mark D. Koch discusses literary and social interpretations of the poor in "The Economy of Beggary in English Literature from the Reformation to the Enlightenment," Ph.D. dissertation, SUNY at Buffalo, 1986.

[24] George, *London Life*, pp. 102, 262.

[25] Taylor, "Impact of Pauper Settlement;" p. 56–68; Wrightson, *English Society*, p. 167; Wrightson and David Levine, *Poverty and Piety in an English Village*, New York, pp. 173–85; and Marshall, *The English Poor*, 236–7, consider the distancing effects of the attempts at codifying and managing the poor.

[26] Jacques Donzelot, *The Policing of Families*, trans. Robert Hurley, New York, 1979, p. 59.

distrust of beggarly distress in Thomas Sheridan's biography of Swift. Sheridan reports that Swift, no lover of unbadged beggars, disguised himself as a blind fiddler to attend a beggar's wedding ceremony. Both Swift and Sheridan watched the crippled and blind sing and dance, tell stories, make jokes "in a vein of humour more entertaining to the two guests, than they probably could have found in any other meeting on a like occasion." The next day, the Dean and the Doctor encountered their beggarly companions who were now "begging their charity in doleful strains . . . some upon crutches, who had danced very nimbly at the wedding; others stone blind, who were perfectly sighted at the feast." Swift, "who mortally hated those sturdy vagrants, rated them soundly."[27] Sheridan's tale suggests a radical – and typical – distrust of need made visible. In fact, the more visible the sores and twisted limbs, the more inauthentic the sight was deemed to be.

In committing their frauds, swearing to clean bills of health or pretending bodily deformations, the poor tried to put themselves forward in an unreceptive world. The three men from Wapping, in search of their rightful settlement, find that they must resort to more and more spectacular assertions of "health" and power that they do not in truth possess to be "seen" at all. When they arrive at Walthamstow leading a tiny band of fellow fugitives, to make themselves visible they need not only pretend soundness, but sound numbers, bodies enough to "raise the County." They pretend to be an army of "near 200" complete with "Arms and Tents like Low Country Soldiers" (p. 142). To be seen, the band must threaten, even while they argue to the good people of Walthamstow (who want to turn them away) that "It is you that threaten, not we" (p. 137). They speak the truth, for as Defoe demonstrates, refusal to see need threatens the reciprocal core of a society that, in theory, depends upon mutual subordination. The band's distress in the fact of the plague absolves their fraud and justifies their posture. "We are not thieves," the baker insists, "but poor people in distress." To open the "shut up . . . Compassion" (p. 138) of the town, fantastic strategies become necessary, even commonplace.

In presenting the band's strategies, Defoe indicts the society that demands to be fooled. His resolute band overturns the "ideological fictions" that their enemies, their society, depend upon. For there is not, nor will there be "room enough" unless sadlers from Wapping and Molls from Colchester bend the more conventional rules that can only apply to the privileged few. He also complicates the moral in every part that H.F. promised. For when it is time to deliver his pattern to follow, H.F. issues a disclaimer instead: "I give this Story thus at large, principally to give an Account of what became of the great Numbers of People which immediately appear'd in the City as soon as the Sickness abated" (p. 150). By shifting his moral to a general consideration of the "great numbers," H.F. leaves the victory of his three men, who arrive home safe and sound, suffering only colds and distempers, to tell instead a more difficult tale of great numbers.

This textual shift reveals one final time the uncertainty of poor bodies progressing through a hostile world. For in closing his tale, H.F. provides an epilogue, the stark story of the poor bodies "that in great Numbers, built themselves little Hutts and Retreats in the Fields and Woods, and liv'd like Hermits in Holes and Caves, or any Place they cou'd find." These huts were often discovered empty after the great plague summer, "nor is it unlikely but that some of the unhappy Wanderers might die so all alone." While it can be argued that Defoe introduces such a desolate, solitary account to reinforce his insistence upon solidarity and movement, it is still difficult to discount the pensive, bleak tone that inserts itself into his final cautionary tale.

We are left at the end not with a tale of triumph, but with the description of one particular hut and one particular man found dead, "and on the Gate of a Field just by, was cut with his Knife in uneven Letters, the following Words, by which it may be suppos'd the other Man escap'd or that one dying first, the other bury'd him as well as he could":

> O mIsErY!
> We BoTH ShaLL DyE,
> WoE, WoE. (pp. 150–1)

H.F.'s pattern for all poor men to follow is reduced textually to a *memento mori* unevenly carved. The words of solitary woe anticipate the final lines of H.F.'s *Journal*, the sincere but coarse lines of his own making that call attention to the alienated cost of being "yet . . . alive" once the plague has disappeared. When Defoe insists that attention be paid to the cost of survival, the miracle of being "yet . . . alive" while one hundred other bodies are swept away, he points to the greater problem of survival in his own age. The three men from Wapping and their sturdy band could play soldier to work their little fraud on a suspicious public, but their extraordinary success undercuts any moral to their story. "Great Numbers" were, would, and will be, swept away, in the attempts to find a rightful settlement. The unevenly carved testament to the "mIsErY" tells the true story, intimating in its Hobbesian, solitary woe the disconnection and alienation of modern life.

We are left with a perplexing vision in the *Journal* of a city too large to be managed, and a populace too large and needy to be relieved. Defoe offers two radically different solutions to the problems he calls up. In one, the poor can be provided for by "some pious People daily" who will

pay "great Sums of money" to assist the poor distempered people. For
they "that give to the poor, lend to the Lord, and he will repay them."
But this utopian scheme, which overturns some of Defoe's own pro-
nouncements about charity, is not, either in 1665 or in 1720, as efficient
as Defoe's more dependable "Dead Carts" waiting to carry off the poor
by the thousands; for "had they been left," the poor bodies would "certainly have been an unsufferable Burden by their Poverty" (p. 98).

H.F.'s silent, shut-down London of 1665 is as dismal as the "little
Huts . . . often found empty" strewn across the countryside. In its stillness, it becomes a city empty not just of bodies, but of need, fulfilling the
longings expressed by the mother of *Due Preparations*. No movement, no
visible bodies, just dead quiet enveloping all until the occasional mob, so
many atoms colliding, bursts out of the odd alley. The vision of a
devastated city safe from urban need will be called up often in the eighteenth century. Swift will modestly propose to eat up superfluous children
while he plans to turn Ireland herself into a grazing land for horses.
Pope will close down all moral and intellectual activity, replacing motion
increasingly frenzied with the dead level of stillness dullness promises.
Blake will translate all to heaven where bodies are something else entirely.
Such dreams of annihilation address most excessively the dilemma of the
city marked with "mIsErY" and "WoE."

Schemes of riddance were entertained from the start. It would be
better, Sir William Petty mused, working on the problem of recalcitrant
bodies difficult to fit into a physical economy, if plagues were more dis-
criminating in their effects. Were a plague able to distinguish the drone
from the worker bee, the lazy poor from the energetic workers, the dead
limbs on the body politic could be pruned.[28] Defoe approaches such a
final solution in his *Journal* by wiping out a problem in fiction that proved
impossible to solve in reality. Carrying off "useless mouths" that could
only be fed in his pastoral idyll of the three men from Wapping, an idyll
undermined by its context of necessary fraud, Defoe forces H.F. to tell a
moral tale overwhelmed by its mortal circumstances. It is a tale he keeps
on telling, using in other versions of mortal need the figure of the cannibal
to uncover the complicated workings of a consumer society that devours
its own children.

[28] George Wittkowsky, "Swift's *Modest Proposal*: The Biography of an Early Georgian Pamphlet," *Journal of the History of Ideas*, 4 (1943), p. 84.

7

Consumptive fictions: cannibalism in Defoe and Swift

In a Word, The Nature and Experience of Things dictated to me upon just Reflection, That all the good Things of this World, are no farther good to us, than they are for our Use. *Robinson Crusoe*, p. 129

I had settled my little Oeconomy to my own Heart's Content. . . I soaled my Shoes with Wood which I cut out from a Tree, and fitted to the upper Leather, and when this was worn out, I supplied it with the Skins of Yahoos dried in the Sun. I often got Honey out of hollow Trees, which I mingled with Water, or eat it with my Bread. No man could more verify the Truth of these two Maxims, *That Nature is very easily satisfied; and That Necessity is the Mother of Invention.* *Gulliver's Travels*, p. 276

The insular life possesses its simple virtues, as Crusoe and Gulliver readily admit. Fish are jumping, the Yahoos are nigh, and so long as you are able to content yourself with rough fare, Gulliver's oats and whey, Crusoe's goat stew, with an occasional enemy thrown in for variety (Yahoos melt down into a rather serviceable tallow), you will agree that on the whole "Nature is very easily satisfied." Swift and Defoe, on the other hand, fleshing out the more problematic aspects of such modest economies, do not allow such pastoral dodges. They call attention in their fiction to "*the Dearness of things* necessary to Life." Both Swift and Defoe insist in their explorations of physical economy that the cost of life may in fact be so dear that to survive we may find ourselves consuming each other.

"If we were but seen by the people of any other country," Defoe complained, we would be taken for "if not cannibals, yet a sort of people that have a canine appetite" (*DP*, p. 37). Both Defoe and Swift set moral tales in strange lands to abstract the cannibal nature of their own physical economy. They use the cannibal to explore the savage "other" that becomes incorporated into the civilized being, that part that exists "by necessity" in a consuming society grown complex and interdependent. Defoe demonstrates Crusoe "civilizing" his savage to make him part of a

149

system he controls. But the savagery Crusoe combats turns out to be located as much within as outside his own nature. He proves himself to be the most professionally savage inhabitant of his island as he feeds needs that grow increasingly complicated. Swift also insists upon exposing the savagery implicit in his straining physical economy. To protect himself from his yahoo "nature," Gulliver skins the Yahoos he so fears, and melts them down for tallow, making use of their bodies to separate himself from their needs.

In their cannibal fictions, Swift and Defoe represent an imperialistic society that compromises their most compassionate instincts. Both writers, however fundamentally different, united almost ironically in their service to a mixed government of Harleys that inevitably disappoint. They reveal their shared distrust of a system that consumes its subjects, a system that they nonetheless depend upon. They use the cannibal as the emblem of a physical economy that requires an infusion of new blood to revitalize (and subsequently threaten) an ailing body politic. Just as "Moloch" London depended upon an influx of fresh bodies to grow faster than its death rate, England depended upon its colonized bodies to feed the "necessary" needs that resulted from its expansion. Hating the crews of butchers and pirates that insure that after three navigations of the globe Mrs. Gulliver could enjoy her dish of tea, Swift exposes the luxurious "needs" of an economy of consumption. Defoe, ostensibly the professional booster of such a vigorous economy of expansion, points repeatedly to its cost, its dependence upon slavery, upon violence, and upon death. "To feed on Man's Flesh is lamentable, but not sinful," he observes, exposing in his charity the struggle implicit in the civilizing process.[1]

It is generally agreed, Defoe notwithstanding, that eating people is wrong. The cannibal provides a convenient benchmark of civilization, that place we like to think that we depart from. Yet, at the same time, the cannibal has long been used as an index of the barbarity of its civilized observer. Montaigne offered the cannibal as a morally neutral model, arguing that "there is more barbarisme in eating men alive, then to feed

---

[1] Cannibalism enters into Defoe's most vivid fantasies of a Hobbesian universe. Maximillian Novak, *Defoe and the Nature of Man*, Oxford, 1963, gives examples of Defoe's idea of "extremes of necessity." In *The Farther Adventures of Robinson Crusoe* a serving maid aboard a damaged ship is so hungry that she confesses herself "tempted to bite her own arm." "Had she been a mother she might have eaten her own child in her delerium . . . would have eaten her [mistress] with 'Relish'." Defoe, like Pufendorf, decided that to "feed on Man's Flesh in the desperate Extremity of Famine" is a lamentable "but not sinful Expedient," p. 71. Paula Backscheider, *A Being More Intense: A Study of the Prose Works of Bunyan, Swift, and Defoe*, New York, 1984, describes the "disastrous and perilous" state of a "mulatto" captured by Magadoxans so fierce in their hatred of white people that "they seize them, rip the flesh, and consider the chunks prizes to be exclaimed over or as tasty morsels to be savored," *The General History of the Pirates*, p. 49.

upon them being dead."[2] The idea of cannibalism can support a society's analysis of itself in complicated, often contradictory ways. The cannibal can be the neighboring enemy, the barbaric "other" that defines social worth. It can also serve as a mythic marker in the history of a civilization. We *used* to eat each other in the shadowy past before we knew better. Again, the cannibal may exist within the bounds of contemporary society as a reminder of that society's capacity for suffering. Thus the report of an Irish mother literally devoured by her hungry children – they feed off her flesh for twenty days – emphasizes the misfortune that determines the Irish problem Swift faces in *Modest Proposal*.[3] And finally, the cannibal may stand as victim, visceral representative of larger and more powerful systems of consumption that mechanically reproduce its consumptive patterns.[4]

Swift and Defoe employ the cannibal not just to explore a reprehensible "other," but to make that "other" part of the corporate sensibility that includes "ourselves." While both writers express a strong impulse to annihilate the need that the denatured and cannibalized bodies of the poor represent, they complicate their yearning for order. The desire to cleanse and rid the earth of its irritating and offensive burden is subsumed by a more basic need to incorporate the need that cannot be denied. This chapter will first look at Defoe's cannibalistic strategies, concentrating on Crusoe's domestication of Friday, and will then consider Swift's use of the cannibal in *Gulliver's Travels* and in his Irish Tracts addressing the problem of the bodies of the Irish poor. In calling attention to the price of survival, in designing complex economies that depend upon the commercialization of human flesh, enslaved, pickled, or fricaseed, both writers expose a world of mutual dependency as they tell the cost that must be paid to sustain the fiction of a "Nature . . . very easily satisfied."

---

[2] *The Essays of Montaigne Done into English by John Florio* (1615), 3 vols., ed. George Saintsbury, London, 1892, I, p. 226.

[3] W. Arens, *The Man-Eating Myth: Anthropology and Anthropophagy*, Oxford and New York, 1980, considers the mythical implications of cannibalism, pp. 139–62. Arens is perhaps most extreme in his view that cannibalism itself is a fictional construct imposed upon civilization's "other" to enable the "civilized" people to subjugate their "cannibal" enemies and victims. Claude Rawson considers the theoretical implications of cannibalism in fiction in two long pieces in *Genre*: "Cannibalism and Fiction: Reflections on Narrative Form and 'Extreme' Situations," 10,4 (1977); and "Cannibalism and Fiction," 11, 2 (1978). His reading of "A Modest Proposal," *Augustan Worlds*, ed. J. C. Hilson, M. M. B. Jones and J. R. Watson, Leicester and New York, 1978, pp. 29–50, reprinted in *Order From Confusion Sprung*, is also valuable.

[4] See Peter Hulme, *Colonial Encounters*. Peter Linebaugh discusses the slave trade in his forthcoming *London Hanged*.

My savage: Defoe orders his fictional world

After his fourth year of confinement, Robinson Crusoe examines his insularity and finds it relatively good. The happiness he can manufacture depends upon his isolation. Removed from "all the Wickedness of the World," he is freed from "the *Lust of the Flesh, the Lust of the Eye, or the Pride of Life*," As Lord of his solitary manor, he becomes almost embarrassed by riches, "Tortoise or Turtles enough; but now and then one, was as much as I could put to any use."//Pastoral circumstances protect him from the bustle and wickedness of a more complex economy, for although he has wood enough to build a fleet and grapes enough to have overloaded his ships with wine and raisins, Crusoe the speculator is prevented all too materially from carrying out visionary schemes of commerce.//The mother of *Due Preparations* would have applauded his self-enforced austerity.

Sounding like Gulliver among the Houyhnhnms, Crusoe decides that nature is very easily satisfied as long as we temper our desires. "All I could make use of was All that was valuable," he muses as he contemplates the moldy parcel of money, that "nasty sorry useless Stuff." As often noted, the nasty stuff has its uses later on, but in the fourth year on the island, it remains hermetically sealed off from a world of consumption. "I had no room for desire," he decides, "except it was of Things which I had not, and they were but Trifles, though of great Use to me." Desire comes in the back door in this sequence, for while his circumstances do not allow the room for its presence, the absence of things of "great use" yet "trifling" conflate luxury and necessity, need and desire.[5] Without the "room" for desire, Defoe sets out to build traps of necessity.//His Crusoe would give a handful of gold and silver for a gross of tobacco pipes, "nay . . . all for a Handful of *Pease* and *Beans*, and a Bottle of ink." Enumerating the "things" wanting, Crusoe strips away a desire that nevertheless represents itself in his self-denying act of accountancy.//

//Crusoe's stoicism depends upon his confined state/Yet even secured on his island, kept from his desires, he still depends upon a complex physical economy outside the island. Crusoe spends "whole Days" contemplating the inevitability of a Hobbesian descent into "Nature" had God not provided him with a foundering boat to gut. Without the proper tools, had he killed a goat or bird, he would have had "no way to flea or open them, or part the Flesh from the Skin, and the Bowels, or to cut it

<hr />

[5] Sekora argues that luxury "was probably an idea born of psychological necessity. . . It provided its users with a powerful measure of self-worth, for it identified all they *were not*," *Luxury*, p. 51. Just as significant, however, is the way luxury measured all that its critics could be, enlarging their sense of power while implicating them in a desire that needed to be curbed.

up; but must gnaw it with my Teeth, and pull it with my Claws like a Beast" (pp. 128–30). Trapped in his simple pastoral, Crusoe is saved from his natural state by goods belonging to other "civilized" men providentially sacrificed for his sake. To protect himself from his "Claws like a Beast," Crusoe constructs his "necessary" umbrella and fashions jerkins from animal skins that must have rubbed his skin raw. Inevitably the skins connect him to the state he is trying to contain.

Even as he disguises his savagery with the skins of fellow creatures, Crusoe worries more about the savage without. The "idea" of the savage causes him to limit the size of his economy, for his physical safety depends upon his relative invisibility. A larger physical plant would not only be unwieldy (remember his first attempt at boat building), but would call attention to itself. Greater visibility requires more bodies to defend against encroaching "enemies." Yet he cannot risk becoming too insular or he will become "swallowed up" by a self-enclosing, self-reflexive landscape.

Burrowed into his "delightful Cavity or Grotto," Crusoe imagines himself "one of the ancient Giants." In his womb-like cave, Crusoe can boast that "if five hundred Savages were to hunt me, they could never find me out" (p. 179), but nursery fantasies of potency quickly turn into nightmares. Even in his cave, a maternal structure that punishes as it entices, Crusoe frightens himself with visions of a personal nature both savage and frail. The presence of a "monstrous, frightful old He-Goat" fills him with terror.[6] Sighing loudly, "like . . . a Man in some pain," the goat undercuts Crusoe's presumption of strength, for all the while the "ancient Giant" pretends power, the dying goat signifies solitary, self-enclosed frailty. Crusoe tries to rationalize the goat's condition, deciding that "could I have but enjoy'd the Certainty that no Savages would come to the Place to disturb me," he would happily lie down and die in the same fashion. But his fear, even here, of being "disturbed" by the savages complicates his stoicism (pp. 177–80).

When Crusoe investigates his cave, a refuge for ancient giants and dying goats, he uses a candle made from goat tallow. The tallow might very well be a circumstantially realistic detail, but its presence jars a reader preparing to sympathize with the sighs of a fellow creature sounding like a "Man in some pain." Swift will more self-consciously elaborate upon this juxtaposition in *Gulliver's Travels* when he blandly reports Gulliver's expropriation of Yahoo hides. It is more shocking here in its relatively unironic state. While Gulliver hates the Yahoos he skins, Crusoe tends to identify with the animal. Traditionally associated with the unregenerate qualities of fallen man, restless, unruly, and "in some pain," the goats on

---

[6] Homer O. Brown, "The Displaced Self." pp. 572–3, and John Richetti, *Defoe's Narratives*, p. 50, consider the significance of the goat as a version or reflection of Crusoe.

Crusoe's island reflect his vulnerable condition. They are the first "poor Creatures" that he thinks of after he takes courage "to peep abroad" after hiding from the single footprint – he thinks of them "in great Pain" for want of milking – and they are the first "poor Creatures" he sacrifices to feed his colonized savage's "hankering" for human flesh. The immediate erosion of Crusoe's sympathy, once he fears being eaten, calls attention to the luxury of feeling in his precariously balanced physical economy. Fearing that the savages "would have seiz'd on me with the same View, as I did of a Goat, or a Turtle; and have thought it no more Crime to kill and devour me than I did of a Pidgeon of a Curlieu" (p. 197), Crusoe demonstrates the compromises that become necessary to preserve life.

When he separates himself from the goats to save his own skin, he does so to remain intact, to preserve his own most vulnerable body from dismemberment. By insisting upon his relatively high position on the eating chain, he reveals a fear of disconnection all the more threatening in light of the cannibalistic threat, for the cannibal actually scatters the body itself into discrete parts. No wonder Crusoe feared that even dead, he would be "disturbed" by savages, for in his primal savage scene, he sees the shore "spread with Skulls, Hands, Feet, and other Bones of humane Bodies" (p. 165). Early illustrators of cannibalistic scenes exploited just this fear. The earliest known representation of American Indians "depicts one of the characters contentedly gnawing away on a human arm while other parts of the body are roasting over a fire." The seventeenth-century engraving of the natives of Española offers glimpses of an odd foot and hand waving from the mouth of a primitive kettle. Fundamental to the illustrations is the dismemberment made graphic, the limbs drying in sheds, the bones scattered across the page.[7] To separate himself from the vulnerable material condition that connects him to the threat of such disconnection, Crusoe must separate himself from the savage-animal world that can eat him up. If there is to be an eating chain, he must be the one ordering it. For not to order it is to become consumed.

Crusoe faces the same problem that shaped Moll's and Roxana's lives – how to exert control over a system that depends upon – even as it disavows – human consumption. Defoe's characters are not by nature ruthless, but when pressed to eat their neighbor, or even their child, they comply, balancing precariously acts of savagery and restraint in the name of civilization. In his attempts to master his physical circumstances, Crusoe more than compensates for his frailty by "seizing upon" others, notably Friday, a compliant savage ready to be colonized. His first description of Friday reveals the unstable, ambiguous nature of the savage "other" Crusoe is attempting to contain. However cannibalistic by habit,

---

[7] Arens, *The Man-Eating Myth*, pp. 24, 27, 29, 52, provides fascinating illustrations of cannibals, viewed through colonizing eyes, severing and scattering limbs.

Friday demonstrates "all the Sweetness and Softness of a *European* in his Countnenance . . . especially when he smil'd." Showing his savage teeth in a gesture of friendship, Friday proves through his geniality, his willingness to offer signs of "Subjection, Servitude and Submission," that he possesses a mild and affectionate nature. Yet he also eats people when he gets the chance. Just this juxtaposition of sweetness and savagery complicates his character, suggesting that Friday might be another victim of another, perhaps simpler, physical system that eats up its fellow creatures, no more or less guilty than Moll Flanders laying her snares (pp. 205–6).[8]

The fact of the cannibal upsets the notion of order for Crusoe and his world. Montaigne could philosophically rationalize his presence, but even late in the Enlightenment, long after the Chain of Being had lost its organizational power, witnesses to cannibalism had difficulty fitting the man-eater into any proper system of physical economy.[9] Crusoe's attempt to curb his captive's appetite reveals the high cost that civilized restraint demands. When Crusoe confronts gentle Friday's "hankering Stomach" for "some of the Flesh" still scattered around the sacrificial ground, he expresses "Abhorrence at the very Thoughts of it." His abhorrence is so strong, in fact, that Crusoe lets Friday know "by some Means" that he "would kill him if he offer'd it" (p. 208). This is pure Defoe, for just as Moll abhors a sexuality she employs, so Crusoe threatens murder to make his savage civil. To separate his savage from his "nature," Crusoe "falls to work" to cover over Friday's nakedness. Stitching up a soul for his savage out of goat and hare skins, Crusoe works seriously here with materials that Swift parodies in both *Tale of a Tub* and *Gulliver's Travels*. Just as Gulliver skins Yahoos to cover over his own yahoo nature, Crusoe covers over Friday not only with skins taken from another version of himself,[10] but with linen drawers looted from a dead man's chest. His investment links his savage to the civilized world of commercial consumption that the "poor Gunner" defended in life. Friday complies with this sacrifice awkwardly enough, for "the Sleeves of the Wastcoat gall'd his Shoulders, and the insides of his Arms," but in time, he accommodates himself "very well" to civilization and its discontents (p. 208).

Although the denatured Friday no longer looks savage – and probably looks more than a little ridiculous – he still possesses the "Relish" of a

---

[8] Hulme argues that this description is a "classic case of negation," *Colonial Encounters*, p. 205.

[9] Joseph Banks, exploring and botanizing with Captain James Cook, describes the Maori people as creatures who by their abnormality put into question the notion of the chain of being. *The Endeavour Journal of Joseph Banks, 1768–1771*, 2 vols., ed. J. C. Beaglehole, Sydney, 1962, volumes I and II.

[10] Homi Bhabha considers "the technique of camouflage" implicit in colonial discourse in "Of Mimicry and Man: The Ambivalence of Colonial Discourse," *October*, 28 (Spring 1984), pp. 125–33.

cannibal stomach. To alter his savage's hankering, Crusoe displays his talent for fire power to impress the benefits of civilized virtue upon his savage.

Crusoe shoots down a goat to separate Friday from the savage nature that threatens Crusoe's physical economy. But in the action, he makes further connections between man and animal. In the goat stew episode, Defoe links together the "fellow Creatures," the goat that is eaten, the savage that will eat anything, and Crusoe, who must resist being "seized" upon. Perhaps it is simply the way Crusoe casually picks off his random goat, a young kid sitting next to the "She Goat lying down in the Shade," that jars. His action violates both pastoral expectations and sporting ethics. The sitting goat is not even the animal that Crusoe intended to kill, but a random creature made personal in its description.

Friday's response to the kill connects him to the sacrifice. It becomes difficult to separate "poor Creature" Friday from poor victim goat in the following passage:

I presented my Piece, shot and kill'd one of the Kids. The poor Creature who had at a Distance seen me kill the Savage his Enemy, but did not know, or could imagine how it was done, was sensibly surpriz'd. . . He did not see the Kid I shot at, or perceive I had kill'd it, but ripp'd up his Wastcoat to feel if he was not wounded, and as I found, presently thought I was resolv'd to kill him.   (p. 211)

Friday's fears are not misplaced. When Crusoe recalls "the Savage his Enemy," he alludes not only to Friday's enemy, but to Friday himself, that natural savage that so disturbs Crusoe's sense of civilization. Wearing the "poor Gunner's drawers," Friday represents the consumption of not just one goat but an entire shipload of goods that preserves him and Crusoe from his "savagery." Friday even wears a "wastcoat" constructed from the skins of a goat, that version of Crusoe's other self. It is not surprising within such a tangled context that Friday tries to rip away his clothing to separate himself from that which is being destroyed "for his sake."

Crusoe destroys more than a goat for Friday's sake. To convince Friday of his benevolence, Crusoe continues the carnage in killing a parrot. Shooting the goat, no matter how flashy the display of powder and power, can be rationalized as a way to replace human with animal flesh. But killing the parrot is an act of luxury. Even Crusoe seems to recognize the gratuitous nature of his deed, for on Crusoe's island, parrots are made not to be eaten, but to speak. Crusoe's own Poll "would sit upon my Finger, and lay his Bill close to my Face, and cry, *Poor* Robin Crusoe,

Where are you? Where have you been? (p. 143). Out shooting parrots, Crusoe would have to answer, for the edification of my savage.

The murder of the parrot seems almost accidental. His gun loaded, Crusoe sees a great fowl, alerts Friday, and discharges his weapon. Crusoe is guilty and not guilty of the action. After all, he mutters, it could have been a hawk. Crusoe might call upon dull organs to justify the killing of a fellow creature, but Defoe refuses easy absolution. For when Friday runs to fetch the parrot, we learn that the "Parrot not being quite dead, was flutter'd away a good way off from the Place where she fell" (p. 212). Pronouns tell. "She" fell. Verbs tell more. "Flutter" suggests a nervous presence, a tremulous emotion sympathetic in its neurological connections. Crusoe himself experienced "fluttering thoughts" (p. 154) after viewing his primal footprint on his deserted shore. Insistent upon computing the cost of living, Defoe makes his readers know the creatures they consume: the idle kid sitting next to its mother in the shade, the sentient parrot picked out of the tree, beings sacrificed to make safer the idea of civilization.

To protect himself from savagery, Crusoe must repeat acts of mastery, colonizing more and more subjects to feed his growing needs. By the time he leaves his island, it contains a mixture of Spaniards and Mutineers. Their "story," filled with agreements and disagreements, union and separation, until "at last the *Spaniards* were oblig'd to use Violence" to subject and "use" the villains honestly, exaggerates Crusoe's own attempts to manage an island that depends upon interdependency and subjugation. In his discussion of "improvements," he records the "Attempt" his colonials made on the mainland, and how they "brought away eleven Men and five Women Prisoners, by which, at my coming, I found about twenty young Children on the Island." Crusoe does his part to stock the island with "Supplies" including "seven Women, being such as I found proper for Service, or for Wives to such as would take them: As to the *English* Men, I promis'd them to send them some women from *England*, with a good Cargoe of Necessaries" (pp. 305–6).

Slavery – physical and sexual – becomes "Necessary" here, sustaining not just life, but Crusoe's jaunts around the world. While Defoe repeatedly presents the rigors of the slavery system – Crusoe, Colonel Jack, Roxana and Moll all endure some sort of literal or figurative forced labor – he remains oddly outside of his own analysis of the system. Peter Earle ruefully notes that Defoe "went so far as to hope that one day all Englishmen might be masters, wishing for his country's good 'that it might please God that all our people were masters and able to keep servants, tho' they were obliged to buy their servants, as other nations do'."[11] The contradictions of such a wish for an equality based upon a greater inequality is

[11] Peter Earle, *The World of Defoe*, p. 170

never entirely absent from Defoe's attempts to explore "mutual subordination." Wallowing in wealth, Crusoe reports that he is "in a Condition which I scarce knew how to understand, or how to compose my self for the Enjoyment of it" (p. 285). Just that lack of understanding allows him to continue his attempts to control that nature that threatens him.

Once composed, Crusoe sets out to commit his final act of mastery over the savage within and without. He takes part in the most unnecessary shooting of "a very nice Gentleman" (p. 293), a bear. Circumstantially, Crusoe has all the right in the world to kill the bear. He and Friday are in the process of heroically holding off a pack of starving wolves that have attacked their band in the Pyrenees. Making connections between the "Kind of two-legged Wolves" that threaten travellers and the "Hellish Creatures" (p. 291) that physically assault their party, Crusoe interrupts his narrative of the wolves to report "the greatest Diversion imaginable" – the story of Friday and the bear.

Crusoe describes the bear much as H.F. describes the plague victim who kissed his "poor unhappy gentlewoman" into the grave. For although the bear might be dangerous, he appears weak, the victim of his own weight. He is "a heavy, clumsey Creature, and does not gallop as the Wolf does." Men are not even "his proper Prey." If you meet him in the woods, and don't meddle with him, "he won't meddle with you; but then you must take Care to be very Civil to him." This cumbersome gentleman will, however take affront, and "will have Satisfaction in Point of Honour."

Friday takes on this gentlemanly prey with "Joy and Courage":

O! O! O! Says *Friday* three Times, pointing to him; O Master! *You give me te Leave! Me shakee te Hand with him: Me make you good laugh.*

I was surpriz'd to see the Fellow so pleas'd; *You Fool you,* says I, *he will eat you up: Eatee me up! Eatee me up!* Says *Friday,* twice over again; *Me eatee him up: Me make you good laugh: You all stay here, me show you good laugh.*

Friday's joy in mastering Mr. Bear has been interpreted to reflect Crusoe's own confidence in his ability to triumph over circumstances that had once threatened to swallow him up. While this is true, Crusoe's mastery is compromised by a disturbing sadism central to the encounter. For the bear "was walking softly on, and offer'd to meddle with no Body," the hapless victim of Friday's and Crusoe's need to assert domination to be "safe." Friday plays with the bear not to protect himself, but to "show us some Laugh as he call'd it."

Throughout the episode, the painfully human characteristics of the animal confuse the purpose of the bear-baiting. At one point, pursuing what even Crusoe suspects to be "Folly," Friday lures the animal on to the large limb of a tree:

Ha, says he to us, *now you see me teachee the Bear dance*; so he falls a jumping and shaking the Bough, at which the Bear began to totter, but stood still, and begun to look behind him, to see how he should get back; then indeed we did laugh heartily. But *Friday* had not done with him by a great deal; when he sees him stand still, he calls out to him again, as if he had suppos'd the Bear could speak *English; What you no come farther, pray you come farther*; so he left jumping and shaking the Bough; and the Bear, just as if he had understood what he said, did come a little further, then he fell a jumping again, and the Bear stopp'd again.

A bear with a hand to shake, a bear who can learn how to dance on the shaking limb of a tree, a bear that appears to understand English, and not only totters, but consciously "look[s] behind him" for his bearings might make his immediate audience "laugh heartily," but his confusion reflects Defoe's less than hearty appreciation of Friday's play. "We could not imagine what would be the End of it, and where the Jest would be at last," Crusoe recalls uneasily, "But *Friday* put us out of doubt quickly."

Giving his audience "*one more laugh*," Friday draws the bear into his immediate vicinity, creating in the shooting an intimacy between victim and victimizer difficult to "laugh" at. While the bear, thinking his enemy gone, comes back from the bough "mighty leisurely, looking behind him every Step," moving tenuously, "one Foot at a Time, very leisurely," before the animal can set his hind feet on the ground, "*Friday* stept up close to him, clapt the Muzzle of his Piece into his Ear, and shot him dead as a Stone" (pp. 293–6).

"Mighty leisurely," tottering clumsily, betraying at the very worst a gentle curiosity toward's Friday's strategies, the bear, like the parrot, falls victim to Crusoe's need for mastery. That Friday, first civilized victim to Crusoe's rage for order, who learned from his master how to shoot fluttering parrots out of the sky, expresses Crusoe's desire for mastery and demonstrates just how well Crusoe has established his "natural" physical economy. But Crusoe's complacency, his own pleasure in Friday's play, is not entirely Defoe's. For all his love of mastery, Defoe would not stop looking hard at what was being mastered, at the cost of life dearly maintained. Just as Moll and Roxana are compelled to assert their material presence over a system that in the end absorbs their desperate energies, Crusoe compulsively ranges about the world to order an economy bigger than himself, one that incorporates fear into its triumphs and demands that freedom depend upon slavery. It becomes indeed a place to run from.

Nature is easily satisfied: Swift's reluctant cannibalism

Swift did not need to travel half way around the world to find savages, not when they could be found lounging on dung hills of their own making, crowding "the *Streets*, the *Roads*, and *Cabbin-doors*" (*PW*, XII, p. 109) with all too visible evidence of material need. The Yahoo insinuating savagery into gentle Gulliver's consciousness was in fact Swift's home-grown Irish native, that combination of "the savage beast, the degenerate man, and the indocile creature" that the English loved to hate. "A man in station in Ireland," explained Lord Clonmell, colonial administrator, "is really like a traveller in Africa, in a forest amongst Hottentots and wild beasts." The cautious man might defend himself, but only if he be "eternally on the watch and on his guard against his next neighbours, men and beasts, at every step he takes, at every thing he does, at every word he utters."[12]

Swift never let down his guard against his "neighbours, men and beasts," nor against the most vexing enemy of all, the Yahoo within. Not that Swift cares to investigate "within," that place where maggots and guts wait to expose themselves to the unwary dissector. Unlike Defoe, whose relatively elastic narratives allow the space for indeterminate investigation, Swift does not care, or perhaps is unable to care to use his narratives to explore the interdependence between world and self, outside and inside, consumer and consumed. He might send his Gulliver off to "Several Remote Nations of the World," but Swift already knows the truth waiting for his gull at home in the stable.

To be at home in the stable is not properly speaking to be home at all. With money in your pocket, you are home anywhere, Moll infamously boasts. Just this sort of accommodation galls Swift, who tries to undermine in his fictions assumptions of easiness he delights in blowing up. While Defoe is not as complacent as Moll, and through her narrative insists that we pay attention to the cost of her easy settlement, Swift cannot even allow such a fiction to spring up. When he strands Gulliver on foreign shores, his pockets loaded with "Bracelets, Glass Rings, and other Toys, which Sailors usually provide themselves with in those Voyages" (*GT*, p. 223), Swift makes sure that we are to laugh at Gulliver's mistaken notions of what conveniently serves.

Gulliver bearing glass rings parodies the colonizing impulse to exert control through manufactured artifacts which imitate value. For Swift, the real culture has become implicated in its chains of consumption. The whole globe needs to be navigated at least three times round "before one of our better Female *Yahoos* could get her Breafast or a Cup to put it in,"

---

[12] Donald T. Torchiana, "Jonathan Swift: the Irish and the Yahoos: The Case Reconsidered," *From Chaucer to Gibbon: Essays in Memory of Curt A. Zimansky, Philological Quarterly*, 54 (Winter 1975), p. 199.

while Gulliver required "the Workmanship of an Hundred Tradesmen," and Mrs Gulliver five times the number to "be dressed as [they] ought to be" (*GT*, pp. 251–3). Montesquieu was not alone in observing the "arduous" sensuality of civilization, where "for one man to live elegantly, a hundred must labor ceaselessly." Addison might crow that "the Muff and the Fan come together from the different Ends of the Earth," that the "Brocade Petticoat rises out of the Mines of *Peru* and the Diamond Necklace out of the Bowels of *Indostan*,"[13] but Swift saw more clearly that the muffs and fans came from rents "squeezed out of [the] very Blood and Vitals" not only of Indostan, but of Ireland and the Irish natives (*PW*, XII, p. 11). Swift employs the cannibal to call attention to a need that his contemporaries preferred not to own. There is more barbarity in eating a man alive than in eating him dead, Montaigne argued earlier. Swift starts from this premise, demanding that his reader recognize the cost of "civilized" life.

Not all of Swift's gentle readers wanted to know what he had to say. In his attempt to call attention to the cost of things, Swift confronted a blindness carefully cultivated, the product of generations. Lord Orrery, for instance, a man careful not to look too carefully at the bodies in the way, writes Swift in 1735 about a custom in Cork "from Time immemorial" with "its hideous Consequences." What he reports reveals the refined effort it took not to see what blocked the path. On the day of the mayoral election, the "black Guards" – bootblacks dedicated to keeping better feet clean – assemble in High Street, "their Pockets full of Meal and Flower, which they throw into harmless Peoples Eyes as plentifully as Beggars at Paris bestow holy water in Churches." Unexpectedly on foot, Orrery meets a "ragged Groupe of Shoe Boys" who blind him "in a most furious

---

[13] *The Spectator*, No. 69 (1711) ed. Donald Bond, 5 vols., Oxford, 1965, I, p. 295; Earle describes Defoe looking at the world "as something designed by God to provide an intellectual obstacle race for man. The globe on which men lived had been originally an intellectual blank. Man had been left by the Creator to discover its secrets." As John Ray decided, "materials so fit to serve all the necessities and conveniences" of life demonstrate "that they were created intentionally, I do not say only, for these uses." Defoe sees: "How wonderful . . . that Providence had adapted nature to trade by making things float. How much more difficult life would have been if 'a ship that swims in one sea, would immediately sink to the bottom in another'. What sort of a world would it be if 'the horse would not be rid; nor the ox draw, nor the cow be milk'd'?" (p. 48). George Lillo demonstrates the confidence in imperial right in his praise of trade, that which "improve[s] mankind by love and friendship . . . taking from [savages], with their own consent, their useless superfluities, and giving them, in return, what, from their ignorance in manual arts, their situation, or some other accident, they stand in need of." While the "populous East, luxuriant, abounds with glittering gems, bright pearls, aromatick spices, and health-restoring drugs," the west "glows with unnumber'd veins of gold and silver ore" waiting for "the industrious merchant to collect the various blessings of eatch soil and climate, and with the product of the whole, to enrich his native country." *The London Merchant or the History of George Barnwell*, introd. Bonamy Dobrée, New York, 1952, Act III, scene i, p. 42.

Manner with this Emblem of Snow." The outraged Earl confesses his
temptation to "drive the ragged Regiment" into the river, but decides
instead to decline and pass by inoffensively, "shaking my Ears and bowing
at the same time; not perhaps unlike my Dog Hector who, when he is
corrected, growls, fawns and wags his Tail." These "flowery honours"
are paid to all Christian souls; "the higher your Rank, the greater your
Quantity of meal," he explains, almost preening himself on his dusty
significance (*Corr*, IV, pp. 401–2).

Much is going on here that Orrery seems determined to avoid bringing
into consciousness. Even as he attempts to turn the "flowery honours"
into an emblem of snow, its homely materiality cannot be dismissed. For
the blackguards fling *food*, "Oat-meal," into "harmless Peoples Eyes" that
prefer blindness to clear sightedness. Making the connection between
squandered "holy water" and meal, Orrery plays with the sacerdotal quality of the "Tribute," but nonetheless refuses the responsibility thrust upon
him so rudely in the street. For flour not only bakes bread, but powders
my lord Orrery's wig. The blackguards are making visible in this carnival
of misrule obligations not being met, calling attention to their betters'
consumption of themselves. Orrery's metaphoric escape from their
assault is particularly telling. The Earl will become the Earl's dog, classically titled, but "inoffensive." Hiding out on the food chain, Orrery takes
on the characteristics of something even lower than the Irish "animals"
he makes use of.

In confronting his assailants, Orrery employs irony to defuse their
energy. The shoe boys, of course, neither know nor care that their victim
is trying to contain them with classical allusions; they are participating in
a drama of their own. Mock-heroically, Orrery wishes that he could drive
his attackers not just into the river, but into the "Scamander," fitting
waters for a diminished Hector. Just this sort of polished blindness is
what Swift attacks. When he employs the mock-heroic, he does so to be
identified, not to be disguised. Even more significantly, in his various
tracts and satirical works, he "wastes time" clarifying just the sort of social
issues that Orrery hides from. His *Directions to Servants*, for instance, a
nervous, edgy, incomplete work addressing the uses and abuses of the
servant system, cranky as Defoe's *Conjugal Lewdness*, examines perhaps
too closely the inconsistencies and difficulties implicit in a system that
depends upon subordination, depends in fact upon "cleanly girls" being
hungry enough to "dabble" in "other Folks' urine" (*PW*, XIII, p. 61).

Orrery had no use for the *Directions*. "A man of SWIFT's exalted genius
ought constantly to have soared into higher regions. He ought to have
looked upon persons of inferior abilities as children whom nature had
appointed him to instruct, encourage, and improve." Swift should have
"jest[ed] with dignity . . . leaving poor slaves to *beat their porridge* or *drink*

their small beer in such vessels as they shall find proper."[14] The lower classes should "pass on unnoticed," Orrery decided, speaking for his age and his class at a time when great pains were being taken not to notice what was in the street. To open "harmless Peoples Eyes," dull organs steadfastly closed to visions of need, Swift takes to throwing not just flour and meal into his audience's face, but resorts finally to piling up bodies in the public way, making his reader eat the bodies of "children whom nature had appointed him to instruct, encourage, and improve."

Swift insists above all that his readers understand the waste that would send blackguards into the streets, their pockets crammed with flour. There is an irony in the consumption made visible, for although corporeality threatens the economy, it is the empty gut that can never be brought to a "reasonable Compass." The bodies that most disturb Swift are the "half-diminished" beggars frightening not in their bulk – for they are wasted -- but in their number. The author of "A Letter to the People of Ireland" reported that Dublin's public thoroughfares were "crowded with living Spectres, Bodys of our Species with half Life, rambling about for Sustenance. . . Infinite are the Numbers." Driven from "dreadful scene" to "dreadful scene" of destitution, "If they happen to hear of the Death of a Horse," they "run to it as to a Feast." The beggars become reduced to the animals they rush to consume, part of the species of "those animals" that Swift records "come in my way with two legs and human faces, clad, and erect."

Forced to eat each other to sustain their "half-life," the yahoo Irish become incorporated into an eating chain that determines and depends upon their state of near starvation. Writing for the *Intelligencer*, Sheridan relates the most extreme tale of need, citing an account of Tyrone's Rebellion in which a poor widow literally fed her starving children with pieces of herself. Having died of despair, she was eaten by her children. Sheridan cites the Elizabethan account of the historian Fynes Moryson, in which the children are discovered:

all eating and gnawing with their Teeth the Entrails of their dead Mother, upon whose Flesh they had fed 20 Days past, and having eaten all from the Feet upward to the Bare Bones, roasting it continually by a slow Fire, were now come to the eating of her said Entrails, in like sort roasted, yet not divided from the Body, being as yet Raw.[15]

[14] John Boyle, Earl of Orrery, *Remarks on the Life and Writings of Dr. Jonathan Swift*, London, 1752, *Swiftiana*, 9, 1974, pp. 282–4.

[15] Oliver Ferguson, *Jonathan Swift and Ireland*, Urbana, 1962, pp. 170–3; David Nokes discusses Swift's mixed sympathies for the beggars of Ireland in "Swift and the Beggars," *Essays in Criticism*, 26 (1976), pp. 218–35, arguing that "None of his Irish tracts reveal any real sense of identification between Swift and those he claimed to represent," p. 232. The connection may be strained, but it is always painfully and graphically present.

More desperately, Swift wonders how poor bodies retain any matter at all; entrails cost too much to maintain. Observing the "immense Number of human Excrements at the Doors and Steps of waste Houses, and at the Sides of every dead Wall," he observes slyly that they might be spectral, fraudulent, or even imported: "Heaps . . . laid there privately by *British Fundaments*, to make the World believe, that our *Irish* Vulgar do daily eat and drink" (*PW*, XII, p. 220).

To possess waste of their own, the poor would be guilty of a consumption they could not afford. Paradoxically, reduced to the minimum body, they still stand in the way. Swift records their bleak progress as well as his energetic exasperation towards their condition in much of his work, presenting a "melancholly Object" pressing its need upon those who "walk through this great Town" (*PW*, XII, p. 109). The ubiquitous presence of poor bodies dismays and offends, pushing the viewer back into an awareness of bodily need made personal. Swift doesn't much like the sight, but he offers it obsessively and aggressively, forcing his reader to see what stands in the public way.

The poor . . . we want them not

On Brobdingnag Swift magnifies the need twelve times over in one of "the most horrible Spectacles that ever an *European* Eye beheld," the beggar woman's cancerous breast "swelled to a monstrous Size, full of Holes, in two or three of which I could have easily crept and covered my whole Body" (*GT*, p. 112). Inverting the nurturing associations of the breast, Swift's monstrous breast is offered not to be sucked, but to suck up the reader. There is something perversely compelling about Gulliver's fantastic return to the breast, his embryonic body tentatively creeping back into the flesh, but in the end, the cancer itself keeps us outside the rotting flesh drained of maternal fluids. Turning need into spectacle, Swift forces us to stare hard at a sight that he confesses "perfectly turn[s] my Stomach" (*GT*, p. 113).

Staring hard at least exercises our eyeballs (*Tale*, p. 185) and might even sharpen dulled sensibilities. Swift provokes us into recognizing a need too large to absorb that he would just as soon wish away. "But why all this concern for the Poor," he grumbles, "We want them not," for "where the Plough has no Work, one Family can do the Business of Fifty, and you may send away the other Forty-Nine" (*PW*, XII, p. 22). The poor are with us always, but sometimes it would seem that Swift, however lacerated by a compassion finely felt, would rather they go away. Fantasies

Wittkowsky, "Swift's *Modest Proposal*: The Biography of an Early Georgian Pamphlet," pp. 92–3. In his study of crowds and power, Canetti observes that "A mother is one who gives her own body to be eaten." "The Entrails of Power," p. 258.

of annihilation occur with bleak regularity in his work. When he is not wishing the beggars well fed, he is wishing them good riddance.[16] He can dramatize their victimization, wondering how his Irish Israelites can make bricks without straw (*PW*, XII, pp. 11–12,), but then he will stop to turn on his charges, the wretches. "There is hardly one in a hundred who doth not owe his Misfortunes to his own Laziness or Drunkennes, or worse Vices" (*PW*, IX, p. 191). Nineteen out of twenty "did not become so by what Lawyers call the Work of God . . . but meerly from their own Idleness, attended with all Manner of Vices, particularly Drunkeness, Thievery, and Cheating" (*PW*, XIII, p. 135). Just as Orrery's blackguards squander flour and meal to make their unruly demands, Swift's wastrels pour good broth out of their pitchers into the kennel as they whine for alms to spend on spirits and ale (*PW*, XIII, p. 140). The entire "profligate Clan of Thieves, Drunkards, Heathens, and Whoremongers" are "fitter to be rooted out off the Face of the Earth, than suffered to levy a vast annual Tax upon the City" (*PW*, XIII, p. 139).

Swift's rage to root out offenders cannot be denied, yet at the same time, he is driven to enter the condition that so offends him. Taking on the disreputable voice of Ebenezor Elliston, a street robber condemned to be hanged for his sins, Swift presents a world "like Hell." "I know not what it is," Elliston confesses, "that we are never easy till we are half drunk among our Whores and Companions, nor sleep sound, unless we drink longer than we can stand" (*PW*, IX, pp. 40–1). Locked into a system that extorts bribes for concealment, treble ale-house reckonings for protection, "Cloaths for our Whores . . . every Moment threatening to inform against us," the street robber exploits others to be consumed in turn by the economic system that makes use of his transgressions. His reward is oblivion sought in a place of "continued horrible Noise of Cursing, Blasphemy, Lewdness, Scurrility, and brutish Behaviour; such Roaring and Confusion: that *Bedlam*, in comparison, is a sober and orderly Place" (*PW*, IX, p. 41). "The Misfortune is," Elliston understates, "that we can never be easy till we are drunk, and our Drunkenness constantly exposes us to be more easily betrayed and taken." Not that Swift can ever allow things to be "easy," but the ambivalence in the "Confession" complicates his anger towards his improvident poor. Elliston, preparing to "die like a Man, the Death of a Dog," while urging his audience to "root out" him and his kind "like Wolves and other mischievous Vermin," exposes in his impotence a world of need that cannot be entirely reduced to irony. Swift's entry into that world, however qualified, allows, for a moment, exasperated sympathy, not the dramatic involvement Defoe would pro-

---

[16] As Ferguson argues, "The Answer to the Craftsman" proposes "the annihilation of Ireland herself," *Jonathan Swift and Ireland*, p. 180.

vide in his tales of Moll and Colonel Jack, those "Vermin" on the body politic, but not satiric dismissal.

In "Bulk," the beggars and thieves, a most "undeserving vicious Race," should be rooted out, but individually, however briefly, one Elliston, dying like a man the death of a dog, cannot be so easily reduced. Swift approaches the problem that the beggars present with a nervous energy that propels him through the streets that his contemporaries ride over. In his "Proposal to Give Badges to the Beggars," as one who walks through streets filled with need both offensive and material, he addresses the problem that the gentry, easy riders accustomed to employing cushioned strategies, attempt to evade and deny. His anger is deeply felt and broadly distributed in this proposal, complicated by a sense of "persecution" from rich and poor alike. Suffering a compassion rubbed raw, he battles both the "Persons in Coaches and Chairs" as well as their wretched, victims "guilty" of need, and attempts through his prose to create an awareness somewhere in between, to create in his "brother walkers" the ability to see what blocks their way (*PW*, XIII, p. 135).

The mediation is necessary, for to recognize the need, you need to be in the street to jostle beggarly shoulders. Swift both identifies with and distances himself from the problem, neither a Defoe entering into the circumstantial scenes that shape his narratives nor an Orrery blinded by showers of meal. He is a Yahoo, whether he likes it or not, dropped "by a perfect Accident" on an Irish shore, " A *Teague*, or an *Irishman*, or what People Please" (*PW*, XIII, pp. 111–12). The negligent irony of the last phrase undercuts the urgency of his identification, but it also emphasizes the traps he is building, for as he insists, in Ireland nobody escapes playing the slave, the knave, the fool, unless they happen to be "Bishops and People in Employments." Carole Fabricant tends to locate Swift squarely in the Dublin streets where he became "King of the Mob"[17] that he would also like to keep at arm's length. Her shrewd awareness of Swift's connection to the lower classes provides an important corrective to traditional interpretations of Swift's "Tory" position. It is also important to remember, however, that Swift is never squarely anywhere. Although he insists upon smelling his poor, he also insists upon announcing that their fragrant need perfectly turns his stomach.

Jousting with the powerful, jostling improvident shoulders, Swift exposes himself to the demands others try not to see. As early as "A Description of a City Shower," his "Poet" could not sit boxed up impotently in a chair safe from the rain, but stood "needy," stained by the urban dirt swirling in the air (*Poems*, I, p. 138). Driven to advertise a need that seemed impossible to relieve, Swift even seems to have internalized

[17] Fabricant, *Swift's Landscape*, p. 244. Her entire chapter, "The Drapier-Dean in his Landscape," pp. 210–68, emphasizes Swift's strong sense of identification with the poor.

his dread of public and private poverty, confessing in a letter to Pope that "I know not any man who is in a greater likelyhood than my self to die poor and friendless" (*Corr*, IV, p. 104). Such malaise is no more artificial than his notorious stinginess, expressions both, I suspect, of a fear of consuming what others lack. The more "doses for the dead" Swift wrote, the more threatened he became by destitution made personal that could only be attacked through words.

The problem becomes rhetorical: how to present distress impossible to be dismissed, how to topple the gentry out of their soft-cushioned chairs into the street. Just as Laputans need flappers to be forced to attend to concrete reality, the senseless reader needs to be stung into a moral awareness. The resistance the reader could bring to the problem was not merely traditional at the time Swift started writing his tracts. It was hardening. In his own writings, Swift demands a "mutual subjection" to maintain the body politic, "that there may be no Schism in the Body," yet even as he ordains a dependency upon the needs of the poor, he resents it. While he can rationalize "Things in a State of Imperfection" ingeniously enough, arguing on one occasion that God put them there, "to stir up human Industry" (*PW*, IV, p. 245), he also views the lower classes as a threat to the commonwealth. "If we consider the many Misfortunes that befal private Families," he warns, "it will be found that Servants are the Causes and Instruments of them all," those wretched embezzlers of goods who burn to set fire to the house itself through "Sloth . . . Drunkenness, or . . . Villainy" (*PW*, IX, p. 204). The public is too often "at the mercy of the meanest instrument" (*PW*, IX, p. 237). Chafing at the control exerted by those below, Swift hates depending upon such "instruments," revealing in his farcical struggles with the recalcitrant servant Patrick the extent of his notorious irritation.[18]

Harmless eyes

Swift's battles with his objects of compassion and consumption place him within the context of a more general social conflict. The poor and serving classes were being resented for their awkward intrusion into "civilized"

[18] We can find evidence of Swiftian exasperation almost too easily. Sheridan discusses his anger towards servants, *Life of Swift*, p. 387. Swift's own record of his masterly skirmishes with Patrick is hilarious and disturbing: "Oh, ho. [Patrick] was damnably mauled one day when he was drunk; he was at cuffs with a brother footman, who dragged him along the floor upon his face, which lookt for a week after as if he had the leprosy; and I was glad enough to see it." *JS*, I, p. 302. Accidentally locked out of his chamber by Patrick, he cools his heels in the cloisters till after ten: "then came in Patrick. I went up, shut the chamber-door, and gave him two or three swinging cuffs on the ear, and I have strained the thumb of my left hand with pulling him, which I did not feel until he was gone. He was plaguily afraid and humbled." *JS*, II, pp. 375–6.

life. The serving class, long considered part of the "little family" of the greater household, each servant being an integral member subject to reciprocal accommodation, was being put in a new "place" back stairs – out of sight. In the process, the servant class became by nature of its location, more utilitarian, more instrumental. A serving maid was likely to find herself sharing quarters with the chamber pot she carried in and out of her lady's chamber.[19] Such denial of consciousness in an insistence upon function could not have been accidental, could even have been considered "necessary." As Mandeville perversely observes, "No Body will do the Dirty Slavish Work, that can help it."[20] Or as Swift asks more nastily, indicting in his question the system as well as the parts of the system, "What cleanly Girl would be dabbling in other Folks' Urine" in the first place? (*PW*, XIII, p. 61).

While servants were being turned into utensils, the poor were being categorized and codified as deserving or useless. In his proposal to badge his "original poor," a necessary procedure to keep his needy separate from the infamous "sturdy" beggars on the stroll, Swift resembles the sort of model projector that he could satirize so wickedly. But all the while, his own compassion strains against his efficiency, for when he is not classifying his objects of compassion as beasts clad and erect, dubiously possessing "the intelligence of a dog or horse" (*PW*, XII, p. 88), he is thrusting their pain upon us.

He locates much of the pain in the body itself, suggesting in his prose a terrible mutilation that undercuts his anger turned against guilty, beggarly need. "If he be not quite maimed," he proposes in his scheme to badge the poor, the beggar "and his Trull, and Litter of Brats (if he hath any) may get half their Support by doing some Kind of Work in their Power." What is it to be "not quite maimed?" Does one lack half an eye, part of a limb? Derogatory slurs like "Trull" and "Brat" become complicated, subverted by their context. Why wouldn't he have "any," one wonders? Has the beggar "not quite maimed" been rendered sterile? By the time Swift laconically alludes to the possibility of beggars "doing some Kind of Work in their Power," he has demonstrated too well the absolute impotence of his subject (*PW*, XIII, p. 133). But pity turns to gall, to hard anger towards the powerlessness itself. Within such a tangled context, Swift's most radical suggestion in his proposal to badge his beggars, presents real problems in interpretation. For Swift decides that to be

[19] See Trumbach, "Patriarchy and Domesticity," *Rise of the Egalitarian Family*, pp. 119–50, on servants being put in their place. Flandrin discusses the ways in which the servants were gradually dismissed to the back stairs, *Families in Former Times*, pp. 92–3, and also considers their employers' distrust of their inevitable promiscuity, pp. 142–3. Mark Girouard traces the growing invisibility of the servant in *Life in the English Country House*, Harmondsworth, 1980, p. 138.

[20] Mandeville, "An Essay on Charity and Charity Schools," *The Fable of the Bees*, p. 307.

"useful," the badged, parish poor should be made to drive foreign beggars away from the church door.

The solution is a crazy one, almost as unbalanced as the problem itself of infinite need made visible. If the parish beggars were forbidden to suffer sturdy "Foreign Beggars" to invade their Parish, "they would prevent interlopers more effectually than twenty Beadles." Swift's modest solution calls up a vision of properly badged beggars armed with their crutches and blankets, badged beggarly brats at badged beggarly breasts, big bellied trulls sallying forth to earn their alms by beating off their rivals. In his violent attempts to solve the problem, Swift lurches between positions benevolent and malevolent, but whatever his stance, he is thrashing about in the thick of things even as he tries to detach himself from a need that he, fellow Teague in spite of himself, too clearly recognizes is coming from his own vitals. "If your little Finger be sore, and you think a Poultice made of our *Vitals* will give it any Ease, speak the word, and it shall be done," he offers, making deadly his desire to serve the body politic (*PW*, II, p. 114)

In its dire efficiency, Swift's desperate solution addresses the greatest difficulty the poor present. In their deep, integral, corporate need, they become too easily absorbed into larger structures, made invisible by hunger that becomes predictably boring. Orrerys are always ready to avert "harmless Eyes" from public assaults on their complacency. Mandeville takes on the problem of public catastrophe become commonplace in his "Essay on Charity and Charity Schools." While he grants that bared sores exposed to the cold air might shock the viewer the first time, he warns that even the most sensational beggars never get sufficient alms, for the "more we are conversant with Objects that excite [Pity], the less we are disturb'd." The only resort for the "industrious beggar," – if he can walk – is to follow behind his patrons "close and with uninterrupted Noise teaze and importune them to try if he can make them buy their Peace. Thus thousands give Money to Beggars from the same motive as they pay their Corn-cutter, to walk Easy." Mandeville's poor, aching corns on the body politic, are reduced to superfluous flesh that can be lopped off without too much pain. Swift refuses to allow such painless detachment, but incorporates the pain into his tracts.

To render from a class both vexing and threatening a claim both intimate and compelling, Swift must be able to overcome not only Orrery's blindness, but also Orrery's impulse to hurl his beggarly assailants into the river. Without turning heightened sensibility into anger against the object of pity, Swift must still keep his reader's sympathy alive. Pity, Mandeville argues, can only be raised when the sufferings of others become vital enough to make us uneasy. If any of us were locked in a room adjacent to a yard containing a two year old at play, and were we to see

the child threatened by presence of a "nasty over-grown Sow," we would
be made "uneasy" by the child's predicament, and with menacing noises
would try to drive the sow away. But were we to witness more extreme
threats, the sow opening her "destructive Jaws, and the poor Lamb beat
down with greedy Haste," were we to witness "tender Limbs" torn
asunder, "the filthy Snout digging in the yet living Entrails, suck up the
smoking Blood," were we to hear the crackling of bones, we would be
moved to a state of pure pity to ache at the sight "as no Language has an
Epithet to fit it."[21] In his *Modest Proposal* Swift goes one better by turning
his reader *into* the "nasty overgrown sow" that is digging into yet living
entrails that turn out to be too familiar for comfort. He makes us cannibal-
ize ourselves.

The forging of such an indelicate sense of identity between consumer
and consumed requires a strategy subtly aggressive. Montaigne
approaches the self-identification implicit in cannibalism when he
recounts the taunts of a prisoner being fattened up by his captors. He
sings defiantly that when his enemies eat his flesh, they will also be eating
the flesh of their fathers and grandfathers, who "have served his body
for food and nourishment." The muscles, flesh and veins "are your owne
. . . know you not that the substance of your forefathers limbes is yet tied
unto ours? Taste them well, for in them you finde the relish of your owne
flesh." After connecting most intimately victim to victimizer, Montaigne
reports, almost off handedly, the cannibals' questions about the more
refined examples of civilized cannibalism. The visiting savages wonder at
the large numbers of the poor, "hunger-starved, and bare with need,"
begging at the doors of the city of Rouen while other men were "full
gorged with all sortes of commodities." While they don't mind eating up
an enemy, the cannibals cannot understand a society in which some men
stuff themselves while other men starve. But then, Montaigne adds flatly,
the savages "have a manner of phrase wherby they call men but a moytie
one of another."[22] In his own attempt to force a consciousness of interdependence, of human connection, upon his reader, Swift will be less
urbane.

To force sluggish consciousness into being at the expense of a cultural
easiness, to make his reader recognize that one half of the world was
eating up its other half, Swift employed a form of cannibalism complicated by his own aggressive needs. In *Modest Proposal*, his satiric structure
seems generated from an exasperation so lethal that the literary product
violates the most generous generic norm. When Swift dehumanizes the
children of the poor, turning them into animals dropped from improvi-

[21] *Ibid.*, pp. 268, 265
[22] Montaigne, I, p. 231.

dent dams, he translates them out of their natural wretchedness while hating them for their condition. His plan should increase mothers' tenderness and care towards their children. It should also discourage their men from "offer[ing]" to "beat or kick" their wives "for fear of a Miscarriage" (*PW* XII, p. 115), for now the burthen in the belly has become a commodity not to be wasted. In such a context, the insensible mother and brutish father, regardless of their own victimized state, almost deserve to be eaten for their moral indifference. Even more deserving of butchering are the plump young girls who cannot stir without the aid of their chairs. Swift gloats over their natural end as he uses cannibalism punitively to check the "natural" yahoo propensity to satisfy indolently and violently a debauched appetite. That for Swift is the problem. We are cannibals because we are Yahoos driven by desires, craving what we think we need.

Luxury lurks beneath the baldest need. Gulliver, for instance, "needs" to skin Yahoos to shoe himself. How else will he separate himself from the fallen nature he is working to disguise? Insisting that his natural needs are quite simple, while maunching on oats and whey, Gulliver also melts Yahoos into tallow. The modest proposer recognizes needs no less simple. "Having of late destroyed their Deer," the Gentlemen of this Kingdom might find the bodies of young lads and maidens to their liking (*PW*, XII, p. 113). "*Swines Flesh*" also appears to be rapidly disappearing from the land since "the great Destruction of Pigs" (*PW*, XII, p. 116). The deer are gone, the pigs are going, but still we crave something more to eat. As Swift suggests in his riddle on the meaning of time, "Never finding full repast / till I eat the world at last," locked in time, man restlessly hunts for new ways to feed an old hunger.

To tempt discerning palates, Swift offers Irish babies dressed like suckling pigs "hot from the Knife" (*PW*, XII, p. 113). The phrase cuts both ways, awakening sympathy for the suckling pig as well as for the fattened child, calling up an identification between baby and pig that Lewis Carroll would later exploit with grave delight. For it is a fact that suckling pigs do look like suckling children, especially in Ireland where the pig was known as the gentleman who paid the rent, and is even associated today in certain circles with Hibernian parlors. Swift might be making his own chilling connections between pig and peasant in his account books when he records, in his charitable accounts, giving a shilling to or for a "Pig."[23]

[23] L. M. Cullen notes that as late as 1729, the Irish pig was envisaged as an animal "fed simply on trash" and was regarded all through the century as home produce outside the market context. "Population Growth and Diet, 1600–1850," *Irish Population, Economy, and Society: Essays in Honour of the late K. H. Connell*, ed. J. M. Goldstrom and L. A. Clarkson, Oxford, 1981, pp. 104–5. There are only three references to pork in the account books, all in 1734, under "Small Gifts." One, "given simply as 'Pig' . . . may not even be meat but one of Swift's impatient perjoratives describing the object of a small beneficence," Thompson, *The Account Books of Swift*, p. lxxxiv.

Swift knew what it was to make a pig out of himself. When he was not advising his readers to "bring your Guts to a reasonable Compass," he was remembering the time that he, like the Yahoos who stuff themselves until they burst, gorged himself giddy on one hundred golden pippins. Indeed, one hundred golden pippins seems excessive, for it takes only one to turn need into luxury. Reconstructing prelapsarian innocence, Mandeville looks back with nostalgia to the men of the "first Ages" who were able to feed themselves on the fruits of the earth, reposing "naked like other Animals on the Lap of the common Parent." It is not "natural," Mandeville argues, for a man to kill "perfect Animals as Sheep and Oxen, in whom the Heart, the Brain and Nerves differ so little from ours," without giving way to "Concern." Not one man in ten could even admit the desire to become a butcher, he muses, questioning quite seriously whether "ever any body so much as kill'd a Chicken without Reluctancy the first time."[24]

The "first time" loads Mandeville's discourse with irony that allows a scandalized sensibility the time to become easily hardened. Reluctancy, like virginity, can only be lost once. Even as he probes the motives of the market economy that contains him, Mandeville rationalizes it, stressing that we all "will feed heartily and without remorse on Beef, Mutton and Fowls, when they are bought in the Market," although we will probably be more squeamish about those animals we "took care of." To know what one eats requires a rare consciousness. Perhaps that is why Crusoe shot his sitting goat so unexpectedly, sparing one of his "own" herd for a more interchangeable link on the food chain. Not only do we not want to see whom we are eating, but we don't want to see it butchered. Sir Thomas More, for one, insisted in his *Utopia* that the butchers and their slaughter-house "shambles" be banished outside the city limits, where running water could carry away the blood. Utopian citizens were not allowed to take part in the butchering since "slaughtering our fellow-creatures gradually destroys the sense of compassion, which is the finest sentiment of which our human nature is capable." Swift, less nice, brings the "sham-

---

[24] Mandeville, *The Fable of the Bees*, p. 188. Plutarch emphasises the same reluctancy in "On the Eating of Flesh," *Moralia*, 12, trans. Harold Cherniss and William C. Helmbold, Cambridge MA and London, 1984, p. 993, p. 995. Keith Thomas develops at length the "embarrassment about meat-eating" that enters seventeenth- and eighteenth-century discourse. Arguing that "the concealment of slaughter-houses from the public eye had become a necessary device to avoid too blatant a clash between material facts and private sensibilities," he finds the tentative vegetarianism a sign of ideological strain. "By an inexorable logic, there had gradually emerged attitudes to the natural world which were essentially incompatible with the direction in which English society was moving . . . the confident anthropocentrism of Tudor England had given way to an altogether more confused state of mind." *Man and the Natural World: A History of the Modern Sensibility*, New York, 1983, pp. 287–303.

bles" back into the city limits, into the "most convenient parts of it" where "Butchers . . . will not be wanting" to do their part[25] (*PW*, XII, p. 113).

When Swift brings the shambles into the city, he makes palpable bodily needs he – and we – would rather deny. Uneasy with desires difficult to order, Swift suffers from a fear of being what he calls "crammed" (*Corr*, IV, p. 194). His dilemma is as moral as it is neurotic, for to stuff yourself with good things to eat while the other half of the world starves is to risk ending up eating unawares pieces of your grandfather's flesh. "Cramming" leads to disease both physical and moral. Gulliver, as a physician and surgeon, offers a drastic cure concocted from assorted herbs, excrement, gums and oils, "dead Mens Flesh and Bones, Birds, Beasts and Fishes" to cure the effects of "Repletion." The "abominable, nauseous and detestable" mixture is immediately rejected upon ingestion by the most hardened of stomachs. "This they call a Vomit" (*GT*, pp. 253–4), Gulliver explains mildly, prescribing dead men's flesh in a parodic description of the practices of his own country's physicians. To turn his own reader's repleted stomach, since previous attempts at instruction have ended up in "idle, visionary and undigested" projects (*PW*, XIII, p. 174), Swift resorts in his *Modest Proposal* to creating something "*solid* and *real*," a composition of organic metaphors rendered from dead babies' flesh and bones, pickled, stewed or fricaseed (*PW*, XII, p. 117).

In his transformational act, while he reifies the needs of the poor, he turns objects of contempt – the unwashed poor – into objects of skewed grace. The act of cannibalism becomes an act of communion commercially mass produced. When Crusoe sacrifices a goat to keep Friday from eating his kind, he fulfills a priestly function that the Defoe given to playing with providential patterns would recognize. Swift, "not the gravest of Divines," parodically distributes flesh and blood to his readers, aggressively proposing that we sacrifice babies metaphorically so that we will stop eating each other. As he confesses to Stella, he can be called a "Beast forever after the order of Melchisedec. Did you ever read the Scripture? It is only changing the word *Priest* to *Beast*" (*JS*, p. 154).

When Swift metaphorically distributes the flesh and blood of "his" poor, he exploits their only virtue, their need. Just as the more "savage" cannibals ingest the heroic virtues of their victims, Swift's cannibal readers are made to consume the hunger of their victims, the only way they can come to know the condition they try to deny. One of the advantages of his scheme, the proposer boasts, is that "the poorer Tenants will have something valuable of their own" (*PW*, XII, p. 114). It was commonly believed that the beggar "eats your Meal, and drinks your Milk, and

[25] Sir Thomas More, *Utopia*, trans. and ed. Robert M. Adams, New York, 1975, p. 46. Mandeville also argued that butchers should not be allowed to sit on juries, *Fable of the Bees*, p. 193.

pays you nothing for it. Instead he fills you with more children."[26] Swift
arranges for the poor to pay for their meal with their bodies, and with
their ability to suffer. In their accommodation they resemble Christ,
another historical victim who gave up his flesh to redeem men from a
nature and need he refused to recognize. In sacred systems, somebody's
living depends upon somebody's dying, a truth Swift underwrites with
grim humor.

The sacrificed bodies are also colonized bodies, subject to exportation
the better to serve the crown. Not only can their carcasses be pickled and
barrelled to be sent overseas, but, as Swift argues bitterly in his "Answer
to the *Craftsman*, " their live bodies can support his Majesty's colonies in
the Americas. To sustain a colonial system that depends upon its "Acts of
Inhumanity and Lust, the Earth reeking with the Blood of its Inhabitants"
(*GT*, p. 294), Irish beggarly bodies can be exported to serve as a "Screen"
between English subjects and the "savage" Indians being domesticated
(*PW*, XII, p. 176). This sacrifice recalls Christ's own submission to his
father's will. By absorbing the world's arrows and spears, Irish bodies
would redeem their own colonizers from destruction, while back in Ireland, a minimum colony of natives could tend their diminished paradise.
Over seventeen million acres of grazing land would become a veritable
Eden where the few Irish bodies remaining could sit beneath black berry
bushes and preside over potato beds as comfortably as Mandeville's first
parents napped on the lap of nature. "This happy island will become a
new *Arcadia*," Swift predicts, pointing wryly to the expensive nature of
such pastoral schemes. The bodies of the Irish poor can only be incorporated as commodities into a system that depends upon their consumption.
Nature is very easily satisfied. All we need to do, when we're not skinning
Yahoos, is cut out our vitals to make poultices for our wounds.

Never sparing of his own vitals, his own flesh "eaten up" by the villainy
and corruption of men in power,[27] his sensibility "torn to pieces by pamphleteers and libellers" (*Corr*, II, p. 279), Swift turns his own words into
flesh and blood in a parodic communion between reader and writer. Pope
recognizes the aggressive act of communion implicit in his writing when
he writes Swift that even after death, he would not be "quite in peace,"
but would no doubt "rather be employ'd as an Avenging Angel of wrath
to break your Vial of Indignation over the heads of the wretched pityful
creatures of this World; nay would make them *Eat your Book*, which you
have made as bitter a pill for them as possible" (*Corr*, III, pp. 107–8).
Forcing words down his reader's throat, Swift makes us eat not just his
book, but the need he calls up. His reification is typical, the strategy of a
writer compelled to make literal reductions.

[26] Wittkowsky, "Swift's *Modest Proposal*," p. 104.
[27] Delany, *Observations*, p. 148.

I will discuss Swift's habit of reification at greater length in the following chapter. But we can see the reductive process at work comically in a parody of social communion acted out between Pope and Swift. Pope and Gay visited Swift for an evening of talk after they had supped. (Swift was a notoriously stingy host.) But, protested Swift, if you had not supped, I would have been required to get in something for you. A couple of lobsters would have run two shillings, tarts another shilling, a bottle of wine two shillings more. "Two and two, is four; and one is five: just two and six-pence a piece. There, Pope, there's half-a-crown for you; and there's another for you, sir: for I won't save any thing by you I am determined."[28] Turning bodily and social need into shillings and pence, turning the supper he doesn't give into half crowns he bestows, Swift insists upon the solid hunger of luxury even as he insinuates a skepticism toward the need that more conventional exchanges prompt. In this transformation, Swift employs an irony that protects him from the physical nature that so threatens to compromise the ideal of communion. And in the process, the Priest/Beast enforces a mock communion between himself and his satiric victim.

In his insistence on the cost of things, pickled babies and uneaten lobsters, Swift turns the chain of being into an eating chain. His poem "The Day of Judgement" presents an apocalyptic vision that links him even more to Pope's "Avenging Angel." The work is particularly disturbing in its neutral portrayal of an economy that consumes itself. In "an horrid Vision," the poet sees the graves give up their dead before a "nodding" Jove who sits to pass judgment on the "Offending Race of Human Kind." The God who is eaten sacramentally in the act of communion becomes in this poem the God who eats his offending, blockhead children. The world's mad business over, this God damns his blockheads and fools to send them off "bitten," performing a final act of consumption that cuts off possibilities of transcendence. "I damn such fools! – Go, go you're bit," Jove, "armed with terrors," roars, dismantling a system of heavenly compensation. For in the end, this Jove consumes them all, victims and victimizers alike (*Poems*, II, pp. 578–9).

In the act of communion, the communicant literally eats the conditions of the contract, reconstructing in the real the sacrifice made in the ideal. As priest of St. Patrick's, Swift, while playing with this eucharistic form, demands that his parishioners, his readers, recognize through the ritualistic reconstruction exactly what makes up their physical economy. If the problem of the body cannot be resolved, if the useless mouths Defoe rids through desperate plague measures, cannot be fed in reality, Swift insists that the body remain in language. Transcending downward, he

[28] Joseph Spence, *Anecdotes, Observations and Characters of Books and Men*, ed. Bonamy Dobrée, Carbondale IL, 1964, pp. 43–4.

reduces soul to body to make it known as material that must be accounted for. In the process he brings the "shambles," the slaughter-house, into the sacred place, mixing profane blood and guts with the holy wafer and wine to alter the consciousness of a people who would just as soon not know the stuff life and death is made of. While Mandeville thinks that butchers should not be allowed to sit on juries, Swift insists that the jurors are butchers, that the citizens maunching their swine's flesh and sipping their coffee are also eating their children.

It was difficult not to make the connections between consumer and consumed in the eighteenth century. It took great effort not to see the fifty artisans laboriously constructing ball dresses that would press against the cushioned interiors of chairs bearing burdens of silk and lace. McManners calls particular attention to the visceral quality of the street that the chairs skimmed over:

> Reminders of the crudeness of death were evident in the crudeness of living – blood on the pavements from the butcher's shops, slivers of corpses thrown out into the street from the lecture rooms of the anatomists, dead animals in the gutters.[29]

McManners could be describing a typical corner of the urban landscape Swift and Defoe make their own. The blood, the corpses, the dead animals sending up their "nauseous" stinks control the fictional visions of both writers. Dead cats tend to give off a "double Stink,"[30] dead parrots flutter in the sacrificial consciousness, while babies are butchered to fill the needs of a society dedicated to consumption. In their careful attention to embodied need, both Swift and Defoe refuse to spare their readers such a "speaking sight." The spectacle of need, the cost of life itself, informs their work.

---

[29] McManners, *Death and the Enlightenment*, p. 59.
[30] "A Description of a City Shower," *Poems*, I, p. 137, line 6.

8

Vital parts: Swift's necessary metaphors

> For when we opened him we found,
> That all his vital parts were sound.
> "Verses on the Death of Dr Swift" (*Poems*, II, p. 559,
> lines 175–6)

His delight was in simplicity. That he has in his works no metaphor, as has been said, is not true; but his few metaphors seem to be received rather by necessity than choice. Samuel Johnson on Swift's "Life"[1]

The Earl of Orrery had little use for *Gulliver's Travels*, that "irregular essay" full of trifles and optical deceptions. He particularly disapproved of what Swift does with proportion in the *Travels*:

> Lemuel Gulliver has observed great exactness in the just proportion, and appearances of the several objects thus lessened and magnified: but he dwells too much upon these optical deceptions. The mind is tired with a repetition of them, especially as he points out no beauty, nor use in such amazing discoveries, which might have been so continued as to have afforded improvement, at the same time that they gave astonishment.
> (*Remarks on the Life and Writings of Dr. Jonathan Swift*, pp. 135–6)

Swift, Orrery complains, accentuates the deformities rather than the beauties of nature, and debases in the process a human nature that an enlightened dean of the Church of Ireland should be exalting. He is right to be uneasy, for Swift indeed employs his optical "deception" not to regularize and harmonize nature, but to deform it, and he does so not out of perversity but out of necessity. Well might Orrery complain that there is not much beauty in the work. For when you stare as hard as Swift, ghastliness becomes predictably regularized.

In all of his work Swift addresses the problem of making intelligible an opaque world of matter. Not only is form difficult, perhaps impossible to perceive, but the language he uses to describe that form proves predictably unstable and threatens to collapse possibilities of meaning altogether.

[1] Samuel Johnson, *Lives of the English Poets*, III, p. 51.

To make meaning, Swift creates a world of descending metaphors, deflating in the process possibilities of transcending through language the matter in the way. Comparison, therefore, tends to reduce rather than expand opportunities for growth; enlargement just makes bigger that which blocks us in the first place. Thus, when Gulliver tries to describe the (first) "monstrous Breast" that so nauseates him on Brobdingnag, he "cannot tell what to compare it with, so as to give the curious Reader an Idea of its Bulk, Shape and Colour" (*GT*, p. 91). Comparing spots, pimples and freckles to Lilliputian smoothness, and finally to his own skin observed by the Lilliputians, so full of bristles and holes, Gulliver closes with an unsettling generalization about proportion, recalling that Lilliputian courtiers, those doll-sized models of physical perfection, were able to identify their own deformities, the wide mouths and large noses impossible for far-sighted Gulliver to detect. Therefore, Gulliver begs, the reader should not imagine that his Brobdingnags, "those vast Creatures," were actually deformed, no more so than the Lilliputians, no less than Gulliver himself. "For I must do them Justice to say they are a comely Race of People" (*GT*, p. 92). As comely as us all made monstrous under microscopic scrutiny. We all become in this exercise "vast Creatures," deformed victims of Swiftian tricks in perspective.

Even after he has rationalized Brobdingnagian regularity, Gulliver returns to contemplate their (natural) deformity, the coarse uneven skins of the Maids of Honor, their moles "as broad as a Trencher, and Hairs hanging from it thicker than Pack-threads" (*GT*, p. 119). Worse still, he adjusts his lenses to make even more ghastly *real* deformation. The unsightly beggar "Fellows" that crowd against regal coaches produce "the most horrible Spectacles that ever an *European* Eye beheld," while the familiar cancerous breast literally engulfing Gulliver makes it difficult for the reader to regard a "normal" breast with equanimity. By insisting upon a deformation undetected by Gulliver on Lilliput to be impossible for Gulliver on Brobdingnag to avoid falling into, Swift forces the reader again and again into the body.

When Swift concentrates on the frailties of the body, when he exposes the pains his Celias take to patch themselves together, and uncovers the material beneath the flayed woman that flatly asserts itself, he presents the maimed body as every body. This body becomes an object of satire, but at the same time, in its universally imperfect nature, it resists satire. Or rather Swift, hating and caring, and hating to care about what he must see, cannot sustain a classically satiric detachment of a mind less complicated. He doesn't possess the plastic urbanity of Charles Boyle, for one, later the fourth Earl of Orrery, who in his *Examination of Bentley's Dissertations on the Epistles of Phalaris* quite revels in the possibilities physical deformities offer the satirist. For "nothing is so Divertive, or raises Laughter so much as Deformity, especially when Wit goes along with it." This detachment eludes Swift, although there are times when he seems to enjoy his play with deformed matter well enough. In his *Tale*, as pert as any modern in his assumption of the satirically fashioned mantle, he tries in his "Dedication" to Lord Somers for just such a diverting tone, bantering that he has "expected indeed to have heard of your Lordship's Bravery" in battle, "or of your wonderful Talent at Dress and Dancing." Somers was a cripple, far from likely to cut a good figure "mounting a Breach or scaling a Wall." Swift satirizes here the outrageous puffery bloating most dedications, and one hopes that Lord Somers, wealthy, powerful, good humored, in spite of his "body such as is generally united with a peevish and irritable mind" could take the joke.[2] At the least, he possessed the resources. The deformity of the wretched becomes more awkward.

The unsightly beggar fellow who crowds Gulliver's coach, the one with the wen in his neck, who turns "perfectly" his observer's stomach, neither diverts the viewer nor offers the slightest opportunity for urbane laughter. His presence forcibly intrudes upon our carefully cultivated blindness. We can, if we must, take the beggar as representation of fallen man, our "fellow," an urban fellow twice driven out of paradise, symbol of London itself, that greater wen where misshapen men huddle together. But the matter of the man remains, a body that won't go away. "VISION," Swift reveals in one of his "Thoughts on Various Subjects," is "the Art of seeing Things invisible" (*PW*, IV, p. 252). The utter palpability of the beggar with the wen in his neck makes us fear even more those deformities we don't see, the vision of the "invisible," where even greater defects wait to reveal themselves.

Angels, not so violently intrusive, are invisible, perhaps part of that "vision" of the invisible that Swift looks to. It would be nice to think that when Swift shoves us into matter, he, as befits his clerical position, can see beyond the matter signs of transcendence. But we only have what he allows, visions of those "altered" for the worse, pain delineated beneath flayed skin, guts leaking onto the Beau's new suit of clothes, prodigious quantities of blood that course through veins and arteries ready to "spout up" once a malefactor's head is severed cleanly from his body. The invisible tends to become lost in matter made gross in its visibility, matter without a soul, while "Defects" made palpable "encrease upon us in Number and Bulk" to block transcendence (*Tale*, pp. 173–4).

The senses cannot be denied even when they promise to mislead. To avoid the truth of the body is to end up as crazy as Jack of the *Tale*, blindly bouncing against posts to fall into the kennel. Jack argues that the eyes of understanding see best when shut, for when opened, the eyes, "*blind*

2 *Tale*, pp. 19–20, n. 4; p. 25.

Guides," tend to "*fasten upon the first Precipice in view, and then tow our wretched willing Bodies after . . . to the very Brink of Destruction; But, alas, that Brink is rotten, our Feet slip, and we tumble down prone into a Gulph.*" Making a venereal joke here, Swift implies that eyes offer "the fairest Way of losing . . . frail Noses." But he is also insisting upon the necessity of sight, no matter how fallible, to replace Jack's more skeptical reliance upon "inner vision" (*Tale*, pp. 193–4).

Swift's own visionary imperative becomes complicated by his personal history. For as his own vision failed, in making what Johnson calls his "mad vow" never to wear spectacles,[3] Swift became radically dependent on senses which would inevitably decay. This determined immersion into matter itself gives special poignancy to Delany's anecdote about his friend's fierce desire to "see" the materials of his fiction even if he had to tumble over the rotten brink into the gulf below. In an attempt to gather visual materials for a poem on the Carberry Rocks, Swift, like H.F. straining at the edge of the plague pit for enlightenment, extended himself over the "brink" of a "dreadful precipice."

Not content with what information his eyes could give him, as he stood over it, he stretched himself forward at his full length upon the rock to survey it with more advantage. And attempting to rise up again when his curiosity was well gratified as it could; he found as he told me, (for I had it from his own mouth), that he lost ground, which obliged him to call, in great terror, to his servants who attended him (for he never travelled or even rode out, without two attendants) to drag him back by the heels; which they did, with sufficient difficulty and some hazard.

So determined here to get to the empirical edge of things, driven by that very curiosity he is so often compelled to satirize, Swift, in this instance, appears to be taking part in an exercise that sounds habitual. As Delaney emphasizes, he never even rode out without "two attendants . . . to drag him back by the heels" from precipices dreadful and necessary to measure. Not to wear spectacles is to chastise such an unruly spirit, and to locate even more solidly a ferocious imagination firmly in a body that will always betray. For if vision is the art of seeing the invisible, the rage to measure matter merely gets in the way of the spirit. Unless the matter is all that there is.[4]

---

[3] Johnson, "Swift," *Lives of the English Poets*, III, p. 47. Pat Rogers discusses Swift's refusal to wear spectacles in "Gulliver's Glasses," *The Art of Jonathan Swift*, ed. Clive Probyn, London and New York, 1978, pp. 179–88.

[4] Delany, *Observations*, pp. 135–6; In 1733 Swift, Sheridan, and Orrery observed a stream of water running through a rock from a hill outside of Dublin. Catching the water in a milk pail, Swift computed that if a two-gallon pail could be filled in a minute, 2,880 gallons would stream out in 24 hours. "This multiplied by 365 produces 1,051,200, and shows

For feeling hath no fellow

When Swift stretches his body over the precipice, he is extending himself into matter that he plans to order through poetry.[5] Much of Swift's work reflects a struggle to impose form upon matter, and concerns itself with the stubbornness of matter itself always intruding upon thought, spirit, and the text itself. We can see Swift working with the matter of the body in two particular works, one familiar and one lesser known. Book III of *Gulliver's Travels* dwells on the stuff of existence that cannot be shed without strategies bound to become ridiculous. Gulliver's observations of the Laputan's attempts to transcend body reveal Swift's hostility to their strategies, but not to their struggle. To understand the desperate nature of their attempts, it helps to look at an even later work where Swift presents a domestic world at war with matter that cannot be contained. Faced with such a reality, Laputans might well keep one eye on heaven. This work, *Directions to Servants*, calls up a world of matter that threatens to overcome literary form.

Although Swift told Pope he had been working on the *Directions* for twenty-eight years, only fragments of the "seriously incomplete" piece were published posthumously. The *Directions* became one of the works that his contemporaries least admired, inspiring Orrery to wax lyrical on the reason the dean shouldn't have been dabbling in such lowly matters.[6] And although Swift himself thought the piece "very usefull as well as humorous," the fragmentary account of the workings of a domestic household delineates a material world that cannot be contained "usefully." All matter threatens as weapons in the perpetual warfare between master and servant, purity and pollution. Consider the candle, that tool of illumination, and where to stick it.[7]

You may conveniently stick your Candle in a Bottle, or with a Lump of Butter against the Wainscot, in a Powder-horn, or in an old Shoe, or in a cleft Stick, or in the Barrel of a Pistol, or upon its own Grease on a Table, in a Coffee Cup or a Drinking Glass, a Horn Can, a Tea Pot, a twisted Napkin, a Mustard Pot, an Ink-horn, a Marrowbone, a Piece of dough, or you may cut a Hole in a Loaf, and stick it there.   (*PW*, XIII, p. 14)

---

the quantity that runs from the rock in a year; so that in three years, about the 15th of November, he computed that it must burst the body of the mountain, and emit an inundation which will run to all points of the Boyne, and greatly endanger the city of Dublin." Ehrenpreis, *Swift*, III, p. 755.

[5] Orrery reports that Swift "was extremely solicitous," that "Carberiae Rupes," Swift's Latin poem describing the "Rocky Ruins," should be printed, and "mistakenly" "assumed to himself more vanity upon" the Latin poem "than upon many of his best English performances," *Remarks*, pp. 130–1.

[6] *Ibid.*, pp. 283–5.

[7] Candles in the *Journal to Stella* frequently take on a sexual connotation; they become quite literally "scandalous candles," *JS*, p. 149.

It is not enough to stick candles into marrowbones, for every evening they must be put out entirely. Swift offers many ingenious methods of extinguishing their flames. Enlightenment dies hard in this passage, becoming as stubborn a material as the snuff it leaves in its wake:

You may run the Candle End against the wainscot, which puts the Snuff out immediately: You may lay in on the Floor, and tread the Snuff out with your Foot; You may hold it upside down until it is choaked with its own Grease; or cram it into the Socket of the Candlestick: You may whirl it round in your Hand till it goes out; When you go to Bed, after you have made Water, you may dip your Candle End into the Chamber-Pot: You may spit on your Finger and Thumb, and pinch the snuff until it goes out: The Cook may run the Candle's Nose into the Meal Tub, or the Groom into a Vessel of Oats, or a Lock of Hay, or a Heap of Litter; the House-maid may put out her Candle by running it against a Looking-glass, which nothing cleans so well as Candle Snuff: But the quickest and best of all Methods, is to blow it out with your Breath, which leaves the Candles clear and the readier to be lighted.   (*PW*, XIII, pp. 14–15)

Sexual innuendo notwithstanding, snuff, grease, breath itself become agents of contagion both dangerous and useful, for "nothing cleans so well as Candle Snuff."

The calculated lunacy of Swift's *Directions* emphasizes the primacy of matter. The servants compelled to run candle ends against wainscots and looking glasses become trapped by materials that they and we cannot control. I say we, because, satirically, Swift does not so much direct servants as frighten masters and mistresses, his gentle readers, victims of their servants' compulsion to spread snuff and spittal and grease and urine throughout a household always under attack. Swift's strategies to contain the matter just make things worse. "Put your Finger into every Bottle to feel whether it be full, which is the surest Way; for Feeling hath no Fellow" (XIII, p. 24). Swift is instructing here his most engaging and vexing of servants, the butler, who is also guilty of pressing the salt with his moist palm, and is "accustomed to filling [his] Mouth full of Corks, together with a large Plug of Tobacco" when he bottles the wine. Of course this is satire, not social history. One is supposed to read the *Directions* knowing that servants should avoid committing the outrageous violations of decorum that Swift sends up. But Swift, a master known to break his knuckles cuffing incorrigible valets, and driven in at least one instance to clean (clandestinely) his muddy gown with his own hands to test the perceptions of a less than zealous servant,[8] is not in this instance writing satire as much as recording the vexations of a world all too real. And in the process, employing a prose double-edged and wary, instructing

[8] *Holyhead Journal*, *PW*, IV, pp. 206–7.

servants not to stuff beans up their noses, he incites, on at least one level, domestic riot.[9]

Swift's *Directions* indict the master and mistress along with their servants, establishing a domestic space impossible to fill without discord. To cure the pretensions of a proud and lazy mistress who cannot take the pains of "stepping into the Garden to pluck a Rose," but keeps instead an "odious" chamberpot for her needs, Swift suggests that the housemaid carry the offensive utensil openly down the "great" stairs, avoiding the more seemly backstairs to expose the filthiness of her mistress to the entire household. The housemaid is instructed to answer the street door with brimming chamber pot in hand, for "This, if any Thing can, will make your Lady take the Pains of evacuating her Person in the proper Place, rather than expose her Filthiness to all the Men Servants in the House" (*PW*, XIII, pp. 60–1). The easy word, "proper," jars here. The art of living is to evacuate one's Person in the "proper" place, to pluck a rose, a physical action as simple and complex as proper actions in Eden itself. For even in the garden, servants will swarm, Strephons will hide, and Swift will lie in wait to catch the body in the act.

In the *Directions*, as in much of his work, Swift creates a world crammed with unpleasant bodies crowding, shoving, spying, in vain attempts to assert themselves. "Now, in all Assemblies, tho' you wedge them ever so close, we may observe this peculiar Property; that, over their Heads, there is Room enough; but how to reach it, is the difficult Point," Swift cautions in his *Tale* (p. 55). Worrying over his chances for "Fame" in "after times," he complains to Bolingbroke, that effortlessly "great Lord," that "the house is so full that there is no room for above one or two at most, in an age through the whole World" (*Corr*, III, p. 355). The illusion of "room" lures cramped sublunary poets and cracked projectors to their doom. Only Gulliver's Houyhnhnms, four feet on the ground, ready to die when the body wears out, can find room enough to satisfy their nature as they approach a utopian ideal impossible for humans to reach. The Laputans, on the other hand, those creatures that so anger Swift in their benighted arrogance and their willful blindness, resemble more the human species in their attempts to provide for their corporeal selves a space overhead, a room for one's own expansion.

The problem of embodiment shapes the sprawling third book,[10] written last, of the *Travels*. As rational readers, we like to read the satire

---

[9] Janice Thaddeus considers "the position of servants . . . Swift's attitudes toward mutual subordination . . . and the literary background" of *Directions to Servants* in "Swift's 'Directions to Servants' and the Reader as Eavesdropper," *Studies in Eighteenth Century Culture*, ed. OM Brack Jr., Madison WI, 1986, pp. 107–23.

[10] See Marjorie Nicolson and Nora M. Mohler on Book III in "Swift's Flying Island in the *Voyage to Laputa*," *Annals of Science*, 2 (1937), pp. 405–30; and "The Scientific Background of the *Voyage to Laputa*," *Annals of Science*, 2 (1937), pp. 299–335.

straight, as an indictment of the hubris of the new science, Swift the Ancient tilting at pert Moderns no better or worse than the vivisectionists of the Royal Society. But the satire turns immediately complex. Gulliver observes Laputan efforts to deny the body with real animosity, but Gulliver also yearns for freedom, however it can be attained, from the material world.

For one thing, this Gulliver, unlike a less reflective wanderer of Books I, II and IV, appears depressed from the start by the grim desolation of his physical circumstances. On Lilliput, tied to the ground by his insistent hosts, he spends more time measuring, observing, and recording a strange land than he does meditating upon his condition. On Brobdingnag, Gulliver is even harder pressed to react to his gigantic masters than to contemplate his own condition. Responses almost always reflexive and automatic determine his narrative. And even in Book IV, even after all his years of shipwrecked arrivals, showing no signs of wear, Gulliver can still, after a brief rest on a desolate shore, brush himself off, check his supply of bracelets, glass rings and other baubles, and set out with confidence barely qualified into another strange country to meet the natives. Such mechanical resilience is curiously missing from Book III.

Not that Gulliver doesn't work at keeping spirits high. After five days of exploring, he berths at a "convenient Place," where he gathers "Plenty of Eggs," a "Quantity of dry Sea-weed," and makes a Crusoe-like inventory of his quantity of "Flint, Steel, Match, and Burning-glass." But snug in his cave, sleeping on "the same dry Grass and Sea-weed which I intended for Fewel," Gulliver is nonetheless able to sleep "very little":

for the Disquiets of my Mind prevailed over my Wearyness and kept me awake. I considered how impossible it was to preserve my Life, in so desolate a Place; and how miserable my End must be. Yet I found my self so listless and desponding, that I had not the Heart to rise; and before I could get Spirits enough to creep out of my Cave, the Day was far advanced.   (*GT*, p. 156)

Underslept, overwrought, man reduced to sleeping on his fuel, Gulliver appears paralyzed by the physical extremity of his situation. Yet he possesses in his cave those materials that would normally raise his spirits, the plentiful eggs, the sweet-smelling herbs, the dry seaweed, things that please a nature "very easily . . . satisfied." His listless despondence reflects not the impossibility of preserving "life," but the impossibility of escaping life in a Hobbesian nature, "solitary, poore, nasty, brutish, and short."

Oppressed by these material considerations, Gulliver responds to the appearance of a cloud overhead with "Inward Motions of Joy." Clouds traditionally promise transcendence, although as early as Aristophanes, they do not always promise what they deliver.[11] Gulliver, gazing at the vast, opaque body overhead, may show himself "ready to entertain a Hope, that this Adventure might some Way or other help to deliver me from the desolate Place and Condition I was in," but Swift quickly reasserts the solid, intractable circumstances Gulliver so wants to shed. Waving his cap at Laputan anglers, for his hat was long since worn away on other adventures, Gulliver is "drawn up by Pullies" into a cloud all too material (*GT*, pp. 157–8).

Once in the cloud, Gulliver is surrounded by a crowd, for room is difficult to come by even overhead. Those nearest him, appearing to be of "better Quality," fill him with wonder, for he has never seen till then "a Race of Mortals so singular in their Shapes, Habits, and Countenances." In their desire for disembodiment, the Laputans have deformed themselves into singular shapes, heads reclined to the right or left, one eye turned inward, the other gazing straight up into the Zenith. In their deformation, the Laputans attempt the transcendence Plato hints at when he demands inwardness as the way out of the trap of the body. They only succeed, however, in misshaping matter already cumbersome while losing control over senses they need to survive. Flappers, versions of the servants Swift employs to drag him away from dangerous precipices, multiply the burdens of a body that cannot be denied.

Gulliver hates the Laputans' thwarted attempts to shed the body. While manufactured bladders swat dulled organs and randy wives slide down to Lagado to feed on deformed footmen, Swift mocks most bitterly the ridiculous attempts of crazed philosophers to get out of the body. His anger, ostensibly neutral, seems poised against his own mutated strategies to contain the sexuality that always threatens. How else to explain the absolute revulsion of Gulliver as he describes the Laputan struggles against body? Usually blandly accepting of the most noxious Lilliputian, the grossest Brobdingnagian, Swift maintains that he has never seen "a more clumsy, awkward, and unhandy People, not so slow and perplexed in their Conceptions upon all other Subjects, except those of Mathematicks and Musick." They are, in fact, the *most* "disagreeable Companions" he has ever met (*GT*, p. 163).

I think that Gulliver's contempt for Laputan and Lagadan attempts to achieve transcendence betray Swift's own desire to escape from the desolate circumstances of man in nature sleeping on his fuel. That the experiments themselves prove ridiculous does not detract from their urgency. One noxious projector daubed all over with excrement, "his Face and Beard . . . pale Yellow," is turning into the waste product he works at

[11] See Swift's and Sheridan's exchange of poems comparing clouds to "the Ladies," *Poems*, II, pp. 612–22.

reconstituting. This effort to reduce excrement to its original components, a most heady attempt to deny bodily processes by transforming them, is doomed to fall flat into a "Vessel filled with human Ordure about the Bigness of a *Bristol* Barrel" (*GT*, p. 180).

Brutally materializing the abstract, at the Academy at Lagado, Swift animates in the process metaphors about the "body politic." The not so visionary part of the Academy searches for "effectual Remedies for all Diseases and Corruptions" of the political body. Far from avoiding the body in these experiments, the projector insists upon its physical presence as he purges senators in the interest of public health. Common understanding can become the result of surgical tampering: violently opposed parties can reconcile their differences if they will only put their heads together to be sawed in half and equally divided. Ministers with short memories can be stimulated by 'a tweak by the Nose, or a Kick in the Belly." Sounding like the Swift who disciplined Laetitia Pilkington with "deadly" pinches to correct her reasoning,[12] his projector suggests pinching the arm "black and blue . . . to prevent forgetfulness" (*GT*, pp. 188–9).

The methods of physical correction contradict each other, for while the beshitten projector immerses himself in excrement to deny natural processes, the less visionary social scientist denies the spiritual and intellectual levels of experience to concentrate on the physical ground of political being. "As to the Difference of Brains in Quantity or Quality," he assures Gulliver as he reduces thought to material mash, "among those who are Directors in Faction . . . it was a perfect Trifle." Never able to forget "stink" emanating from the projector's excremental cell, Swift insists upon the truth of the body more responsive to a "Kick in the Belly . . . or a pinch in the Arm" than to reason (*GT*, p. 189). But at the same time, this world of the senses appalls him. Putting himself and his reader in this material bind, he reveals how thoroughly he yearns, even more than his Laputan butts, to unbody himself. This is especially evident in the Struldbrugg episode where Swift most unequivocally rejects such a possibility.

When he first hears of the fabulous Struldbruggs, Gulliver is "struck with inexpressible Delight." He quickly imagines enjoying their fate. First he would amass riches, recognizing it better by far to begin immortality as a "great" Bolingbroke or Temple rather than as a poor parson cousin putting Temple's Epicurean thoughts in order. Once comfortable, Gulliver would apply himself to learned pursuits, granted the time to sift through the minds of the ages for inspiration. For such an "immortal," even mutability hath its charms. The turnover of learned mortals he

---

[12] "Whenever I made use of an inelegant Phrase, I was sure of a deadly Pinch," reports Mrs. Pilkington, *Memoirs*, p. 108.

might invite to dinner affects his sensibility as little as would the "annual succession of Pinks and Tulips," while the various "Revolutions of States and Empires" add exhilarating pleasure to days everlasting. In his Gulliver's reveries, Swift pokes mortal holes in such Olympian detachment, but he is not entirely ironic, entertaining in this fantasy such delight that the reader most likely shares Gulliver's eventual horror when the Struldbruggs' real state of immortality is revealed (*GT*, pp. 207–10).

While the Struldbruggs lose their appetites, their teeth, their sight and hearing, robbed ever so gradually of the senses Swift both insists upon and seeks riddance of, they remain matter irreducible, walking carcasses. "They were the most mortifying Sight I ever beheld; and the Women more horrible than the Men. Besides the usual Deformities in extreme old Age, they acquired an additional Ghastliness in Proportion to their Number of Years which is not to be described." Just as the Laputans, intent on shedding their carcasses, as they scan their inner selves and outer heavens with skewed eyeballs, are the *most* disagreeable of Gulliver's discoveries, the Struldbruggs, in all their "proportional ghastliness" – "and the Women more horrible than the men" – are not only the *most* "mortifying," but in the end, the most indescribable. Dreams of transcendence turn into nightmares of everlasting mortality that cannot even be articulated. But of course, ironically, they can be, to our horror, described, measured, even allotted a proportional ghastliness that Swift insists upon. For Swift, language allows the only way out of the body, but it requires hard strategies that must be grounded in the material that binds (*GT*, p. 214).

The perils of articulation

The other, was a Scheme for entirely abolishing all Words whatsoever: And this was urged as a great Advantage in Point of Health as well as Brevity. For, it is plain, that every Word we speak is in some Degree a Diminution of our Lungs by Corrosion; and consequently contributes to the shortening of our Lives.

(*GT*, p. 185)

The words come from the Lagadan School of Languages' scheme to substitute things for words, an expedient judged "convenient," contributing to the "great Ease as well as Health of the Subject." While calling attention to the cost of language itself, Swift is surely playing here with Lockean notions of language. Locke's exploration of a verbal universe in peril, his essay on an understanding held hostage to the abuses of language that we seem compelled to commit, remains even today a most unsettling document in its casual, elegant dismantling of a system his readers depend upon. Locke himself appeared to have little problem with the "ambush" he sets for his contemporaries and heirs, establishing, as John

Richetti argues, a self that is ironically stable because it is comfortable with radical instability.[13] Thus after particularizing experience in Book III to insist upon the ways individual perception interferes with general meaning, Locke can still soothe his reader with genial common sense most difficult to apply to the problem he uncovers. Locke argues that even though we cannot communicate, strictly speaking, as sociable, civilized beings we must. Although they are specious and deceptive, generalizations and abstractions have after all their uses, and are in fact necessary for men "to consider Things, and discourse of them, as it were in bundles, for the easier and readier improvement, and communication of their Knowledge, which would advance but slowly, were their Words and Thoughts confined only to Particulars" (*Essay*, III, iii, p. 20). Never comfortable with anything easy, especially improvement, Swift literalizes the "easy" bundles Locke depends upon. Words, he will provocatively suggest, not only require bundles to be borne, but "one or two strong servants" to help carry the load of words reified into things.

In his ingenious Lagadan language schemes, Swift plays as relentlessly as Locke with the imperfections of language, but unlike Locke, he refuses to allow the serenity and equanimity the *Essay* experientially offers. Providing a wonderfully comic texture to his discourse, Locke offers "clear" choices after muddying a reality he pretends to see through. To demand more certainties than possible in a world rendered uncertain through unsteady words and fallible memories is simply to be an unreasonable and vain fool, to be guilty of expecting "*Demonstration* and Certainty *in things not capable of it*." For "he that in the ordinary Affairs of Life, would admit of nothing but direct plain Demonstration, would be sure of nothing in this World, but of perishing quickly" (IV, xi, p. 10). Unsettling his own generation with considerations that Swift would insist upon exploring, Locke drove Swift into a pit he never seemed to want to emerge from, the pit of language dissolved, unresolved, composed of signs arbitrary and treacherous.[14] Swift, less generous than Locke, as acutely aware of the dangers of language, the way words (corroding our throats) can even shorten our lives through the process of expression, uses language to fix a reality always coming apart. His irony does not merely qualify the stuff of experience he uses in his discourse; it undermines it.

All the while he labors to make meaning, Swift demands that his readers attend to the arbitrary nature of the metaphoric process even when he locates it most fundamentally within the body itself. Locke had already

[13] "To understand language is to grasp a process that establishes order because it simultaneously reveals disorder and maintains order as a constant possibility." Richetti, *Philosophical Writing*, p. 92.

[14] Paul de Man discusses the "perennial problem" of "figural language . . . a recognized source of embarrassment for philosphical discourse" in "The Epistemology of Metaphor," *Critical Inquiry*, 5 (Fall 1978), pp. 13–30.

considered the significance of the body in the writing process. A sort of proto-Johnson kicking stones to prove his existence, he suggests that the physical act of putting black letters onto white paper allows a "reality" he can verify in the making of his book:

v.g. whilst I write this, I have, by the Paper affecting my Eyes, that *Idea* produced in my Mind, which whatever Object causes, I call *White*; by which I know, that that Quality or Accident (*i.e.* whose appearance before my Eyes, always causes that *Idea*) doth really exist, and hath a Being without me. And of this, the greatest assurance I can possibly have, and to which my Faculties can attain, is the Testimony of my Eyes, which are the proper and sole Judge of the thing, whose Testimony I have reason to rely on, as so certain, that I can no more doubt, whilst I write this that I see White and Black, and that something really exists, that causes that Sensation in me, than that I write or move my Hand; which is a Certainty as great as humane Nature is capable of concerning the Existence of any thing but a Man's self alone; and of God.   (IV, xi, p. 2)

The irony is that the certainty, "as great as humane Nature is capable of," lasts only as long as the process of intuitive apprehension itself.[15] When he calls attention to the fearful fragility of texts pouring out from the vulnerable body of the writer, Swift illustrates just this phenomenological transience of meaning.[16]

When Swift makes his puns and all too solid metaphors, turning his own urine into gravel for Sheridan's walk,[17] opening veins of satire that blot his text, he is forging connections in a post-Renaissance universe empty of correspondences. Similes do not spring forth, but are made, arbitrarily, becoming far too easily "mock similes," perversions of the strategy known as periphrasis, that game preserve, soon cemetery, for words made to signify meaning immediately wearing away. Just as words in a Lockean sense are unsteady, the materials they represent are equally unbalanced. In exploiting this unsettling dilemma by mixing morals and bagatelle, "impos[ing]," to use Orrery's word, "wilfully and wantonly" upon the world a mixture of materials "so different – so incongruous" that they overturn the notions of canon while undermining genre altogether, Swift could exercise his formidable powers to create and uncreate

[15] Richetti, *Philosophical Writing*, p. 113.

[16] See Everett Zimmerman's discussion of Swift's "Language of Self," *Swift's Narrative Satires*, Ithaca and London, 1983, pp. 143–59. Rosalie Colie weighs the relativity of Locke's rhetoric in "The Essayist in his *Essay*," *John Locke: Problems and Perspectives*, ed. John Yolton, Cambridge, 1969, pp. 234–61.

[17] Sheridan describes Swift's transformational powers in the following anecdote. Arbuthnot had been "scribbling a letter in great haste, which was much blotted; and seeing [Swift] near him, with a design to play upon him, said, 'Pray, Sir, have you any sand about you?' 'No,' replied Swift, 'but I have the gravel, and if you will give me your letter I'll p–ss upon it'." (*Life of Swift*, p. 47).

meaning on anything at all. As Stella pointed out with at least partial
interest when reminded of the beauties of "Cadenus and Vanessa," it was
"well known that the Dean could write finely on a broom-stick."[18]

Such prospects for invention can turn a poet giddy. It seems to me that
one of the central problems for the eighteenth-century poet lies not in
the limitations of being bound in a unheroic universe where Miltonic
flights and epic celebrations are embarrassingly out of place, but stems
from the terrible freedom to create meaning out of nothing at all.
Schemes to fix the language, to clamp down the rules of genre to limit
imaginative flight mark the realization of just how far the artist could go.
While the philosophical ambush, the "pit," awaits the writer, so does the
unbounded universe free of essential meaning. Swift (as well as Pope and
Defoe) invents energetic strategies to stay free even while they become
implicated in their fictions of necessity, maintaining an uneasy poise with
materials that threaten to give way.

We can watch Swift address the problems a free language presents in
"A Proposal for Correcting, Improving and Ascertaining the English
Tongue," the first work he put his name to. Arguing that the English
language is less "refined" than that of Italy, Spain or France because it
has been harrassed by "cruel Inroads" from outsiders, he accuses the
conquerors of "scattering" meaning in their wake. William the Conqueror
is deemed particularly guilty of polluting the barbaric mixture called
English when he "scattered" vast numbers of French speakers in every
monastery. There is no doubt from the tract that the additions add "corruption" to the language tantamount to the "great Corruption of Manners, and Introduction of foreign Luxury, with foreign Terms to express
it." But Swift is not looking back at an original purity or perfection that
needs to be recovered; on the contrary, the *English* tongue "is not arrived
to such a Degree of Perfection, as, upon that Account to make us apprehend any Thoughts of its Decay" (*PW*, IV, pp. 6–8). Subject to tampering
from without and from within, the unstable tongue threatens to spoil
Swift's own chance at "Immortality" as an author.

While the threat of contagion and mixture dominates the *Proposal* (for
the licentiousness of the Restoration infected not only our religion and
morals, but our language itself), Swift as writer appears as victim of the
sins of his fathers. The *others*, those wits and poets weak-willed and prodi-
gal should be blamed for their negligence in rendering *his* language useless, unintelligible to future readers. Men of wit and learning, "instead of
early obviating such Corruptions, were too often seduced to imitate and
comply with them," just as those poets, "another Set of Men," have spoiled
the tongue with their abuses (IV, pp. 10–11). How, Swift asks plaintively,
as he prepares to set down his history of his times, "shall any Man, who

18 Orrery, *Remarks*, p. 80. Delany, *Observations*, p. 58.

hath a Genius for History, equal to the best of the Antients, be able to undertake such a Work with Spirit and Chearfulness, when he considers, that he will be read with Pleasure but a very few years, and in an Age or two shall hardly be understood without an Interpreter? This is like employing an excellent Statuary to work upon mouldring Stone." When the style of "the best *English* Historian" grows antiquated, he runs the risk of being "only considered as a tedious Relater of Facts; and perhaps consulted in his Turn, among other neglected Authors, to furnish Materials for some future collector" (IV, p. 18). One of Swift's most characteristic terrors dominates this passage. So fearful of being scattered, he is threatened by the vagaries of his language as he runs the risk of being misinterpreted by readers without the powers to comprehend his meaning. He will instead be reduced to his materials, the mouldering stone and odd facts, that he can supply, reduced to Gulliverian tasks of measurement and computation that lose significance without aids to understanding. His own thoughts on this matter are self-consciously "scattered," he confesses in a closing blaze of puffery to Harley, noble subject of his putative histories.

Swift's actual proposal, although he confesses himself turning projector, is fairly mild, calling for a certain degree of "*Ascertaining* and *Fixing* our Language" (IV, p. 14) which should nevertheless still be allowed to grow. He comes out most strongly against spelling reforms which would allow writers to "spell exactly as we speak; which besides the obvious Inconvenience of utterly destroying our Etymology, would be a Thing we would never see the End of" (IV, p. 11). Swift learnt his letters well from his old nurse, and he insists that others follow his path. "Let the world go how it will," he warns Stella, guilty of fourteen errors at least, "I will have you spell right." But spelling aside, most of the proposal expresses Swift's own fears of being left to moulder in decaying materials, of being "swallowed up in succeeding Collections" of "our *English* story," dependent upon the labors of other obscure drudges for partial resuscitation. When he warns Harley that in two hundred years, his turbulent career will be reduced to a bland sentence manufactured by a "painful Compiler" (IV, p. 18), Swift looks to his own fate as well. And it would be remedied not by writing more proposals to fix the language, but by employing more radically the materials of language itself.

To bring scattered meaning down to earth, Swift creates a poetic of necessity, incorporating metaphors that inevitably descend. Even in his first odes, high on his pindaric stilts, Swift grounded his poetry in the stuff of existence. The villain of his celebration of King William, the giddy tyrant Louis XIV, may appear to be a gilded meteor, but his glories flow out of unnaturally high spirits stimulated by a fistula on the anus; he has stolen his "Plagiary Light" from "the worst Excrements of Earth." All we need do is wait, "and down again 'twill come, / And end as it began, in Vapour, Stink, and Scum." Suggesting a mechanistic interpretation of ambition that would shape much of "A Digression Concerning Madness," Swift leaves his *"Restless Tyrant"* predictably trapped in the body. Grown "Giddy," and hurled down, proved "Mortal to his *Vile Disease*," Louis is destined to fall "sick in the *Posteriors* of the World."[19] Aggressively, Swift reduces the great man striving for posterity, turning him into the victim of a schoolboy's pun. Swift's angry, punitive humor seems self-reflexive, typical of the times that he seems to achieve satisfaction in cutting down to size the grandiose entities that threaten his sense of self. A giddy self certainly knows why to censure other vaunting spirits, and since, as we have already seen, Swift attributed his own giddiness to the eating of forbidden fruit, Louis' Lucifer-like descent approximates Swift's own fear of falling metaphorically and metaphysically.

For ascending bodies ultimately descend. Pindar could soar like an eagle, but Swift's fancy falls flat, "like a dead Bird of Paradise, to the Ground" (*Tale*, p. 158).[20] But although flight was out of the question, the idea of flight remained necessary and compelling. Suffering the incurable disease, or "itch" as he would later call it, of poetry, he complains in his ode to Temple perhaps ironically that

> What'er I plant (like Corn on barren Earth)
> By an equivocal Birth
> Seeds and runs up to Poetry.
>
> (*Poems*, I, p. 33, lines 210–12)

The poet may sow herbs, but weeds spring up to be cut down and thrown into the fire. Weeds ascending promise a false flight at most, a defiance of gravity that will only scatter more meaning, corrupting the language itself with significance by nature "equivocal." In his final ode written in the lofty style, one "Occasioned by Sir William Temple's Late Illness and Recovery," Swift notoriously renounces (in metaphor) his flighty muse. The poem reveals a Swift characteristic in his wary bouts with language, worried about coming apart, fearful of the scattering that giddiness can instill in the hardest of souls. When he rails at his "Malignant goddess," he chafes most at the vagueness of this bane to his repose. She is almost as mercurial as the language he longs to fix. Without a being of her own, his giddy muse is "But a wild form dependent on the brain, / Scatt'ring loose features o'er the optic vein" (*Poems*, I, p. 54, lines 94–8). These

---

[19] *Poems*, I, p. 10, lines 119–29, 144–46. William Ober develops the historical implications of Louis's *fistula in ano* as well as Swift's hemorrhoids in "Seats of the Mighty," *Medical Opinion* (August 1972), pp. 53–9.

[20] Claude Rawson discusses the bird of paradise in *Gulliver and the Gentle Reader*, London, 1973, p. 65.

features "dart" in "trembling light" to fly into "antic shapes in dreams."
Their beams cheat "sickly minds," and depend eventually upon "the
breath" of the poet himself. "Thus with a puff the whole delusion ends,"
the adjuring poet writes (lines 149–54), and knowing Swift from the *Journal to Stella*, we can well imagine that he blew his own breath on to the
page as he wrote the words.

When Swift disowns the muse that he himself has formed out of his
own body, his own breath, he not only demonstrates a distrust of the
subjectivity implicit in the creative process, but, on a more personal level,
he seems somehow to connect his own bad health to his own bad art. Sick
minds spew forth sick issue, and Swift, suffering from the mysterious
Ménière's Syndrome, subject to attacks of dizziness and uncertain sight,
locates the problem of his first unpromising poems within his body. A
way to fight against the instability not just of language but of the bodily
process itself is to insist upon keeping true to the materials that get in the
way. He becomes in the process a most physical writer, one who replaces
spirit and trembling light with spittle and flesh and blood.

The strategy requires concrete connection to "things below," a renunciation not just of the lofty style, but of the loft itself. In the later "Epistle
to a Lady, who desired the Author to make some Verses upon her in the
Heroick Stile," Swift explains that he declines "the lofty style" because it
lacks effect[21] (*Poems*, II, p. 634, line 140). Like a rocket, it produces great
light, but reaches only "the middle Air" to burst into pieces. "Thousand
Sparkles falling down, / Light on many a Coxcomb's Crown." The sport
creates mirth, "sindges hair," but, "breaks no Pates." If he attempts such
poetic heights, Swift argues, he too should burst, "and bursting drop. /
All my Fire would fall in Scraps." The antidote to this scattering is a
concentration of energy physically applied, "gentle Raps" to make his
lady's head "smart." Such a dose will please both assailant and victim:

> Then, cou'd I forbear to smile,
> When I found the tingling Pain,
> Entring warm your frigid Brain.

While the lady grows smart from her smarting pate, the teacher will
"laugh" at her newly fashioned wit, her aroused sensibility long dormant.

[21] Rawson discusses Swift's rejection of "loftiness" in "I the Lofty Style Decline: Self-Apology
and the 'Heroick Strain' in Some of Swift's Poems," *The English Hero, 1660–1800*, ed.
Robert Folkenflik, Newark, London and Toronto, 1982, pp. 79–115. Swift's preference
for a sensible poetic has been recognized before. See Paul C. Davies, "Augustan Smells,"
Essays in Criticism, 25, 4 (1975), pp. 395–406 and Robert H. Hopkins, "Swift and the
Senses," *Greene Centennial Studies*, ed. Paul Korshin and Robert Allen, Charlottesville VA,
1984, p. 71. For a discussion of earlier literary embodiment, see Elaine Scarry's "John
Donne, 'But yet the Body is his Booke,' " in *Literature and the Body, Essays on Population
and Persons*, ed. E. Scarry, Baltimore and London, 1988.

This laughter, far from Rabelaisian or even Socratic, unsettling in its aggressive nature, demonstrates just how far Swift would go to reach his audience (*Poems*, II, p. 638, lines 249–74).

Faced with the threat of dissolution, vexed by a "giddy" head, and worse, compelled to pursue an unstable profession of letters when the very words he had to depend upon were being abused, misused, even wantonly misspelled, to make meaning, Swift forced language itself into the physicality that was so difficult to transcend. In the process he created a poetic of hard necessity in which all the words are made to count, made to hurt, even in his bagatelle. He forges connections ironically sustained, using vulnerable materials of the body itself. Not surprisingly, the first poem we find after his renunciation of the Pindaric Muse, is a celebration not just of the precariousness of verse, but of the power of spittle.

The poem is a light occasional piece, "Verses Wrote in a Lady's Ivory Table-Book," offering the poet the opportunity to send up the silly stuff of conversation he characteristically delights in not just demolishing, but recording. The trifles scrawled across the page expose their creator's lack of invention, and their collector's lack of discrimination. As jumbled as Belinda's dressing table, the leaves expose receipts for paint alongside misspelled vows to be "*tru tel death*." As insubstantial as the "breath" keeping Swift's own wayward muse aloft, the tributes are nonetheless reduced to the material that contains them. For they are placed within the "power of Spittle and a Clout" of displeased readers bent on the most drastic revision. God, it is worth recalling, created Adam out of spittle and dust. Swift the poet distrusts his calling enough to reverse the creative act, creating verses at risk, subject to the material world threatening to subsume the "Nonsense" and "Trifles" scrawled over the "hard . . . senseless . . . light" pages of not just the book, but the "Heart" of its reader (*Poems*, I, pp. 60–1).

The reader is in this case specifically one without ears to hear or eyes to see, for the words scrawled over her ivory tablet hold no part against the fitter "tool," the "Gold Pencil tipped with Lead," borne by a wealthy suitor. In much of his work, Swift battles against just such handicapped dolts. Plans to vex the world spring from skirmishes with archetypal dullness, hearts "*waxed gross*," ears "*dull of Hearing*," and eyes closed shut (*PW*, IX, p. 215). The words come from Swift's sermon "Upon Sleeping in Church." He begins that sermon with a verse from the Book of Acts.

And there sat in a Window a certain young Man named Eutychus, *being fallen into a deep Sleep; and while Paul was long preaching, he sunk down with Sleep, and fell down from the Third Loft, and was taken up dead.*   (*PW*, IX, p. 210)

After this ominous beginning, Swift argues against his dull-witted audience's demands to be stimulated by delivery of what "they have heard the same an hundred Times over," when it is actually the tedium of their own vices that deserves abuse.[22] In falling asleep, the auditors turn the sermon itself into "a Sort of uniform Sound at a Distance," the sound itself guaranteed to lull the senses and bind up the "Faculties." The fate of Eutychus suits the crime; falling from the third loft, hurled down from his insensible heights, the sleeping auditor is made to "smart" for his threat to the preacher's own discourse. For if the sermon turns into "Sound," Swift's own meaning scatters. Swift blames the mixture of his audience for its corporate insensibility; taste and judgment differ, "And how to calculate a Discourse, that shall exactly suit them all" (*PW*, IX, pp. 212–13), he asks impatiently, not as genial as Locke can be on the perils of making sense. The answer appears to be abuse, verbal and physical, for all pates smart when rapped, and after railing at the indecent sloth that causes men "dividing the Time between God and their Bellies" to sleep off their dinner in God's house, he warns, invoking the fate of the unfortunate Eutychus, "*He that hath Ears to hear, let him hear*" (*PW*, IX, p. 218).

Or let him fall from the third loft into fitting senselessness. For good listeners need to be brought to their task, need to be spurred, prodded, pulled by "that Ring in the Nose." Readers are lazy, impatient, grunting creatures (*Tale*, p. 203) only made better by the physical abuse Swift pours on their dull heads. As John Traugott argues, he would kill them to make them better.[23]

The abusive muse

One dy'd in *Metaphor*, and one in *Song*.
"The Rape of the Lock," Canto V, line 60

In his study of verbal and visual satire from Pope to Churchill, Vincent Carretta publishes a "crudely executed" engraving that illustrates an anonymous sixteen-page satire on Lord Hervey, and alludes most directly to a duel between Hervey and William Pulteney in 1731. The frontispiece does not delineate the actual duel, but presents instead a dapper Mr. Pope brandishing a sword tipped with a quill pen, the victor of *A Tryal of Skill Between a Court Lord, and a Twickenham 'Squire*. Ink hurled from the quill spatters the space of the page to "daub" with "foul disgrace" Hervey's face (which looks suspiciously pock-marked). This visual maiming is made

---

[22] Delany reports that Swift's voice was "sharp and high-toned," and that he read prayers "rather in a strong nervous voice than in a graceful manner," *Observations*, p. 42.
[23] Traugott, "The Yahoo in the Doll House," p. 149.

verbal through the words issuing from Pope's mouth: "You write! you Sh–te." Carretta uses the engraving to call attention to the "emblematic-expressive depiction" of caricatures of the period. But the print can also be interpreted more literally as a visual manifestation of the aggressive and physical aspects of satire: the ways the poet physically abuses his victim.

What Pope is seen effecting visually, both Pope and Swift do frequently in their poetry and prose. Through their literary apprehension of their victims, they blur the distinctions between art and life. In the engraving, the poet occupies a literary space outside the "real world" of the duel, for while Pope presents his quill, Hervey wields a real sword, and while Pope is waistcoated and wigged, "attired as if to symbolize the ease with which he will dispatch his political and literary enemy,"[24] Hervey is "dressed realistically," since "strenuous dueling demanded unencumbered agility." Through the power of his pen, Pope can cross over literary boundaries to enter a physical reality where he can spatter his victim with actual ink to disturb not just his peace, but his health. In his shirt sleeves, wearing his own sparse hair, and appearing far from agile, Hervey looks sickly, more like Swift's madman or Hogarth's rake howling in Bedlam, than a duellist about to make his mark. And this sickly victim, verbally maimed, is being made sicker through the power of Pope's pen rather than being "healed" by the corrective surgery of satirical art. The strongest satire of the eighteenth century punishes rather than corrects, and it punishes through pain.

In his study of Pope's "Genius of Sense," David Morris probes the problem of pain in eighteenth-century satire to argue that the "muse of pain" punishes its victims without much hope of correction. The Augustan satirists used the body to inflict pain as punishment, looking toward legal and criminal remedies to justify their license to hurt. While "reformation depended ultimately upon the self-improvement of the culprit," the more commonly practiced method of satirical deterrence "required only that the culprit suffer – and that the spectator or reader bear witness." The suffering is both physical and psychological. When Pope not only applies an emetic to his enemy Curll, but commemorates it as well, once in prose and once in verse, he takes his revenge upon the "very body of his victim" literally and figuratively. It could be argued that the published purge hurt more; surely it lasted longer, extending body into text that can be molested with renewed vigor in every rereading.[25] Swift

[24] Vincent Carretta, *The Snarling Muse: Verbal and Visual Political Satire from Pope to Churchill*, Philadelphia, 1983, pp. 57–61.

[25] David Morris, *Alexander Pope: The Genius of Sense*, Cambridge MA and London, 1984, p. 230. The entire chapter, "The Muse of Pain," pp. 214–40, is valuable. Ken Robinson's "The Art of Violence in Rochester's Satre," *Yearbook of English Studies*, 14 (1984), pp. 93–108 and W. B. Carnochan's consideration of the therapeutic nature of Swiftian viol-

not only punishes, but kills off his victims, turning a living Partridge into an "*uninformed* Carcass" (*PW*, II, p. 162). He transforms the unfortunate William Wood, by virtue of his name, into a "Son of a BEECH," the better to be cut down, "*Un-man*[ned] . . . for sake of a *Trope*" (*Poems*, I, pp. 334–5). Once "*Un-man*[ned]," Wood must be "represent[ed] to the Life" in order to be executed in effigy; he is replaced metaphorically by "an old Piece of carved Timber." The "real" William Wood, "a comely and well-*timbered* Man," represented in the account of his mock hanging, turns into wood, his "Breast" of timber "cold and stiff" (*PW*, X, pp. 147–9).

To fix his victim, the satirist transforms him or her physically, using pieces of hair and nail, spittle and blood, to turn "solid and real" that which will otherwise fade into vague abstraction.[26] When Swift banishes the arbitrary blandishments of an abstract muse in his "Ode Occasioned by Sir William Temple's Late Illness and Recovery" and Pope, in his "Epistle to Dr. Arbuthnot," rejects his "soft numbers" for hard measures, both seem to view the body as a place to mete out punishment to fit crimes of nature. For dunces, frequently born, not made, often act naturally in a yahoo manner which is impossible to correct. Lashing such recalcitrant sinners provides at the least some relief for the one who holds the whip.

Swift's punitive strain surfaces early. Arguing in his "Ode to Dr. William Sancroft" that "swords are madmen's tongues, and tongues are madmen's swords" (*Poems*, I, p. 35, line 14), the poet arms himself against an unfeeling world filled with "bloody sins." Each line in his work, he vows, "shall stab, shall blast, like daggers and like fire . . . to make them understand, and feel me when I write" (*Poems*, I, p. 37, lines 89–94). In his "Ode to Mr. Congreve," a work complicated by Swift's own grudge against unreceptive readers, he promises more retribution; his hate, "*whose lash just heaven has long decreed / Shall on a day make sin and folly breed*" (*Poems*, I, p. 47, lines 133–4). These lofty threats seem excessively violent and out of place, spent, even scattered, in the poem itself, on a "finish'd spark" hardly worth the lashing. Swift will learn to point his sword with more finesse, and "let my anger break out in some manner that will not please them, at the End of a Pen" (*Corr*, II, p. 36). Not to please, but to vex, not to inform, but to punish, Swift assumes the scourge with alacrity, and eventually grace. By the time he writes his "Epistle to a Lady Who Desired the Author to make Verses on Her in the Heroick Stile," he has learned how to sweeten spent rage:

ence, "The Consolations of Satire," *The Art of Jonathan Swift*, ed. Clive T. Probyn, London, 1978, pp. 19–42, are both of interest here.

[26] Robert C. Elliott emphasizes the aggressive, killing nature of satire while insisting upon its magical, transformational qualities in *The Power of Satire: Magic, Ritual, Art*, Princeton, 1960.

> Like the ever-laughing Sage
> In a Jest I spend my Rage:
> (Tho' it must be understood,
> I would hang them if I could)

The parenthetical malice points the satire, allowing Swift to "fill his Nitche," attempting "no higher Pitch," by throwing away the histrionics of his position. A mocking, jog-trot rhythm helps, letting the low poet, "tho the Smell be Noisom":

> Strip their Bums; let CALEB noyse em;
> Then apply ALECTO's Whip,
> Till they wriggle, howl, and skip.
>
> (*Poems*, II, p. 635, lines 167–80)

This verse, more concrete than Swift's early declamations of a heavenly ordained lashing to "*Make sin and folly bleed*," reifies sin into arses so material that they must be hoisted before being lashed. Feminine endings and skewed tetrameter tend to deflate Swift's violence, forcing his scourged victims to join in a *danse macabre* of his devising, as they wriggle, howl and skip off the page, to be displaced by the shocked criticisms of his lady critic who wonders "DEUCE is in you, Mr DEAN: / What can all this Passion mean?" (lines 181–2).

The passion is personal and deeply felt. One has only to read Swift's marginal scourging of Henry VIII to feel how strongly he burned to apply the whip to those he considered enemies. If we believe his notes, Swift wished that the barbarous hellish "dog dog dog" of a king "had been Flead, his skin stuffed and hangd on a Gibbet, His bulky guts and Flesh left to be devoured by Birds and Beasts) for a warning to his Successors for ever. Amen" (*PW*, V, p. 251).

By hanging Henry VIII in metaphor, Swift gives vent to anger while locating his notion of "correction" within the legalistic framework of his culture. Swift, after all angered that the assassin Guiscard died before he could be hung in chains, was only slightly mollified to report that the pickled carcass of the villain was on public display for a shilling a peek. Opening decaying carcasses and reporting the condition of flayed women, Swift, like Pope purging and scourging his Dunces, works out of a punitive tradition that exploits the body itself as that material to be hanged, flayed, and trimmed.[27]

Textual self-extension

The aggression inherent in satire is only part of the assertive action of writing itself. Not only is it a way to concentrate energies and avoid frag-

[27] See Arthur Scouten's intriguing suggestion about Swift's real interest in the "instruments of torture" in "Swift's Poetry and the Gentle Reader," *Contemporary Essays*, pp. 46–54.

mentation, but it can be seen as an exploitive search for space itself, space to write over and make intelligible. It only takes "an inch at most," Swift offers blandly in his "Verses on the Death of Dr. Swift."

> Who wou'd not at a crowded Show,
> Stand high himself, keep others low?
> I love my Friend as well as you,
> But would not have him stop my View;
> Then let him have the higher Post;
> I ask but for an Inch at most.
>
> (*Poems*, II, p. 554, lines 15–20)

But as he recognizes early on, an inch is hard to get when "Whoever hath an Ambition to be heard in a Crowd, must press, squeeze, and thrust, and climb with indefatigable Pains, till he has exalted himself to a certain Degree of Altitude above them" (*Tale*, p. 55). As Selby points out, writing for Swift is not only a physical act, but an act of physical aggression, a process "whose goal, paradoxically, is to overcome the limits of corporeal individuality and achieve 'pre-eminence'."[28] For to write at all is to "assert yourself at the expense of others." In his study of writing and the body, Gabriel Josipovici notes that "the words on the page are themselves assertive, elbowing others with an equal right to be there, off the page."[29] Swift pays attention to this phenomenon continuously in his "random" catalogs that juxtapose high and low, ridiculous and sublime, and in his giddy puns that defy meaning even as they make it, forging connections that are speciously compelling, and that become by means of placement literally true. All you need is the right rhyme and you can fix your enemy forever.

The aggression inherent in "mock" rhythm and rhyme imprisons its victim by the arbitrary management of what makes up the self. Just as Partridge could never resurrect himself after Swift put him to rest, one Richard Bettesworth, serjeant-at-law and a member of the Irish parliament inroading on the Sacramental Test Act, remains imprisoned in literary history as the victim of Swift's sly rhyme:

> Thus at the bar the booby *Bettesworth*,
> Tho' half a crown o'er pays his Sweat's Worth.
>
> (*Poems*, III, p. 812, lines 25–6)

Booby Bettesworth's actions fit his name, for he called upon Swift at the Deanery, where he grew "over-warm and eloquent." Sheridan reports that Bettesworth threatened to cut off the Dean's ears, but Swift writes less melodramatically that his assailant had a "sharp knife in his pockets, ready to stab or maim [him]" (*Corr*, IV, p. 220). Swift responded to his

---

[28] Selby, "Never Finding Full Repast," p. 231.
[29] Gabriel Josipovici, *Writing and the Body*, Princeton, 1982, p. 117.

threats with more poetic violence, promising in "The Yahoo's Overthrow" to "*Knock him down, down, down, knock him down,* to crop and slit and oil and powder that body that so offends."[30]

The words themselves make compelling magic, and in fact while Swift wrote his verses, the inhabitants of the Liberty of St. Patrick's resolved to knock down the enemy in real life if he dared threaten the "Life and Limbs" of their dean. The most powerful word in the poetic exchange seems to me not the ranting threats of slicing and slitting, but the simple body word "sweat." By reducing his enemy to sweat, Swift condenses his essence to transform it into something noxious and perishable, something that exists in two states, actively offensive or benignly evaporated. And even then, the stench of the material remains.

We can see Swift acting with particular poetic aggression in his management of the "matter" of the Duke of Schomberg. Turning matter into metaphor, he threatens to turn body into text in an extreme attempt to exact filial piety from an unresponsive heir, to open dull ears with smart raps. If we remember Gulliver's vision of bones bleaching under a Lilliputian sun, his monument to posterity, it is not surprising to see how Swift reacted to the august bones of "the Great Duke," hero of the Boyne and savior of Protestant Ireland. The bones had been buried in St. Patrick's Cathedral since 1690, but in 1729, in a series of letters inviting prominent families to repair or erect monuments to their ancestors, Swift took on with a vengeance the case of "the Great Duke." After a granddaughter, the Countess of Holderness, declined to answer Swift's "desire" that she "would order a monument to be raised for [her grand-father] in my cathedral," Swift wrote to Lord Carteret to complain:

I desire you will tell Lord F[itzwalter] that if he will not send fifty pounds to make a monument for the old Duke, I and the chapter will erect a small one of ourselves for ten pounds, wherein it shall be expressed that the posterity of the Duke, naming particularly Lady Holderness and Mr. Mildmay, not having the generosity to erect a monument, we have done it of ourselves.   (*Corr*, III, p. 390)

Insisting control over "my cathedral," while he reduces the "great" Duke to the "old" Duke, Swift threatens to name names as he metes out public humiliation. Just as he wrote his own epitaph, careful to guard against the posthumous slurs of others, Swift, himself a posthumous poet, knew how to exert living power over the dry bones of his victims, claiming in the process his rights over the bones as well as the spirit of the man. If his combatants "for an excuse . . . pretend they will send for his body, let them know it is mine," he vaunts, "and rather than send it, I will take up

---

[30] Sheridan, *Life of Swift*, pp. 538–40. See also Fabricant, *Swift's Landscape*, pp. 243–5.

the bones, and make of it a skeleton, and put it in my registry-office, to
be a memorial of their baseness to all posterity."

Swift meant what he said, and later erected a modest black slab over
the duke's remains, advertising the lack of his heirs' filial piety: "Plus
potuit fama virtutis apud alienos / Quam sanguinis proximitas apud
suos." Ehrenpreis suggests that the "strength of emotion out of keeping
with the occasion" could reflect a displacement of regret Swift felt for
"being unable to provide Stella with a monument."[31] And that could be,
but I think closer to his "outburst" lie the dead bones themselves, fitting
memento mori of a condition that he can only rail against. His vow to turn
the great Duke into a skeleton to hang in the registry would not only
memorialize the baseness of the old Duke's heirs to all posterity, but
would advertise the perils of posterity to all base mortals. For skeletons,
"articulated" bones extend form to dead matter even as they depend
upon an art almost ironic in its intention that puts together what naturally
falls apart.

The words Swift places over the duke's old bones also matter, for words
displace flesh and blood, bones and vital parts, making sacred matter
which on its own remains base. Swift's elevation of language is never
entirely straight. No Sidney exulting in a world made golden through
prose, he's warier, yet still driven to at least play with the notion of language as that which can redeem. His faith in the word breaks out oddly
at times, marking the most material of exchanges. If the city of Dublin
deems him worthy of receiving a gold box, symbol of his civic virtue, they
need to inscribe it to make it matter, to esteem him "justly" as "the most
eminent patriot and greatest ornament of this his native city and country."
Such graven praises were never issued, and after certain maneuvers
awarding Archbishop Hoadly a gold box as well, the Lord Mayor and
aldermen offered their trinket to a less than enthusiastic recipient. Swift
wished "that an inscription might have been graven on the box, shewing
some reason why the city thought fit to do him that honour," and managed to "crown himself" for the distinction "being usually made only to
chief governors, or persons in very high employments" in a little speech
he circulated among his own friends (*PW*, XII, p. 148).

Swift was even less grateful when the city of Cork awarded him a (hum-
bler) silver box, uninscribed. He sent it back, demanding that the city
corporation "insert the Reasons for which you were pleased to give me
my Freedom, or bestow the Box upon some more worthy Person, whom
you may have an Intention to Honour, because it will equally fit every
Body" (*Corr*, V, pp. 67–8). The council complied, but perhaps weary of
the game, Swift appears not to have been contented by a properly graven
tribute, for he left the silver box in his will to one John Grattan to store

[31] Delany prints the entire epitaph, *Observations*, pp. 274–5; Ehrenpreis, *Swift*, III, p. 622.

the tobacco "he usually cheweth, called Pigtail" (*PW*, XIII, p. 155). By reducing a symbolic container to a most prosaic function, even as he insists upon its value, Swift sends up the notion of honor that he simultaneously seeks. Honor itself becomes a place to store chewing tobacco, but it also becomes an abstraction that must be articulated, even when it is being mocked.[32] David Veith notes that often it is difficult to tell the difference between tenor and vehicle in what he calls Swift's middle-period poetry.[33] Indeed, for Swift, there often is no difference. In a poetic world bounded by the material, the poet can make connections, but he must realize all the while the arbitrary nature of what he has wrought. The "words" engraved upon the gold and silver boxes mean only what Swift will allow them to. Extorted or withheld, valued or parodied, reduced if need be to utilitarian tobacco holders, they impose meaning in flux just as the "words" memorializing the "posterity" of the great Duke impugn him for his base descendants even as they mark his elevated bones. For whether golden box or marble slab, monuments to "posterity" always fall flat into the posteriors of the world.

Clear solutions

> YET from this *mingled Mass* of Things,
> In Time a new Creation springs.
> These *crude* Materials once shall rise,
> To fill the Earth, and Air, and Skies:
> In various Forms appear agen
> Of Vegetables, Brutes, and Men.
> So *Jove* pronounc'd among the Gods,
> *Olympus* trembling as he nods.
> (*Poems*, III, p. 924, lines 89–96)

> And this I take to be a clear Solution of the Matter.
> (*Tale*, p. 170)

To keep from falling into the posteriors of the world, Swift insists upon the posteriors themselves, locating himself and his work within the confines of the body. As early as the "Ode to the Athenian Society," addressing "*Ye Great Unknown*" who later would turn out to be (to Swift's chagrin) pert modern John Dunton, Swift considers along with the melancholy

[32] Ehrenpreis, *Swift*, III, pp. 651–5.
[33] "Metaphors and Metamorphoses: Basic Techniques in the Middle Period of Swift's Poetry," *Contemporary Essays*, p. 60.

posterity of his words, the inevitability of all "Conquest" vanishing to "an empty Title" at last, reduced to carcass:

> For when the animating Mind is fled,
> (Which Nature never can retain,
>   Nor e'er call back again)
> The body, tho' Gigantick, lies all *Cold and Dead.*
>
> (*Poems,* I, p. 25, lines 288–91)

Some "Traces of Wit" may remain, but they too are subject to decay while paradoxically, "*Men, who liv'd and dy'd without a Name, / Are the Chief Heroes in the sacred List of Fame*" (lines 306–7). Swift, the "young and (almost) virgin" poet is thinking on his own nameless condition, as he teases himself with the idea of posterity. But it matters, I think, that even here, just as he locates Louis' fate in the posteriors of the world, he locates his own in a gigantic, cold, dead body, intimating the bleached Gulliverian bones that could some day dominate a Lilliputian landscape. For the fate of his own body fills Swift's personal and public writing.

"Lo here I sit at holy head / With muddy ale and mouldy bread" (*Poems,* II, p. 420) he grumbles in the poem written in 1727 while he waits for the tides to take him back to hated Ireland and a decaying Stella. Holyhead becomes for Swift the point of departure from paradisal England (the place where he fell from grace eating too many apples), and the point also of the separation between the abstract "holy head" and the decaying body, the Christian "vittal" stinking of fish. As he plays with the materials of communion, turning bread and wine into muddy ale and molding bread, Swift dwells on the materials that bind him, "fasten" him to his physical condition, for he is waiting to "reach that slavish hateful shore" to rejoin a "friend" whose body is giving out.

Holyhead becomes for Swift a transfer point between mortal states, that place he must pass through to help Stella die, and also a place for his own bones to rest. "Now I must tell you," he writes Pope in 1735, "that you are to look upon me as one going very fast out of the world; but my flesh and bones are to be carried to Holy-head, for I will not lie in a Country of slaves" (*Corr,* IV, p. 408). The directions mock the posthumous arrangements Swift makes for his mortal self, the famous epitaph placing him securely within an Irish context he pretends to dismiss, the plot reserved next to Stella in "his" cathedral. But his panic about flesh and bones also betrays an uneasiness. "I would if I could get into a better [world] before I was called into the best," he tells Bolingbroke, "and not die here in a rage, like a poisoned rat in a hole" (*Corr,* III, p. 383). The body matters enough for him to muse in his *Journal* to Stella that if the Whigs triumph, he, unlike the Lord Treasurer, "should have the advantage . . . for he would lose his head, and I should only be hanged, and so carry my body entire to the grave" (p. 435), where it would decompose into an inarticulated skeleton, bones to be pieced together and hanged in somebody else's registry office. Surely part of the fury Swift demonstrated in his treatment of the Duke of Schomberg's bones reflects his own fear of losing control, of being managed posthumously.

To retain personal control, Swift fixes himself within that which decays. It's not just a matter of not wearing spectacles, although his mortification of the flesh points to the process. It's a question of measurement itself. "As to Mortality," he tells Pope, "it hath never been out of my head eighteen minutes these eighteen years" (*Corr*, IV, p. 134). "I was 47 Years old when I began to think of death; and the reflections upon it now begin when I wake in the morning, and end when I am going to sleep" (*Corr*, III, p. 354), he writes Bolingbroke, yet even still, one must enumerate and distinguish "the reflections." Swift reckons that he pays out his lease on life with a tooth every year,[34] pressed down as he is by life's "dead weight" (*Corr*, V, p. 138). In a letter to Swift, Bolingbroke almost parodies his correspondent in the enumeration of bodily ills as he describes his severe "defluxion of Rhume on both . . . eyes" that he took away by "cupping yesterday fourteen ounces of blood." Good God, he wonders, "what is man?"[35] (*Corr*, III, p. 216) Swift doesn't answer the question directly, but in his wish "often" made that God would "be so easy to the weakness of mankind, as to let old friends be acquainted in another state," one of his giddy, wild Utopian schemes, for he will no longer have "sick friends," we can see the germ of a reply (*Corr*, III, p. 242). As he relentlessly reduces himself to body, Swift presents a world in which "man" becomes ultimately that rheum on the eye, that material that blocks utopian schemes of transcendence. Enclosed by such fleshly limitations, he burrows further in to find the way out.

Since I have already discussed cannibalism at length, I will not labor its significance for Swift, but I need to return to Swift's consideration of verbal consumption. The writer is in peril by the nature of his work of being consumed by his reader; in fact, to be read at all, he must be ingested. If the "corruptions and villainies of men in power . . . eat [your] flesh, and exhaust [your] spirits,"[36] one solution is to feed the enemy with charged pieces of a self bound to "turn perfectly the stomach." In his "Letter Concerning the Sacramental Test," he literally offers pieces of himself to the body politic: "If your little Finger be sore, and you think a Poultice made of our *Vitals* will give it any Ease, speak the Word and it shall be done" (*PW*, II, p. 214). "Torn to pieces by pamphleteers and

---

[34] *The Correspondence of Jonathan Swift, D.D.*, 6 vols., ed. F. Elrington Ball, London, 1914, V, p. 246.

[35] Contextually, the question pertains to Gay's difficulty in attaining patronage.

[36] Delany, *Observations*, p. 148.

libellers" (*Corr*, II, p. 279), Swift turns his body back on his devourers. When the "zeal of Liberty" eats him up, left with nothing "but ill thoughts, ill words, and ill wishes . . . of all which I am not sparing," he turns those ill words upon his enemies, "and like a roaring in the gout, they give [him] some imaginary ease" (*Corr*, III, p. 405).

Imaginary ease is the best one can do, and to gain it, Swift embodies himself, his imaginary self, into his writing. Parodically, Peter turns his father's parchment into meat and drink (*Tale*, p. 190); more seriously, Swift the divine turns bread into body, wine into blood. Somewhere in between, Swift the writer turns blood into ink, similes into chickens to be swallowed by ravenous readers. "Sir," the operator of the Mechanical Spirit begins, "it is now a good while since I have had in my Head something, not only very material, but absolutely necessary to my Health, that the World should be informed in" (*Tale*, pp. 261–2). Unable "to *contain* it no longer," making metaphors both "necessary" and "vital," Swift turns airy thought into solid matter, satiric gall coursing through veins that need to be opened. The ink itself, he tells us in *The Battel of the Books* is composed of "two Ingredients, which are *Gall* and *Copperas*, by its Bitterness and Venom, to *Suit* in some Degree, as well as to *Foment* the Genius of the Combatants" (*Tale*, p. 221). When Swift opens his vein to release gall, he parodies the act of communion between writer and reader as he cuts out his vitals to make a poultice. So animated by the properties of ink itself, the pen can move on when "the Subject is utterly exhausted," as the Ghost of Wit delights "to walk after the Death of its Body." And emptied at last, the writer takes pause, waiting to feel the "World's Pulse" and his own before finding "it will be of absolute Necessity for us both, to resume my pen" (*Tale*, pp. 208–10).

The act of writing is both aggressive, as we have seen, and sacrificial, for it entails a constant propitiation of both the reader and the muse. While the reader swallows down similes whole, the muse demands scales from the head and shards of nails:

> Be mindful, when Invention fails,
> To scratch your Head, and bite your Nails
> (Poems, II, p. 643, lines 89–90)

Swift, a poetic practitioner who kept his own nails "pared to the quick,"[37] advises, and at least one time in jest followed his own advice.

All this talk of sacrifice is, of course, comic. Swift appears to mock the hack's productions, the pitiful cost not of writing itself, but of hacking out bad material. The hack's similes are swallowed indiscriminately down, not the bard's. When the *Tale*'s splenetic hack nervously asks his highness so low, prince posterity, what has become of the literary productions of

---

[37] *Ibid.*, p. 173.

his age, we are supposed to laugh at his hubris. But still, pert modern lamentations don't sound that different from the inveterate chafings of a Swift seeking to fix an unstable language, or a Swift addressing "*Ye Great Unknown*" for a nameless place on the list of heroes. And his hack's worry over that "Abyss of Things" threatens to come embarrassingly close to his mature ruminations on the fate of his own "works," tomes overwhelmed by lesser stuff, all to be consigned eventually to a Duck Street pastry cook.

The writing dilemma turns alternately tragic and simple, complicated by the energy Swift himself expends in worrying over it. Too clever and too defensive to expose his fears, Swift employs irony to guard against confessional foolishness. Better to recount with arch enthusiasm tales of "Unhappy Infants, many of them barbarously destroyed, before they have so much as learnt their *Mother-Tongue* to beg for Pity" (*Tale*, p. 33). Pity dissipates here as we contemplate the ineptitude of writers hapless enough not to speak, let alone write, proper English. But Swift continues to dwell on the sacrifice of fledgling works offered to Moloch or consigned to die of "a languishing Consumption," some stifled in their cradles, others frightened into convulsions, bodies flayed alive and torn from limb to limb. By insistently snuffing out offensively weak works, he also extends a degree of carefully hedged sympathy. The tearing of the body itself produces a corporeal connection that complicates mere mockery.

"This *mingled mass* of things"

Much of the urgency shot through this early consideration of the fate of premature works comes from Swift's status, or lack of status, as an author *anxious* to be read. In a consumer economy, lacking name and patron, the writer becomes by circumstance a hack begging to be consumed. Once read, one is excreted, passed through the system, reconstituted into matter for lesser wits to nibble on. Unread, one serves the temple of consumption in less exalted ways as material to wrap pies, more delicacies to be ingested, or as baser matter to wipe the arses that deposit all works to posterity. Fledgling hacks are not alone in their morbid meditations on literary consumption. As late as 1733, in his "Rapsody" on poetry, Swift delineates the perils of his modern Orpheus, perched on top of Parnassus only to become a sitting target for the lesser wits, in peril always of being "bit" by poets of inferior size and merit who "strive to tear you Limb from Limb / While others do as much for him" (*Poems*, II, p. 651, line 333–4). Eat or be eaten, tear or be torn orphic limb from limb, Swift seems to say, as he emphasizes the dangers inherent in words that "shorten life" itself (*GT*, p. 185). The only answer would appear to be more aggression.

Even as he tortures Lagadan words on the rack and erases verses with physical spittle, Swift can still celebrate the power, however fleeting, of the word over the material world. The power is always qualified by body itself. Swift approaches this problem in "The Progress of Poetry," where he compares the poet, "fresh in Pay," to the fat farmer's goose scarcely able to cross over the barn door sill. His belly full of roast beef, "Grown lazy, foggy, fat, and dull," the poet remains earthbound, deep sunk in plenty, "Lumber[ed]" by his mortal condition. The alternative to being "stuff'd with Phlegm up to the Throat" is being hungry, "Guts and Belly full of Wind . . . Flesh brought down to Flying Case." But the transcendence the mock-pindaric artist achieves is deflated immediately. The poet manqué of the exalted spirit rises "like a Vapour / Supported high on Wings of Paper," but only Grub Street responds to his song (*Poems*, I, pp. 230–1). Even tiny Gulliver, pretensions shrunken to six inches, bears too much weight, for after the initial thrust, with "incredible Swiftness" (*GT*, p. 141), he falls flat into the sea, one more bird of paradise brought to ground. To retain Swift's original metaphor, even aloft, lank and spare, a goose sounding harmonious from the skies remains a goose.

If flights out of body turn predictably ridiculous, descent into body darkly inverts the sublime. " 'Tis only infinite below," Swift claims with "sour loftiness."[38] To look below, one needs to "look behind," into "The Gulph of All Human Possessions" (*Poems*, III, pp. 921–4). In his riddle of the privy, Swift plays with the insatiable "Womb" confining "the last Result of all Designs." This devouring womb retains all it receives, reducing thought to matter as it draws in by "NECESSITY" a treasury of learning, "Huge Heaps of never-dying Works." Swift is not unique in turning words into shit. Dryden preceded him in *MacFlecknoe*, and Pope would match him in his *Dunciad*. But in analyzing the "undistinguish'd Mass," going so far as to mythologize what might be excreted potatoes into "six Virgins in a Tomb,"[39] Swift more than any other writer I can think of seems determined to separate himself from the strange mixture drawing him in by carefully distinguishing it, by dissecting the mass and counting the turds themselves, before turning them back into bodies whose "Throats were cut, their Bellies ript." The privy, like Defoe's plague pit, threatens to subsume meaning. The only way out of either place is the way of language itself, the way of enumeration, the way of measurement, the way of myth making. The numbers may be off, the measurements flawed, but the myth, because it is fiction, remains true.

Swift turns his own privy into a fount of fecundity. Just as gaudy tulips spring from dung, so does a "new Creation" spring from this "*Mingled Mass* of Things."

---

[38] Rawson, *Gulliver*, p. 63. See his entire discussion of the inverted sublime, pp. 60–83.

[39] Rogers suggests that "Swift seems to be thinking of potatoes as grown, prepared for the table, eaten, and finally excreted," *Complete Poems*, p. 759.

> These *crude* Materials once shall rise,
> To fill the Earth, and Air, and Skies:
> In various Forms appear agen
> Of Vegetables, Brutes, and Men.
> So *Jove* pronounc'd among the Gods,
> *Olympus* trembling as he nods.

But this apotheosis unsettles. Swift is no Whitman here singing the body transcendent turning to grass. His vision of a mingled mass filling the earth, air and skies, taking on "various Forms" resembles more Rochester's creation myth in "A Ramble in St. James's Park," "Whence rows of mandrakes tall did rise / Whose lewd tops fucked the very skies."[40] Swift eschews Rochester's profanity here, and relies instead on the ominous safety of abstractions. But in the context of the poem itself, a poem filled with deformation and maiming, "mangled Corpses," victims made "The *Food of Worms*, and Beasts obscene," the new creations springing from dung, forms of vegetables, brutes and men, suggest infinite cycles of brute nature designed to feed the "Gulph insatiable" behind it all, the hungry plague pit that Defoe also recognized to be his own final destination.

The riddle itself is a "new Creation," a minor piece balancing ridiculous allusions to virginal potatoes, "Oft in the Train of Venus seen," with sublime allusions to "Sad Charnel-houses." Thought itself becomes matter excreted from the poet's hot brain. In his attempts to distinguish the mingled mass of things, Swift, as much the subjective spider as the sweet smelling bee, mocks a self-reflexive process he depends upon, for he is as compelled to make verses as he is to "make *Oblations* at this Shrine."

The subjectivity of excrement, like the subjectivity of the creative process, can almost be taken as a commonplace. The process itself is completely personal, yet at the same time alien, creating what Maresca calls "the fecal bond"[41] that connects the most rarified presences to their bodies. Children generally like their shit until they are taught not to dabble in offerings not appreciated by an adult world. In this way, children are like the naive order of poets, proud of what they have made because they have made it; it comes from within, that place so vexing to rationalists trying to organize experience. For precisely because the

---

[40] *The Complete Poems of John Wilmot, Earl of Rochester*, ed. David Vieth, New Haven and London, 1979, pp. 40–5.

[41] Thomas Maresca, *Epic to Novel*, Columbus OH, 1974, p. 173. Critics most interested in Swift's "excremental vision" tend either to psychoanalyse or moralize it away. The most successful is Norman O. Brown's classic study of the anal eroticism of Swift's texts, *Life Against Death*, although he does seem to turn Swift unwittingly into Whitman cheerleading the body at the expense of Swift's own splenetic nature. Greenacre, *Swift and Carroll*, goes so far as to imagine the toilet training habits of Swift's overly affectionate Irish nurse to explain his scatology, while, at the other end of the spectrum Jae Num Lee, *Swift and Scatological Satire*, Albuquerque, 1971, argues that Swift "seldom uses scatology for solely meretricious reasons." p. 123.

product comes from within, it cannot be predicted. What comes out comes out, and although the mature poet, one wise enough to appear sophisticated, can prune the product of a "luxuriant" muse (*Poems*, I, p. 31, line 142), while noting ruefully that "Whate'er I plant (like Corn on barren Earth) / By an equivocal Birth / Seeds and runs up to Poetry" (*Poems*, I, p. 33, lines 210–12), even the most calculating creator cannot be sure until it surfaces what "TREASURE here of Learning lurks."

As always, Swift turns on the uncertainty with aggression. *Other* writers, *bad* writers, the *hacks* churn out heaps of badness to be "administered . . . to the Posteriors of ———" (*Tale*, p. 32). But his own pages are also imperilled, destined for Duck Lane where they will wrap pies and presumably wipe bums. Their destiny does not merely reflect the fortunes of the good poet in a bad age. It reflects also an uneasiness with the poetic process itself, with the act of creating something out of nothing but that which lurks within.

Within certainly bothers Swift. Proper words in proper places do not belong within, but need to be kept on the surface of things. That the surface is smoothed over by an irony positively slippery makes the struggle against subjectivity all the more interesting, and all the more desperate. And if the inside is where the words lurk, the outside is where finally they can disappear. For:

> *THERE is in Mankind a certain   *   *   *
> *   *   *   *   *   *   *
> *   *   *   *   *   *   *
>   *Hic multa*   *   *   *   *
>   *desiderantur*   *   *   *   *
> *   *   *   *   *   *   *
> *   *   *   And this I take to be a clear
> Solution of the Matter.   (*Tale*, p. 170)

What is "in" mankind can be cleared out, dissolved into a solution radical in its emptiness. When Swift drives his reader into empty spaces, he opens possibilities of body emptied of matter, and emptied of meaning, but body cleared at last of that which drags down. But just as poetic flight on wings of paper over an admiring Grub Street fails ultimately to satisfy, the lacunae offer thin, brittle solutions to problems that don't really disappear. As Swift wryly suggests, *Hic multa desiderantur*. More would be desirable, more would even be necessary, but more is not possible.

What is possible is verbal play that mocks its own emptiness. Swift was in his letters, his prose, and his poetry, an incorrigible punster. The word Swift alone sent him giddy into verses that strain under the weight of his own name until they "fall with incredible Swiftness" into the abyss he creates. Not the gravest of divines, he cracks his puns in the most serious moments to call attention to the arbitrary meaning that he can control as long as he is doing the making. Make and mock become the same as he determines to "die jesting," able even in the terrible days of his final illness to parody Jehovah himself with the declaration that "*I am what I am, I am what I am.*"[42]

A pun, I think, finds its way into the anatomy of his own dead body, the carcass that dominates the "Verses on the Death of Dr. Swift." The doctors lay all the blame of his demise on Swift himself, who "would never take advice."

> Had he been rul'd, for ought appears,
> He might have liv'd these Twenty Years;
> For when we open'd him we found,
> That all his vital Parts were sound.
>
> (*Poems*, II, p. 559, lines 173–6)

There is a simple irony in the paradox that vital parts now dead can never be "sound." By their very nature, as part of the putrifying carcass, they lose their vitality as the corpse loses its animation. But "sound" can also mean noise, that scattered meaning that Swift's auditors try not to hear. So long devising strategies to penetrate dull ears, Swift has turned into "sound" itself waiting to be delivered, that part of him most vital, most necessary, embodying needs that are translated into text itself. And sound itself becomes metaphor, one that Swift, and later Johnson, would recognize to be most "necessary."

This is not to make Swift content to play modern, filling up an empty belly with wind to express a lack of significance. Meaning exists somewhere for Swift, if he can just fix it. In his assessment of the limitations of language and his recognition that he writes for the consumption of an audience often surfeited, although he plays verbal tricks to force his dull reader to attend, at the same time he tells a straight truth enclosed in an irony we frequently resort to for protection. His fierce faith in the efficacy of language is best seen in the epitaph he wrote for himself. The faith is typically qualified, for the words, written in Latin, are made safer and stronger, less subject to future corruptions of the English tongue. These last words speak one last time to the body itself, a body that Swift finally escapes by once again insisting upon its presence. Swift requested in his will that the memorial be inscribed in black marble, "in large Letters, deeply cut, and strongly gilded." No Duke of Schomberg, Swift assured himself of posthumous control of a reputation that would last as long as the language. In exposing a heart no longer vulnerable because, ironically, it has decayed at last into the abyss of things, in replacing his heart

---

[42] Cited in Orrery, *Remarks*, p. 142; *Corr*, V, p. 214.

with language itself, he embodies his "indignation" to translate a pain freshly felt in each new reading.

> Ubi Saeva Indignatio
> Ulterius
> Cor Lacerare Nequit.
> Abi Viator
> Et Imitare Si Poteris
> Strenuum Pro Virili
> Libertatis Vindicatorem.   (XIII, p. 149)

And in that translation comes a victory qualified by its cost, but written hard and strong in "large Letters, deeply cut."

Afterword

Suppose me dead; and then suppose

Now *Curl* his Shop from Rubbish drains;
Three genuine Tomes of *Swift*'s Remains.
And then to make them pass the glibber,
Revis'd by *Tibbalds, Moore*, and *Cibber*.
He'll treat me as he does my Betters.
Publish my Will, my Life, my Letters.
Revive the Libels born to dye;
Which POPE must beaɪ, as well as I.

"Verses on the Death of Dr. Swift"
(*Poems*, II, pp. 560–1, lines 197–204)

When Dulness, smiling – 'Thus revive the Wits!
But murder first, and mince them all to bits;
As erst Medea (cruel, so to save!)
A new Edition of old Aeson gave,
Let standard-Authors, thus, like trophies born,
Appear more glorious as more hack'd and torn,
And you, my Critics! in the chequer'd shade,
Admire new light thro' holes yourselves have made.

(*The Dunciad*, Book IV, lines 119—26)

The two last lines

That kingdom he hath left his debtor,
I wish it soon may have a better,

I omitted, because I did not well understand them; a *better* what? There seems to be what the grammarians call an *antecedent* wanting for that word; for neither, *kingdom* or *debtor* will do, so as to make it sense, and there is no other antecedent. The Dean is, I think, without exception, the best and most correct writer of *English* that has ever yet appeared as an author; I was therefore unwilling anything should be cavilled at as ungrammatical.

Dr. William King to Mrs. Whiteway on the vexing matter of Swift's "Verses on the Death of Dr. Swift," (*Corr*, V, p. 140)

When Swift writes his own epitaph he is defending himself from the less partial judgment of critics both quick and yet unborn. This attempt to manage his reputation posthumously, paralleled in his own "Verses" on

212

his character, should not be seen as an idiosyncratic expression of anxiety, but rather as evidence of a larger cultural concern. Like Pope's careful and aggressive defense of his artistic career seen in the "Epistle to Dr. Arbuthnot," in the *Satires*, and in the various forms of his *Dunciad*, Swift's labored and strident representation of his best self comes perilously close to the despised Colley Cibber's bid for immortality, the notorious *Apology* for a life in letters. All three writers suffer a sense of injustice that impels them to set the public record straight. When genius and hack alike reveal the same need to make clear their meaning, often in the process defending themselves from each other, it is worth wondering about the reason.

Swift's, Pope's, and Cibber's literary strategies document a fearful skepticism about conventional notions of posterity that reinforces the materiality of their literary careers. No longer confident of providential structures that give shape at last to a life in death, contained by a body that makes spiritual assertions ultimately ironic, and alienated from courtly assumptions of right and privilege that could reward the artist's institutionalized responses, the modern writer was thrown back upon the self. It was a vulnerable self, prone to nervous displays of self-exaltation and fervid attempts to reign in excess. It was a defensive self, wary of being managed. And it was an ironic self – one that knew better than to ask for "much" – only "an inch at most" – knowing all the while the preposterous hubris of such a modest request.

To bring this work to a close, I want to look at two final cautionary tales that give ample reasons for Swift's individual and cultural fears of being matter subject to posthumous revision. In the first instance, Swift appears as subject attempting to control his literary career. His efforts at self-representation in his "Verses on the Death of Dr. Swift" are thwarted by his "friends' " attempt to protect him from his most aggressive, ambitious self. In the second instance he appears as corpse, biographical matter stripped of pieces of himself as he is laid to rest before a public hungry for his remains. In both cases, Swift's attempts to protect himself from bodily appropriation fail as he becomes that material that he was trying so hard to control. In his abortive struggles, he acts out larger cultural anxieties that would motivate the self-promotion of other men and women of letters.

The worry of being posthumously abused that surfaces in much eighteenth-century writing resembles, somewhat parodically, the more urgent fears being acted out at Tyburn Hill on the "tree of glory." Cocking their hats in defiance, crying out greatly "Zounds, who's afraid," the eighteenth-century writers sound more like Fielding's Jonathan Wild than Augustan models of literary propriety in their attempts to die like "the Great." They pretend, of course, more decorum. Pope would not recognize the parallels between his story and the "lives" told to and sold by the Ordinary of Newgate at Tyburn hangings. His career, however, illustrates his dedication to the ordering and distribution of praise and blame. He went so far as to have collected and bound four volumes of virulent, abusive pamphlets that attacked his "shape," his moral, his talents and background. On the leaf beginning the first volume, he wrote, "Job, Chapter 31. Vers. 35. Behold it is my desire, that mine Adversary had written a Book. Surely I would take it on my Shoulder, and bind it as a crown unto me."[1] By appropriating his critics' stories as his own, binding them to him as his crown, he makes their matter his own and enlarges himself as subject of their abuse, a practice he continued in his "List of Books, Papers, and Verses, in which our Author was abused . . ." which he attached to his *Dunciad Variorum*.[2]

As they approach their literary versions of Tyburn Hill, eighteenth-century writers, a notably contentious group, struggle all the harder against being apprehended after death, against being made use of, misinterpreted, hopelessly altered. Defoe stands as a partial exception here. The only writer to have actually confronted the demands of a real mob, in spite of his most public exposure in the pillory, he remains the most private of writers. Stubbornly elusive, "All to Every one that I may Gain some,"[3] Defoe seemed to have possessed a plasticity of character that resisted being "fixed" in editions and letters. His contemporaries, however, appear more consciously worried about being posthumously edited or dissected out of existence, as they invent fearful strategies to express and protect their public and private selves. Felons about to be hanged look to the mob – *their* mob – to justify their deaths and save their corpses from surgical desecration; writers look to the mob of readers that they both need and distrust, the mob that demands, in return, pieces of their literary remains.

Documenting their desire for posterity through self-consciously constructed editions of letters and works, the "modern" writers become objects of consumption, ministering to needs that they would rather eradicate. Unable to rely upon tradition, authority, or court, they look

---

[1] J. V. Guerinot, *Pamphlet Attacks on Alexander Pope: 1711–1744: A Descriptive Bibliography*, New York, 1969, pp. li, xvii.

[2] Richardson's Clarissa makes a similar claim on her adversary Lovelace's attacks when she also quotes Job as her literary model: "And therefore the particulars of my Story, and the base Arts of this vile man, will, I think, be best collected from those very Letters of his (if Mr. Belford can be prevailed upon to communicate them); to which I dare appeal with the same truth and fervor as he did, who says, – *O that one would hear me! and that mine adversary had written a book! – Surely I would take it upon my shoulders, and bind it to me as a crown!"* *Clarissa*, 8 vols., Oxford, 1929–30, VII, p. 48.

[3] *The Letters of Daniel Defoe*, ed. George H. Healey, Oxford, 1955, p. 150. Paula Backscheider's new biography, *Daniel Defoe: His Life*, Baltimore and London, 1989, promises to shed new light on her elusive subject. Unfortunately, her biography came out too late to benefit this book.

instead to the fluctuating appetite of a paying public, and cater to the whims of a fickle, and only occasionally gentle reader. The ironies of this delicate relationship become most apparent in Swift's case. Devoted to dieting the desires of his reader, Swift must nonetheless offer himself as an object of speculation, subject to the imaginative needs of readers necessary for his literary existence.

In their struggles to exert posthumous control, to preserve their literary remains, collecting works and letters, footnoting what has been amassed, in their almost frantic attempts to fix and make permanent that which promises to decay, Swift and Pope lead their contemporaries in strategies that reveal fears about the mortality not just of their carcasses but of their works. The literary corpus can never be safe from violation. Critics like Bentley with his slashing hooks, King with his gentle omissions, can alter the way Swift and Pope are to be read. While the words of their text can be changed entirely, the very material of their work can be transformed into pie wrappers and bum wipes. Meaning becomes located within a body that they know won't last, and who, they ask, will caretake their reputations after they die? They can't even trust each other. That is, of course, the subject of Swift's "Verses" on his death, ironically justified in its London publication, and the subtext of the nervous letters Pope keeps writing Swift about the importance of preserving their epistolary monument.

The struggle for artistic self-definition extends not only into considerations of the correct, authorized editions, but into the idea of the authorized "life" itself. The possibilities for posthumous biographies, staples of the literary marketplace, worried the most sanguine writers of the eighteenth century. Although literary biography existed before their time, going back as far as Suetonius, it took on new urgency once Curll, to quote Arbuthnot's famous line, "one of the new terrors of Death," (*Corr*, IV, p. 101) turned dead lives into fresh profit. Writers and their lives were not just being celebrated, but being apprehended in works that gave pieces of their subject to an audience always hungry for more. Cibber indicates just how hungry the reader could be in a letter to Richardson: "The delicious meal I made of Miss Byron on Sunday last, has given me an appetite for another slice of her, off from the spit, before she is served up to the public table," he writes, promising to "come and piddle upon a bit more of her" tomorrow.[4] Offering up pieces of themselves for popular consumption, writers keep one eye on posterity as they preserve letters and revise editions to sate the appetites of readers always looking for "another slice." Critics, Deane Swift (lesser nephew and biographer) observes, measuring the reading public's taste for objects of consumption,

[4] The *Correspondence of Samuel Richardson*, 6 vols., ed. Anne Laeititia Barbauld, London, 1804, II, p. 76.

are often guilty of greedily devouring the reputation of great men. They should content themselves *"with nibbling at the faults, the superfluities, and the excrescences of books.*[5] Nibbling, piddling, gnawing, the reader exerts a critical power over its objects of consumption.

We can only speculate on the reasons why this was happening, why we know so little about Shakespeare, so much about Colley Cibber and Mrs. Delany, why the literary materials documenting the lives, works, and aspirations of major and minor eighteenth-century writers begin to pile up. Carefully saved letters and manuscripts testify to the weight of a cultural imperative to accumulate proof that the word itself matters. Perhaps a piece of the writer provided a sense of communion often absent in an urban setting; the writer offering to expand the imagination and life of the reader becomes somebody to know, somebody to identify with, somebody to argue against.[6] The endless pamphlets raising and lowering the authors' characters suggest that readers actually cared about the size of Mr. Pope's private parts, the duration of Mr. Cibber's diarrhoea. It could be argued that the "lives" of writers become one more part of the story being told, but the aggression in the telling itself suggests that the writers as well as the readers were asserting a self behind the fictions, a self that refused to go away gently.

It is perhaps fitting that in a consumer economy and a literary market place, the author feeding the print culture gets served up with literary condiments as the last part of the banquet. As Swift predicts in his "Verses," even the uneaten remains are consumed. When "some Country Squire to *Lintot* goes," enquiring after Swift, he learns that he may find Swift in verse and prose in Duck Lane: "I sent them with a Load of Books / Last *Monday* to the Pastry-cook's / To fancy they cou'd live a Year!" But this is just what Swift does fancy – to "live" in his own prose and verse on his own terms, while he parodies the hubris his desire reveals.

"I ask but for an inch at most"

Being drained out of Curll's rubbish, becoming at the end a pie wrapper or bum wipe, was not just a trope for Swift. He began his career with such a fate in mind as he perversely elevated the material aspirations of a hack all too aware of the ten thousand ways that a book, like its author, can go out of the world to return no more. "What is then become of those immense Bales of Paper, which must needs have been wholly annihilate," he muses, too conscious of his inferiority to send "Prince Posterity" "to a

[5] Deane Swift, *Essay*, p. 33.
[6] In "Readers Respond to Rousseau," *The Great Cat Massacre and Other Episodes in French Cultural History*, New York, 1984, pp. 215–56, Robert Darnton discusses the cultural implications of reader identification with Rousseau.

Jakes, or an Oven; to the Windows of a Bawdy-house, or to a sordid Lantern" (*Tale*, pp. 35-6) to learn the fate of his own lost works. Work can be lost because it is by its nature matter subject to the ravages of time itself. Swift's quill has been "worn to the Pith in the Service of the State," his "Head broken in a hundred places by the Malignants of the opposite Factions, and from a Body spent with Poxes ill cured, by trusting to Bawds and Surgeons, who, (as it afterwards appeared) were profess'd Enemies to Me and the Government, and revenged their Party's Quarrel upon my Nose and Shins" (*Tale*, pp. 69–70). Writing to the body, he is compelled finally to exhaust his opened vein "all at a Running" (*Tale*, p. 184), transforming body into text. It becomes, in fact, a text that might possibly never end. Overwhelmed by the material that he attempts to measure and master, having discovered that "the Issues of my *Observanda* begin to grow too large for the Receipts," Swift announces that "I shall here pause awhile, till I find, by feeling the World's Pulse, and my own, that it will be of absolute Necessity for us both, to resume my Pen" (*Tale*, pp. 209–10).

When Swift pauses "awhile" and waits to "feel the World's Pulse," he is satirically predicting the indeterminate state of the early novel while proleptically recognizing the desire both reader and writer share in their attempt to keep that text open. He is writing as a modern confined by "number," by circumstance, and by body, a modern overwhelmed by the materiality of his "*Observanda*." Writing becomes a way of displacing the contradictions of his mortal state. Pausing becomes a way of deferring the inevitable end. Just as "Dr. Swift" lives on posthumously in "Verses" on his death, the hack, always "the last" and the "freshest" writer, waits to resume his pen. Even after his real pulse has stopped, his readers insist upon resurrecting him in their own prose to define and refine his meaning.

The fortunes of Swift's most deliberate bid for posthumous security demonstrate just how tricky Prince Posterity could be. In his study of Swift's "Tory Anarchy," Edward Said argues that the "anonymous" voice that assesses "impartial[ly]" Swift's "remains" in the "Verses on the Death of Dr. Swift" reflects Swift's own "extraordinarily proleptic sense of himself as a problem for the future."[7] More significantly, the poem predicts the problem of the future for Swift. Certainly Swift approached his literary occasions defensively, inventing real and mock strategies to protect himself from being misinterpreted. But even Swift, I would imagine, could hardly have foretold the fate of his calculated defense against time and death. For the poet did not have to wait for the Cibbers and Tibbalds to hack him up to bits. "The Doctor's Friends," notably Pope, that staunch

[7] Edward Said, "Swift and Tory Anarchy," *Eighteenth-Century Studies*, 1, 3 (Fall 1969), p. 64: reprinted in *The World, the Text and the Critic*, Cambridge MA, 1983, pp. 54–71.

defender of poetic justice, and Dr. William King, Swift's bemused editorial choice, were ready with their hooks to improve his incorrect verses.

The drama of the publishing history of the "Verses" turns easily to farce as Pope, "others of the Dean's friends in this country," and King scramble to take charge of Swift's definition of himself. While Swift insists upon extending his personal control over a self which is daily turning into "remains," his friends resist the attempt by asserting *their* idea of *his* character. King confesses himself "very sincerely and sensibly affected by everything that may raise the Dean's character as a writer," even if he has to bend the Dean's meaning in the process. The friends decided that Swift's "Verses" did not properly represent the Dean that they knew. The latter part of the poem dedicated to Swift's virtues proved particularly embarrassing. As King demurred, it might have been "thought by the public a little vain, if so much were said by himself of himself." Such vanity would by its nature be impossible, since "it is well known there is no man living more free from that fault" than Swift. Therefore, to conform to what is "well known," the offending verses had to be sacrificed (*Corr*, V, pp. 137, 139).

When the London printer Charles Bathurst published the sanitized version of the "Verses," he worked from an altered manuscript missing all of Swift's footnotes, 171 out of 484 original lines (including the closing couplet), and padded with over 60 lines from Swift's earlier poem, "The Life and Genuine Character of Dr. Swift." The "Verses," in other words, emerged mutilated, even cannibalized, no doubt gratifying Swift's penchant for the worst. Hadn't he "proleptically" presented the perils of the writing life from the start of his own career, in his creation of a world of hacks being torn limb from limb, of Orpheus ascending only to be "bit"? This vision was confirmed by Pope, equally wary of being misapprehended, not just minced into bits by enemies, but "read . . . dead" by friends.[8] Yet even Pope, in Swift's best interests, laboring to preserve the reputation of a friend too hasty for his own good, reads Swift if not dead at least "improved" at the expense of one or two limbs. For the Dean, it was well known, possessed not a tincture of vanity. How could he say so much "by himself of himself." The Dean, everybody agreed, made no grammatical errors. "A better what?" King asks rather peevishly. No matter, the lines no longer exist; to protect the poet they have been omitted.

Critical apprehension here becomes a seizure of the work itself. Thus, in his own *Remarks of Swift*, Orrery grumbles, "as the two last lines are grammatically incorrect, and as they were not inserted in the first edition published at *London*, I cannot tell how they have crept into a poem, that is otherwise as exactly polished as any of SWIFT's nicest compositions" (pp. 298–9). That Swift himself, through his Dublin publisher Faulkner, later

[8] "Epistle to Dr. Arbuthnot," lines 31–2.

editor of his collected works, restored the offending lines seems not to have fazed Orrery one bit. They are still incorrect. King, on the other hand, upon receiving the Dublin edition, corrected to its originally incorrect state, "was not a little mortified"[9] (*Corr*, V, p. 139).

"Sacred relicks of their posterity"

The body that dominates eighteenth-century discourse is most visible in the "lives" of dead writers being laid to rest. If, in order to escape matter, the writer turns the struggle with material itself into text, that text becomes matter that can turn corrupt, and even turn against its maker. Not only the body of the writer, but the body of the text, threatens to "go off" as awkwardly as Dryden's corpse.

We can find reason enough for fears of literary embodiment in Swift's early biographies, written not by hacks licensed by Curll, but by "friends," gentlemen drafted to defend the cause of Swift himself. As Swift predicted, his death would inspire his "special Friends" to use the event for "private Ends" (*Poems*, II, p. 556, lines 75–6). Swift as writer is suddenly reduced to Swift as material, matter to be revised, reconstructed, and revived to fit the taste of his new maker. Swift exerting form over matter becomes shapeless himself, or rather wrongly shaped, "stuff" to be reworked, re-animated. Just as Pope and King almost wantonly misinterpreted Swift's reasons for writing his "Verses" out of a zeal to "raise" his character, Orrery, Delany, Deane Swift, and finally Sheridan, all personal acquaintances seeking to elevate their friend, raise not his character, but "a character" of their own making. (Only Johnson resists their revisionary methods.) In the process, they not only rewrite the life of their subject, but alter his works, cannibalizing quite unintentionally the "stuff" that was Swift. After briefly considering the early biographers' attempts to order the "heap of writings"[10] that Swift left behind, I will end this work with Sheridan's final representation of Swift on his deathbed, the writer as corpse stripped of pieces of himself, his vexed spirit turned into fetish of a sentimentality that Swift would have satirized rather than endorsed.

As he suggested in his account of Glubbdubdrib, an episode that displeased all of his own commentators, once one becomes a subject to be commented upon, one becomes changed beyond recognition. When Homer and Aristotle appear at the head of their commentators, they

---

[9] Orrery, *Remarks*, pp. 298–9; For a discussion of the publishing history see Williams, *Poems*, II, pp. 551–3; Rogers, *Complete Poems*, pp. 846–8; and A. H. Scouten and R. D. Hume, "Pope and Swift: Text and interpretation of Swift's Verses on His Death," *PQ*, 52 (1973), pp. 205–31.

[10] Delany writes about the "stuff" of Swift, *Observations*, pp. 227–8. Orrery complains about the "despicable heap of writings" that Swift left to be ordered by his critics, *Remarks*, p. 254.

stand as "perfect Strangers to the rest of the Company" (*GT*, p. 197).
Early biographers make Swift a stranger to himself in their struggle
against Swift's vision. Orrery attacks him for his irregular genius, his
indelicacy "that is not agreeable" (p. 132), and his "sarcasms on the structure of the human body." To regularize "this great genius," he moralizes
him, turning him into a *memento mori* being punished for his crimes against
mankind. Expiring a driveler and a show, Swift is represented in a "shocking . . . melancholy account" as the *"poor old man* . . . totally deprived of
reason," paying for his sin of wit.

Delany, ostensibly defending Swift from Orrery's criticism, prefers to
dwell on his friend's errors. Swift forced his muse "to wallow in the mire!
sunk into the character of the basest of all brutes . . . debased below it,
into the gulph (the jakes) of all human possessions" (p. 80). Swift "trifled,"
habituating his mind to insignificant ideas, so that he could "never rise
up to any thing truly great and sublime" (p. 143). Why couldn't Swift
write like Boyle, he wonders, or "gentle Waller"? But no, Swift preferred
to invent filthy Yahoos. Delany corrects him with a "few hints" about the
superiority of the human frame. Man, he tells us, deserves more respect.
He can outrun a horse, outleap antelopes, outswim sharks, carry loads
on his shoulders that would break the back of a horse, dart into the air,
turn somersaults ("inverting the centre of gravity"), and even dance on
ropes (pp. 162–4).

At work is a rather frantic form of repression, created to protect gentle
readers from Swift's work. Replacing the downward spiral of Swift's
materiality with their own lofty visions, "friends" would rather erase Swift
than read him. To cure him of his error, his friends not only render his
vision erroneous, but turn it into the product of a diseased mind. The
direct connection between Swift's bodily decay and mental lapses is one
that will be made frequently by his biographers. Because Swift was bad
(or thought badly of his kind), God, exercising poetic justice, turned
him mad, turned him into the peevish Struldbruggian victim of his own
diseased imagination. As Hawkesworth argues, "his life . . . does not
afford less instruction than his writings, since to the wise it may teach
humility, and to the simple content."[11] Delany is certain that were he
granted one hour of rational reflection, "after the signal chastisement of
his total infatuation," Swift would have repented for his literary follies.
Swift's fearful preoccupation with his posthumous fate seems, within the
context of such friendships, positively mild.

Rereading and reinterpreting, critics eventually erase and rewrite

---

[11] John Hawkesworth, *An Account of the Life of the Revd. Jonathan Swift*, 1755, *Three Biographical Pamphlets, 1745–58, Swiftiana*, 13 (1975), p. 40. Delany argued that Swift saw deformity
and became what he was, *Observations*, p. 144; Orrery says that in painting a yahoo, Swift
became one, *Remarks*, p. 188.

Swift's work. Just as Swift's friends mutilated his "Verses," Swift's nephew, Deane Swift, decided that "properly speaking" the eleventh chapter of the Voyage to the Houyhnhnms should be read as the last chapter of the *Travels*, since the twelfth is "only a sort of a critique, and a very bad one too," one that should be either "burnt or annihilated". To make amends for the mutilation of one manuscript, he adds to another, supplying the curious reader with verses dedicated to the "celebrated MRS. ESTHER VAN-HOMRIGH, that martyr to love and constancy". Neatly incorporating Swift's own language into his production, Deane Swift "Bewail[s] the NYMPH who dy'd to prove, / *That reason was her guide in love*." The subject as well as the style violates Swift's most intimate and defensive representation of himself.

Deane Swift employs a favorite word in Swift biographies – heteroclite – to explain away Swift's writings and life. Swift was irregular because Swift was irregular. "Is there no allowance to be made for the rants and vagaries of an heteroclite genius?" he asks. (*Essay*, pp. 281, 264–5, 252.)

Deane Swift's question trivilizes his subject, for if Swift is a genius, he is not entirely responsible for what he thinks. The reader can escape the implications of his vision while appreciating his "greatness." Only Johnson answers this question negatively, writing, as the one biographer who resists his century's trend to sentimentalize the biographical subject. Perhaps Swift's most critical biographer, Johnson does not so much rewrite his subject as write himself into a subject that he then attacks. His Swift is guilty, not forgiven, for the "singularity" that Johnson so fears in himself. At times the harshness he applies seems prescriptive, Johnson dosing himself with Swift's bad temper and bodily ills, performing home-opathic exercises to chastise his own unruly spirit. Johnson is as hard on Swift as he is on himself, and holds his subject accountable for every extremity of character – even madness.

Johnson, on the other hand, will not be held accountable for Swift's imagination. He will not even attempt to "discover by what depravity of intellect he took delight in revolving ideas from which almost every other mind shrinks with disgust . . . what has disease, deformity, and filth, upon which the thoughts can be allured to dwell?"[12] To discover the allure of filth is to become Swift. To defend against that state, Johnson does not rewrite Swift, but rather flees from his subject's "filthy" vision.

Johnson's rejection of Swiftian material that less rigorous critics were able to revise speaks to the problem that Swift and Defoe presented to their age. The materiality that informs their work was frequently repressed or sentimentalized by readers uncomfortable with the condition that both writers insist upon. We can find the most notable example of sentimental revisionism in Sheridan, a "man of feeling" who manages

12 Johnson, *The Lives of the Poets*, III, p. 62.

to romanticize Swift's "irregular" truths. He is writing, in the year 1784, for an audience eager to find beauties in inconsistency; an audience that has fed upon the misanthropic benevolence of a Matthew Bramble and taken the eccentric brothers Shandy to heart; an audience that has learned from Burke and Boswell that "the great" can be rugged and negligent, disorderly and rude, and that genius, when it deviates, does so with a sublime right. Celebrating Swift's "want of money, want of learning, want of friends," he presents a "forlorn and helpless" Swift, possessing a mind that attained "an unusual size, vigour, and ease." His Swift, like Johnson's, is an "original," but where Johnson distrusted Swift's singularity, Sheridan extolls it.

Sheridan emphasizes the original quality of a mind forged through deprivation and the strength of a sensibility tempered through suffering. Fond of "glorious scenes . . . of Swift's beneficence", he counts up Swift's tender outbursts as assiduously as Swift himself enumerated what he considered to be his own hated "blunders." His Swift weeps at the funeral of his servant Magee and bursts into tears when Dr. Sheridan prepares to move to the country. Like Deane Swift, Sheridan ransacks the damning correspondence between Vanessa and Swift for proof of his tender heart. "In the midst of that bitterness of soul occasioned by his great neglect of her," Vanessa "begins one of her letters in the following manner.[13] 'Believe me it is with the utmost regret that I now complain to you, *because I know your good nature such, that you cannot see any human creature miserable, without being sensibly touched.*' " Sheridan speaks here to a reader more appreciative of the tears that sweeten the indiscretions and "great neglect" of a man of letter's life. The desire for feeling overwhelms moral demands as Sheridan loses sight of the self-protective structures Swift employed to protect a "heart" his biographer is so eager to dissect for benevolent consumption. And in the process, the difficult Swift who hardened himself against fleshly desires is turned into an early Byronic hero, driven to instill bitterness into Vanessa's soul to prove that he owns a heart, a heart that the gentle reader can gnaw on.

When he enumerates the tears Swift shed, Sheridan reifies a sensibility that justifies Swift's genius. Soul becomes matter, material evidence that becomes a measure of the man himself. He takes the process of literalization even further when he presents the reader with an anecdote, probably false, that awakens the most Swiftian fears of posthumous management. In this story, Swift is reduced to a body stripped of its most basic defenses, and becomes for his mourners a fetish of "their posterity," a token not of himself, but of their memory of himself:

[13] Sheridan, *Life of Swift*, pp. 9–12, 458, 490–1.

The citizens gathered from all quarters, and forced their way in crowds into the house, to pay the last tribute of grief to their departed benefactor. Nothing but lamentations were heard all around the quarter where he lived, as if he had been cut off in the vigour of his years. Happy were they who first got into the chamber where he lay, to procure, by bribes to the servants, locks of his hair, to be handed down as sacred relicks to their posterity. And so eager were numbers to obtain at any price this precious memorial, that in less than hour, his venerable head was entirely stripped of all its silver ornaments, so that not a hair remained (pp. 281–2).

Dead to the world, Swift is revived here to die once more for the crowd. The citizens gathered from every quarter exert their presence and their claims on *their* benefactor, Dean, Drapier, hack. By virtue of the shillings they paid for the pamphlets and trifles he wrote, the mob expects its due, suggesting a reciprocal sense of contract between public writer and private reader. This public proprietorial demonstration, like the drunken Lord Jeffreys' grosser acquisition of the bodily parts of Dryden, expired poet laureate, indicates the control that a reading public can exert over the literary product and producer that it consumes. When Swift's spontaneous mourners snatch the "silver ornaments" from his very head, they are claiming pieces of him that they have somehow earned. The material that they snatch will become a "sacred relick" to *their* posterity, fetish of the transaction between reader and the writer of that reader's culture.

This anecdote, like the story of Dryden's mock-heroic interment, cannot be proven, but the mere fact that it exists is significant. For the story of the rape of the Dean's locks tells us about the expectations the death of a writer could raise. Swift's body becomes spectacle, what H.F. would call a "speaking sight." Just as a skeleton articulates form that contradicts, ironically, decay and dissolution, to become intelligible after death, the body of the silenced writer becomes, on its own, a symbol. The very hair of Swift is granted a significance that extends the power of the word into the body itself. Just how potent the representational power of the writer's body can be is revealed in Ehrenpreis's attempt to demystify the "fascinating legends" of Swift's final days. In his more decorous version of the shearing:

The dean was laid out in his own hall, and the people of Dublin crowded to see him. The coffin stood open. He wore neither cap nor wig. On the front and dome of the skull little hair remained. But it grew thick behind, resting like white flax on the pillow. The woman who had nursed him sat at his head. When she left the room briefly, someone cut off a lock of the hair, which she missed on her return. After that day, no person was admitted to see the body.[14]

---

[14] Ehrenpreis, *Swift*, III, pp. 918–19.

But in this simple, stark version, even Ehrenpreis, so determined to mute the melodrama of the event, describes hair "resting like white flax" on its pillow. Mason, the historian of St. Patrick's Cathedral, supplied the original "white flax," but Ehrenpreis "rests" hair that takes on properties organic and anthropomorphic. For the crowd itself, that crowd of readers jostling to snatch its piece, invests the body of Swift with power primitive in its simplicity. It is as if the mortified flesh still contains a spirit that should have fled. And the biographers depend upon just this connection between flesh and spirit as they, to use Deane Swift's words, "gnash with their teeth" and "prey upon their vitals," the materials that become their own version of Swift. The truth of the version becomes incidental, although it is always advertised, for what matters is the banquet itself, the literary remains that the reader can feast upon. In looking at their seizure of the material that was Swift, we can learn just how deeply reader and writer alike grounded themselves in the body that had come to define their existence itself, what Mandeville said we *really are.* But in the grounding, and in the representation, something more is also created. In their struggle against matter that threatened to consume their meaning, Defoe and Swift documented the struggle itself and managed in their resistance to exert form. The materiality that consumed the eighteenth-century imagination also energized it, producing and reproducing a struggle against limitation that we have not yet ended.

Index